MW01625883

Painting Flowers

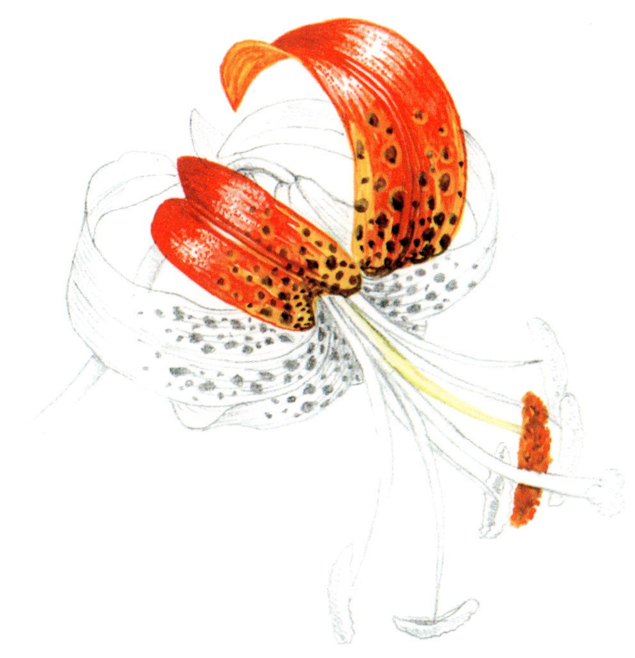

Marjorie Blamey's

Painting Flowers

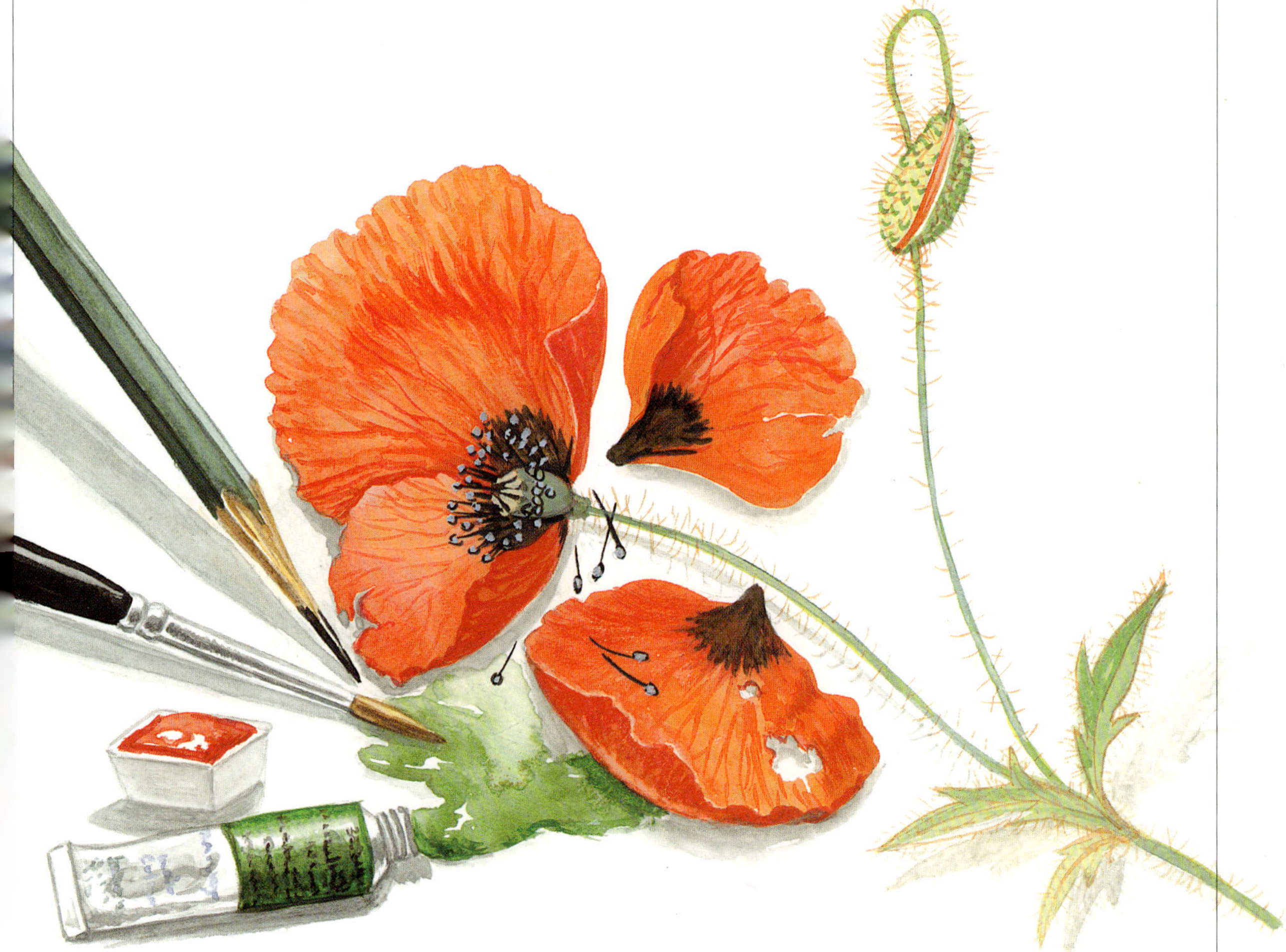

DORLING KINDERSLEY
LONDON • NEW YORK • SYDNEY • MOSCOW

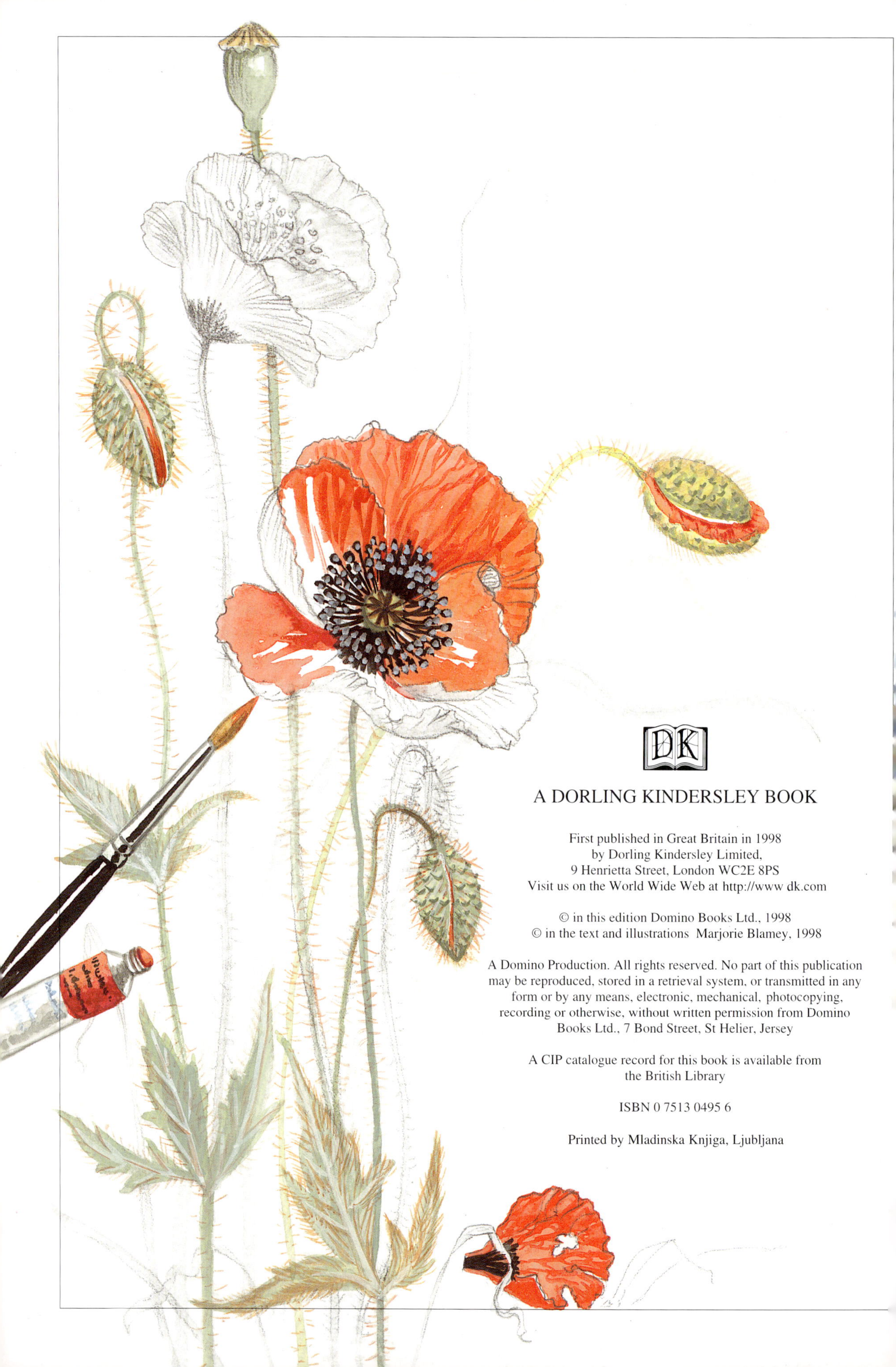

A DORLING KINDERSLEY BOOK

First published in Great Britain in 1998
by Dorling Kindersley Limited,
9 Henrietta Street, London WC2E 8PS
Visit us on the World Wide Web at http://www dk.com

A CIP catalogue record for this book is available from
the British Library

ISBN 0 7513 0495 6

Printed by Mladinska Knjiga, Ljubljana

PAINTING FLOWERS, for me, started at the age of 14. The first flower book I wrote and illustrated, pocket-sized, was entirely copied from other books, as was its sequel on birds. I painted them on paper printed with blue lines that ran when wet, and found that if wetted still more they could make a blue sky, of a sort. This went on until at sixteen a new art teacher at school told me I was wasting my time, and his, with my natural history painting that would interest nobody. In fact, he thought it would be better if I threw away my paints and bought a camera: it could click my subjects in a fraction of a second and produce much better images.

I did as I was told and for £8 got an ancient Leica. It was – still is – splendid for landscapes but not much good for close-ups. But I enjoyed it, and after growing up and finding work as an actress I sometimes wrote for photographic magazines and had my photos exhibited. The war stopped all that. When it was over and I had a husband and later a family and a farm in Cornwall, I took up photography again but painted nothing for 25 years except for whitewashing the cowshed walls.

Then one day I tried painting a clematis flowering by the farmhouse door. It was frustrating: I had done it better as a child. But eventually my paintings in the evenings after farm work got a little better. Somebody saw them in a local show and I got a small book-illustrating commission. Then in 1972 a publisher's editor asked me to paint first some pictures for other books and then a guide to all north-west European wild flowers. He explained that, for helping people to identify plants, a botanical artist needed to be *better* than a camera. The world had gone full circle!

For that book (still in print in 9 languages), over 1000 species were collected for us all over north-west Europe. It was the end of farming and the start of a new life. Other books followed, recently *Wild Flowers by Colour,* which tries to make identifying easier and more fun. This new one, though, is simply on how I paint flowers, whether wild or in the garden. If it helps anyone, I will be really pleased. There is no better hobby. It neither pollutes the atmosphere nor disturbs other people. And having to concentrate on the flowers really makes you see them more clearly and enhances the pleasure they give. It is never too late to start.

Marjorie Blamey

In This Book

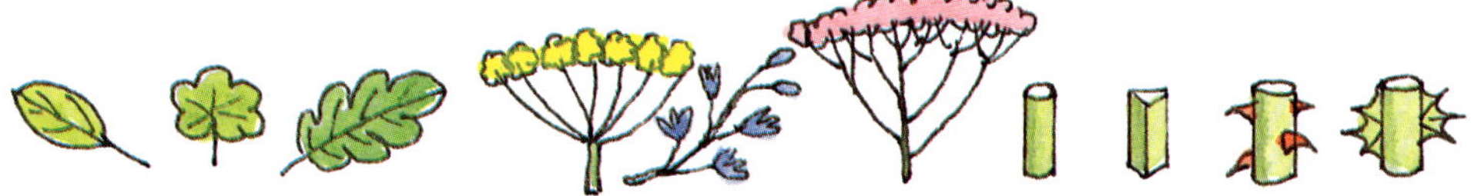

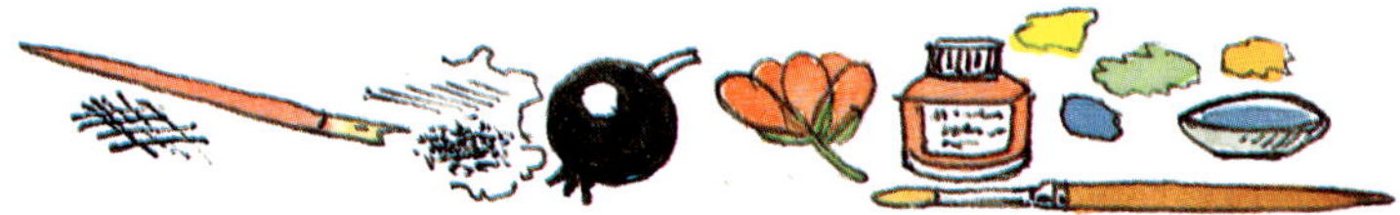

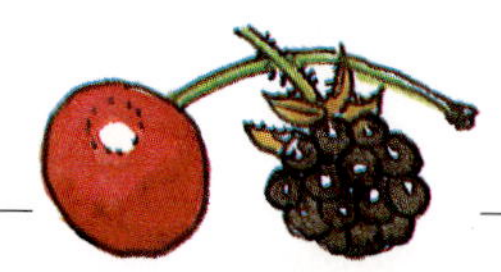

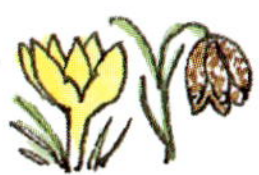

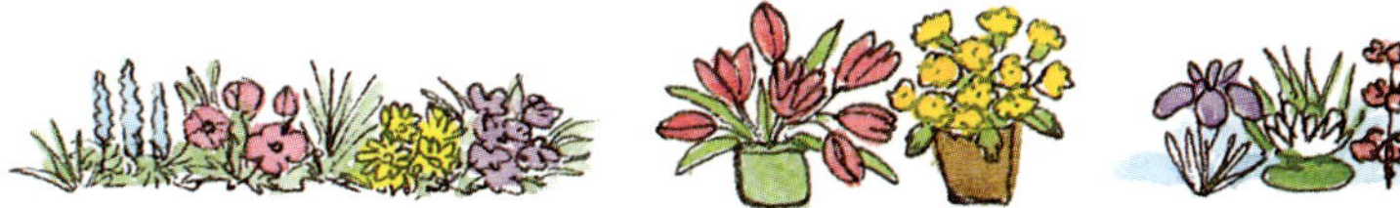

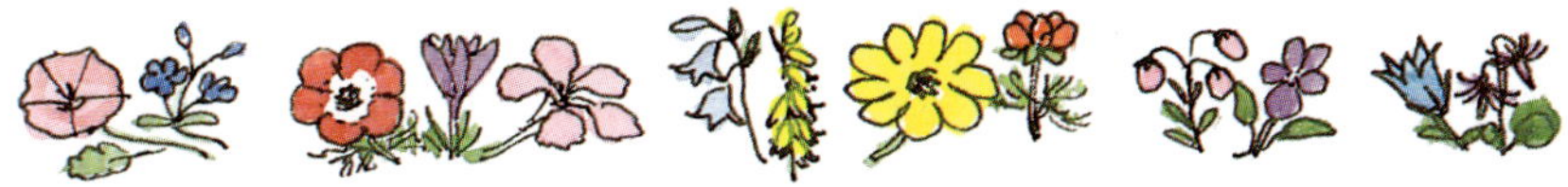

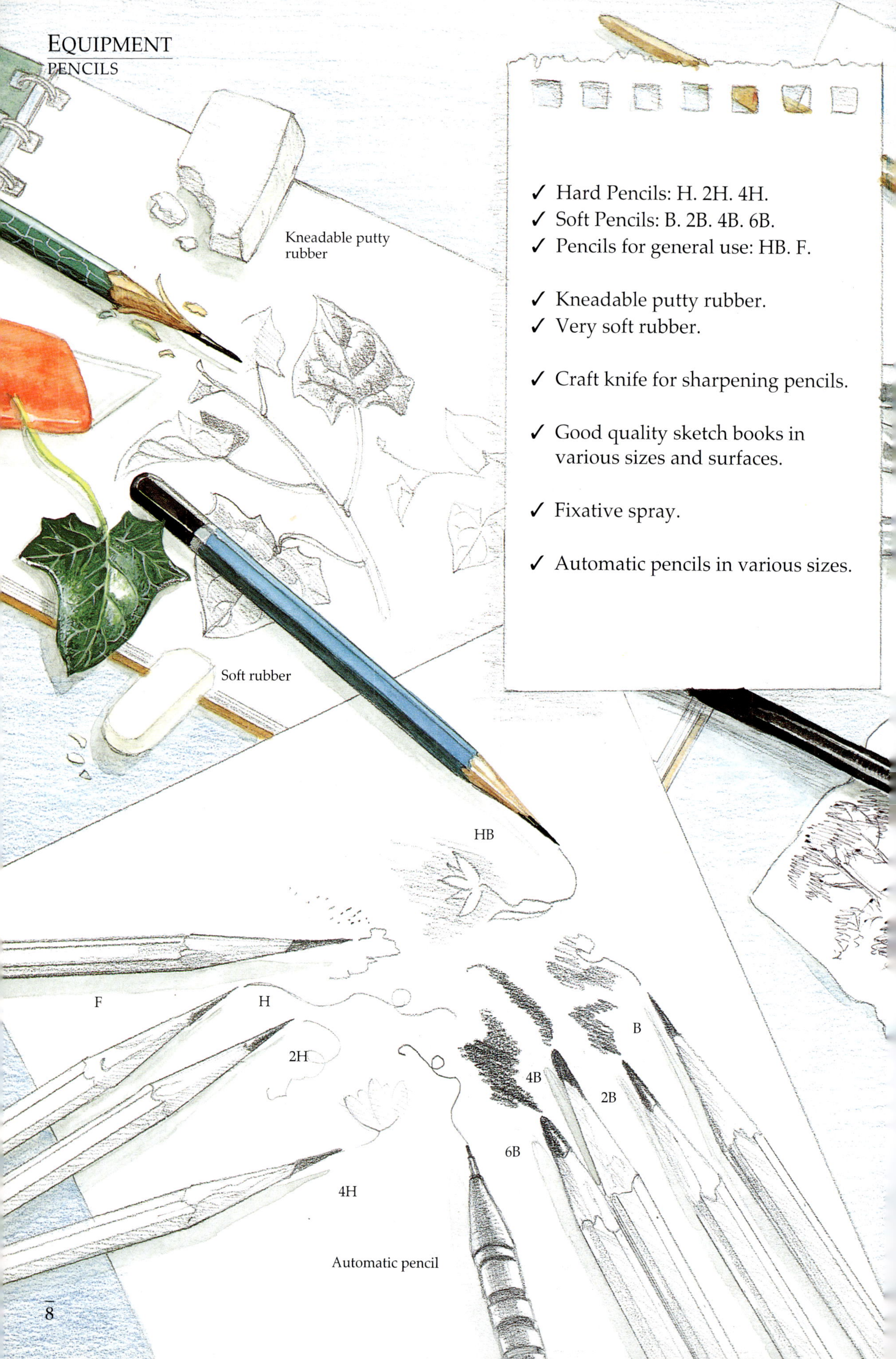

- ✓ Hard Pencils: H. 2H. 4H.
- ✓ Soft Pencils: B. 2B. 4B. 6B.
- ✓ Pencils for general use: HB. F.

- ✓ Kneadable putty rubber.
- ✓ Very soft rubber.

- ✓ Craft knife for sharpening pencils.

- ✓ Good quality sketch books in various sizes and surfaces.

- ✓ Fixative spray.

- ✓ Automatic pencils in various sizes.

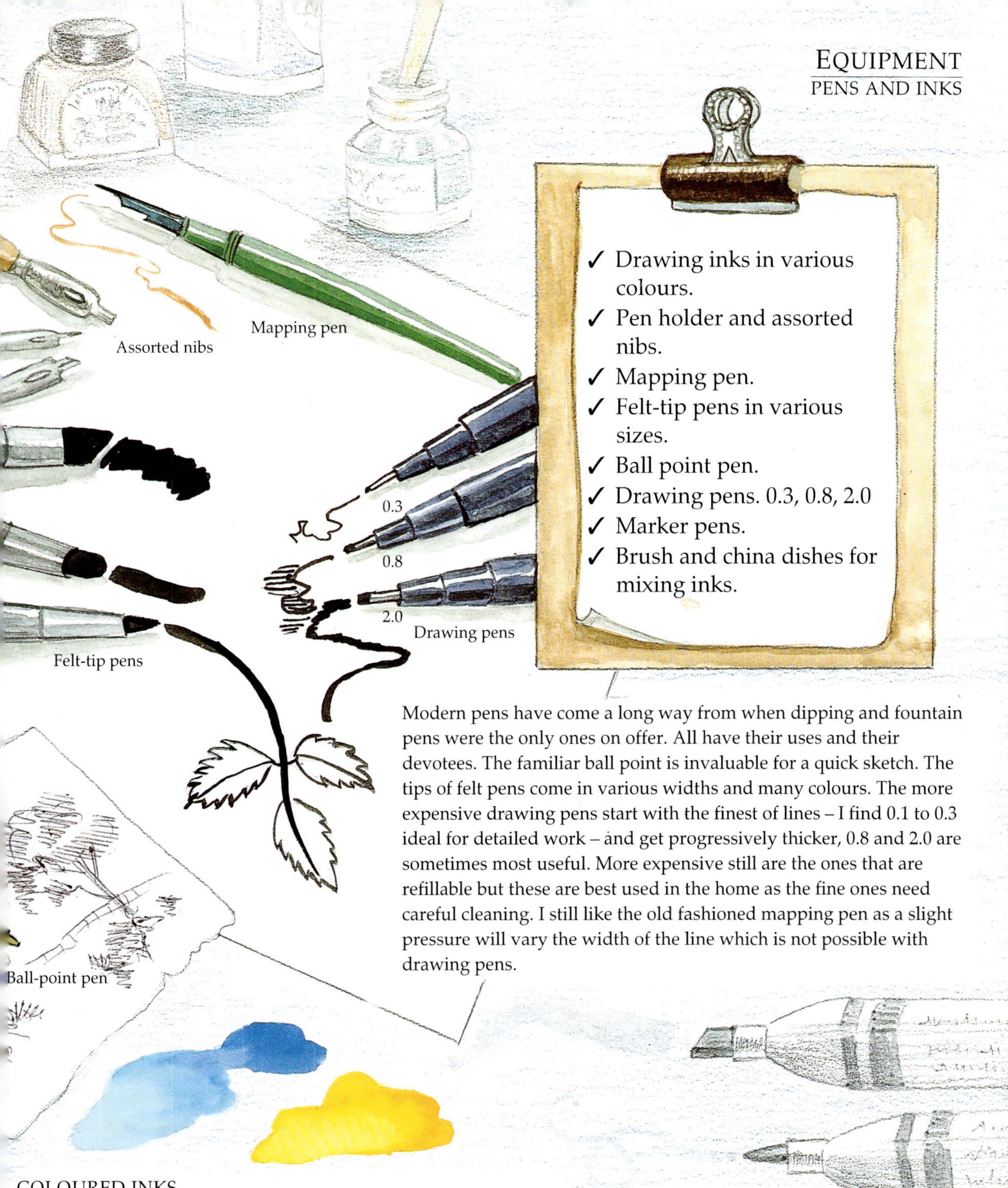

Modern pens have come a long way from when dipping and fountain pens were the only ones on offer. All have their uses and their devotees. The familiar ball point is invaluable for a quick sketch. The tips of felt pens come in various widths and many colours. The more expensive drawing pens start with the finest of lines – I find 0.1 to 0.3 ideal for detailed work – and get progressively thicker, 0.8 and 2.0 are sometimes most useful. More expensive still are the ones that are refillable but these are best used in the home as the fine ones need careful cleaning. I still like the old fashioned mapping pen as a slight pressure will vary the width of the line which is not possible with drawing pens.

Marker pens

COLOURED INKS

Transparent, smooth flowing and as one manufacturer states "the colours are based on dyes chosen for their brilliance rather than their permanence". Brilliant they certainly are, perhaps too bright for some flower painters, but luckily all can be diluted and mixed together to produce softer and more pleasing tones, particularly in the range of greens for leaves. If permanence is not important and bright colours desired then some of the inks can produce shades of purple and cerise that permanent water colour cannot. Besides they are fun to use. Black and white are permanent. All inks can be applied with pens or brushes.

Designer marker pens can be bought at art shops in nearly 150 colours with fine and chisel tips, one on each end of the same pen. They are much like other felt-tip pens and are so easy for rapid sketches. I particularly favour the Cool Grey for adding background grasses to mixed media paintings (p. 41).

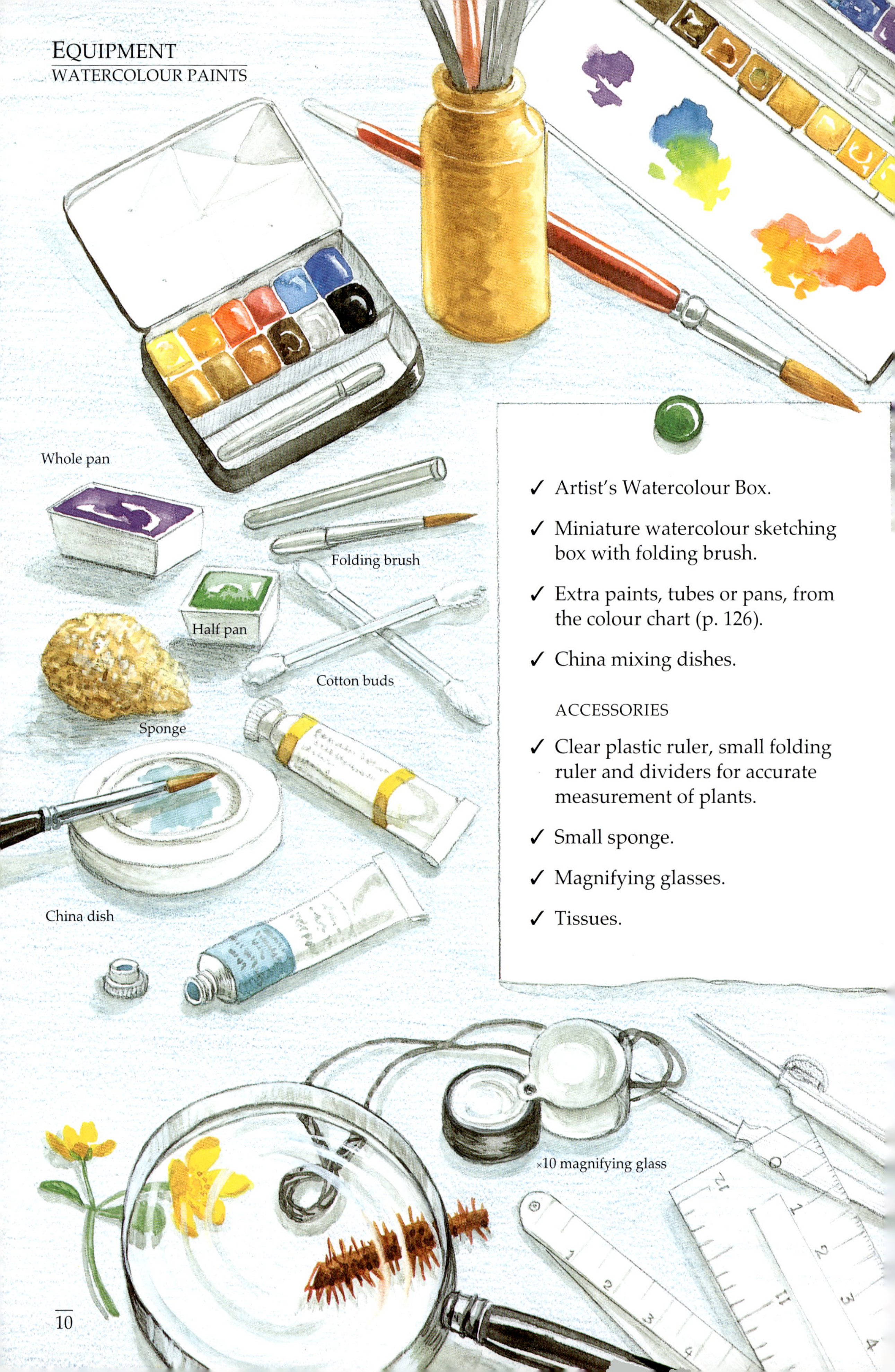

- ✓ Artist's Watercolour Box.
- ✓ Miniature watercolour sketching box with folding brush.
- ✓ Extra paints, tubes or pans, from the colour chart (p. 126).
- ✓ China mixing dishes.

ACCESSORIES

- ✓ Clear plastic ruler, small folding ruler and dividers for accurate measurement of plants.
- ✓ Small sponge.
- ✓ Magnifying glasses.
- ✓ Tissues.

There is a wide selection of brushes all of which are light, well balanced and comfortable to hold. They are also pleasing to look at and I like their smooth tapered handles. There is a choice of natural animal hair or man-made synthetic fibres.

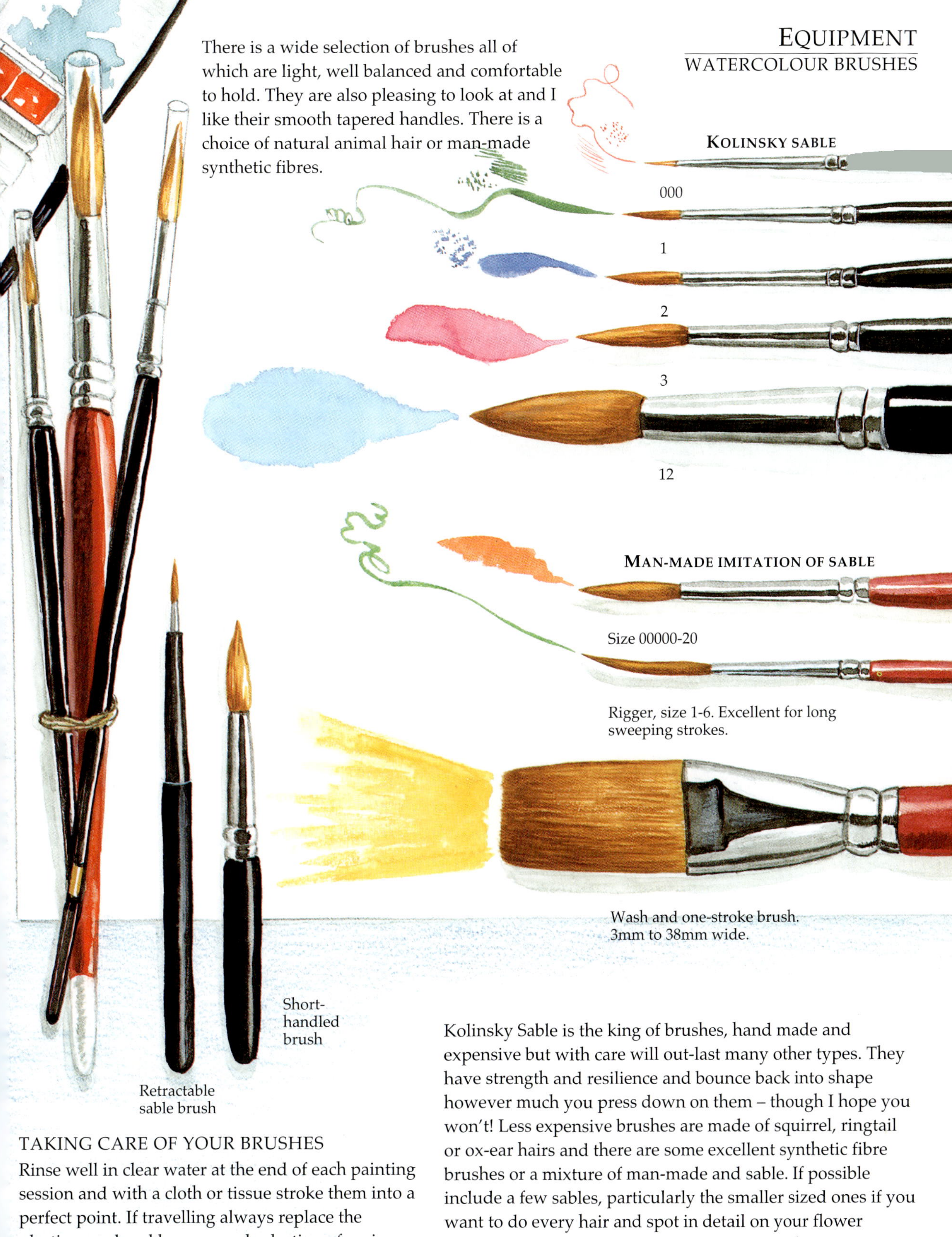

Rigger, size 1-6. Excellent for long sweeping strokes.

Wash and one-stroke brush. 3mm to 38mm wide.

Short-handled brush

Retractable sable brush

TAKING CARE OF YOUR BRUSHES

Rinse well in clear water at the end of each painting session and with a cloth or tissue stroke them into a perfect point. If travelling always replace the plastic guard and keep a good selection of various sized ones handy.

Remember to save the plastic brush guards.

Kolinsky Sable is the king of brushes, hand made and expensive but with care will out-last many other types. They have strength and resilience and bounce back into shape however much you press down on them – though I hope you won't! Less expensive brushes are made of squirrel, ringtail or ox-ear hairs and there are some excellent synthetic fibre brushes or a mixture of man-made and sable. If possible include a few sables, particularly the smaller sized ones if you want to do every hair and spot in detail on your flower painting. Start with size 0, 1, and 3 and enjoy the pleasure they will give you. If you only want to paint flowers in an abstract style or with minimum detail you can leave out the smallest sizes and start with size 3 upwards.

Papers are graded by the weight of a ream – 500 sheets – and every sheet will be marked with that weight. They begin at about 45lbs in sketch books and go up to 300lbs for the very thick sheets which measure approximately 76 × 56cms (30 × 22ins) down to pocket sized pads. 140lbs is a good weight for water colours but even so it may be advisable to stretch it. Heavier papers do not require stretching. Surfaces are HP (Hot Pressed) for maximum detail. NOT (not hot pressed!) with more 'tooth' as it is called which takes colour washes well and ROUGH, beloved by the landscape artist giving great scope for bold effects though less useful for the flower painter who wants detail instead of sweeps of colour. Pale tinted paper is also available for water colour work.

SURFACES & COLOURS

Hot pressed

NOT

Rough

Cream tinted

Grey tinted

Green tinted

WATERCOLOUR BOARDS

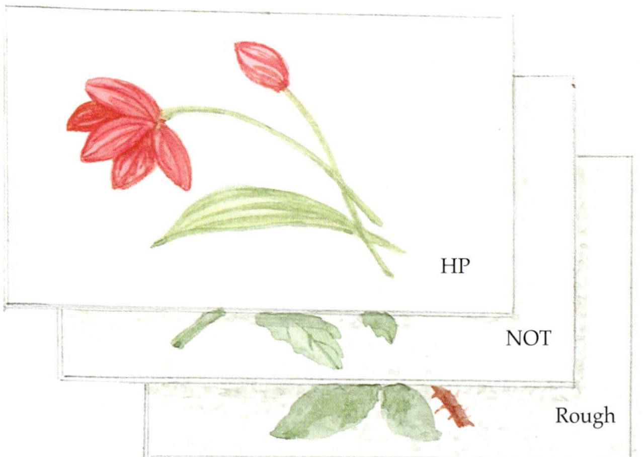

Watercolour boards have various papers mounted on them and are useful for any one not wishing to tackle the stretching process. They are also good for working outdoors as they are firm enough to use without taking another board as a support.

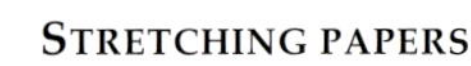

STRETCHING PAPERS

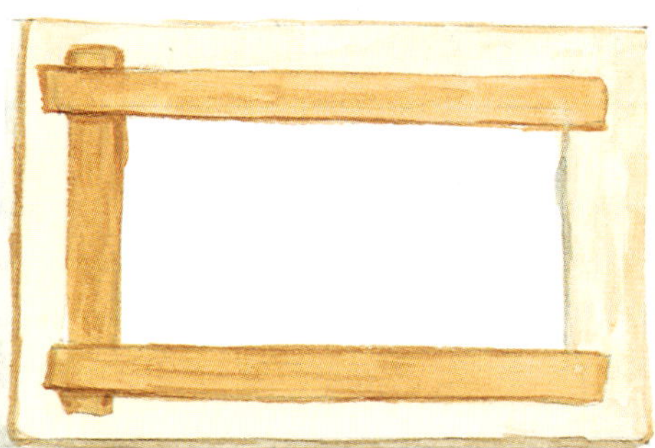

Stretch all but the heaviest paper – and this includes tinted ones. Soak the paper well, preferably in the bath. Hold it up to drip and then lay it on a wooden drawing board which must be considerably larger than the paper. Stick it down all round using brown gummed paper tape 3-5cms wide (1½ to 2ins). Stick half the width on to the paper and half on the board so that it is firmly anchored. Leave to dry thoroughly, preferably overnight, and it will become beautifully flat and tight and stay like this while you paint. Allow plenty of paper around your painting so that you can cut it free when finished.

EQUIPMENT

Papers can be bought in many colours from subtle pale shades to dark greens and browns etc. and are really intended for pastels. However if first stretched (p. 12) or stuck to boards they can be used for water colours and give the artist scope for painting flowers in an entirely different style from the more orthodox way on white paper. By using water colour with added Chinese White to make it opaque, or gouache, you can achieve interesting effects of pale flowers on dark backgrounds (pp. 100-3). Some such papers can be bought already on card for use as mounts.

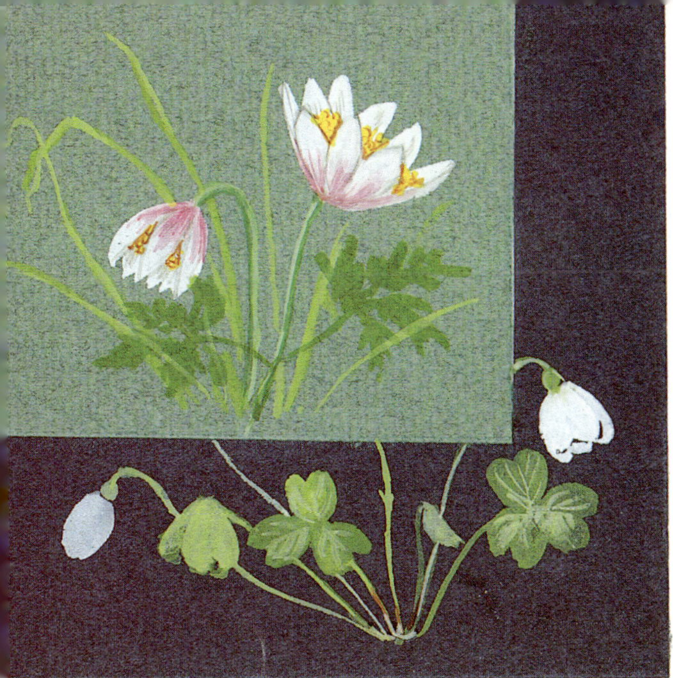

STICKING THIN COLOURED PAPERS

Apply wall-paper glue to the back with a sponge particularly around the edges, allow a few minutes to stretch and place on a suitable card, board or, for large paintings, on hardboard. Smooth out carefully using a soft cloth. Cover with clean paper and literally roll it out as though it is pastry with a rolling-pin. Sponge away any surplus glue around the edges, it wont leave a mark if you do it right away. Allow to dry flat and put weights on the edges if you have used a card that might curl as the paper shrinks. Allow extra paper all round and remember that it will remain on the backing and cannot be removed so choose one suitable in size and strength to take the mount and frame.

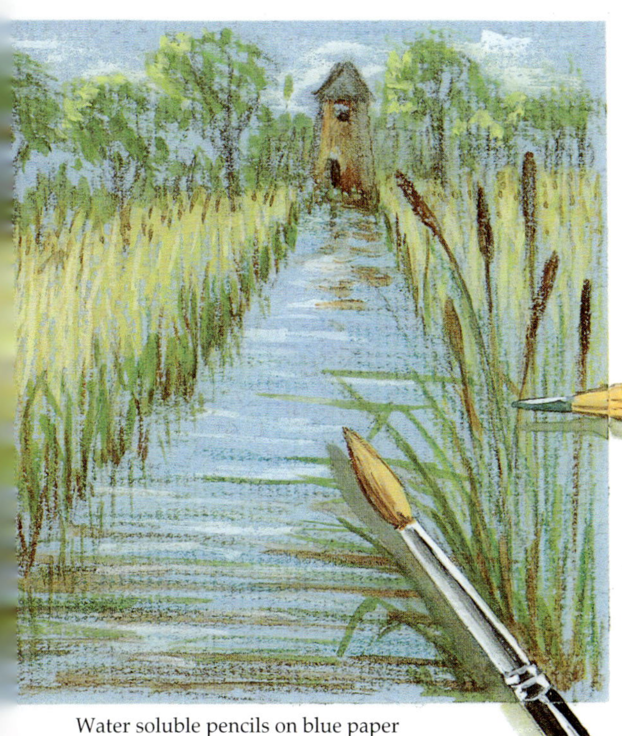

Water soluble pencils on blue paper

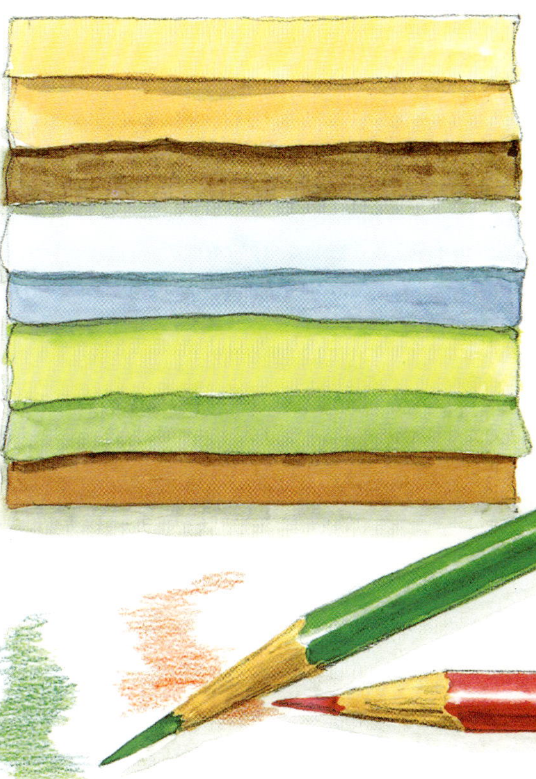

Coloured pencils are especially popular with budding artists from an early age. Clean, cheap, easy to use, available in many colours. Less destructive than charcoal or pastels if trodden into the carpet by young feet!

Water-soluble pencils are very versatile and far superior to the ordinary coloured pencils. They can be used as crayons for doing quick sketches outdoors and when you return home they can be 'painted' over with a wet brush and turned into a water colour. If you want to change a colour slightly you can add a layer of another shade and wash this in too.

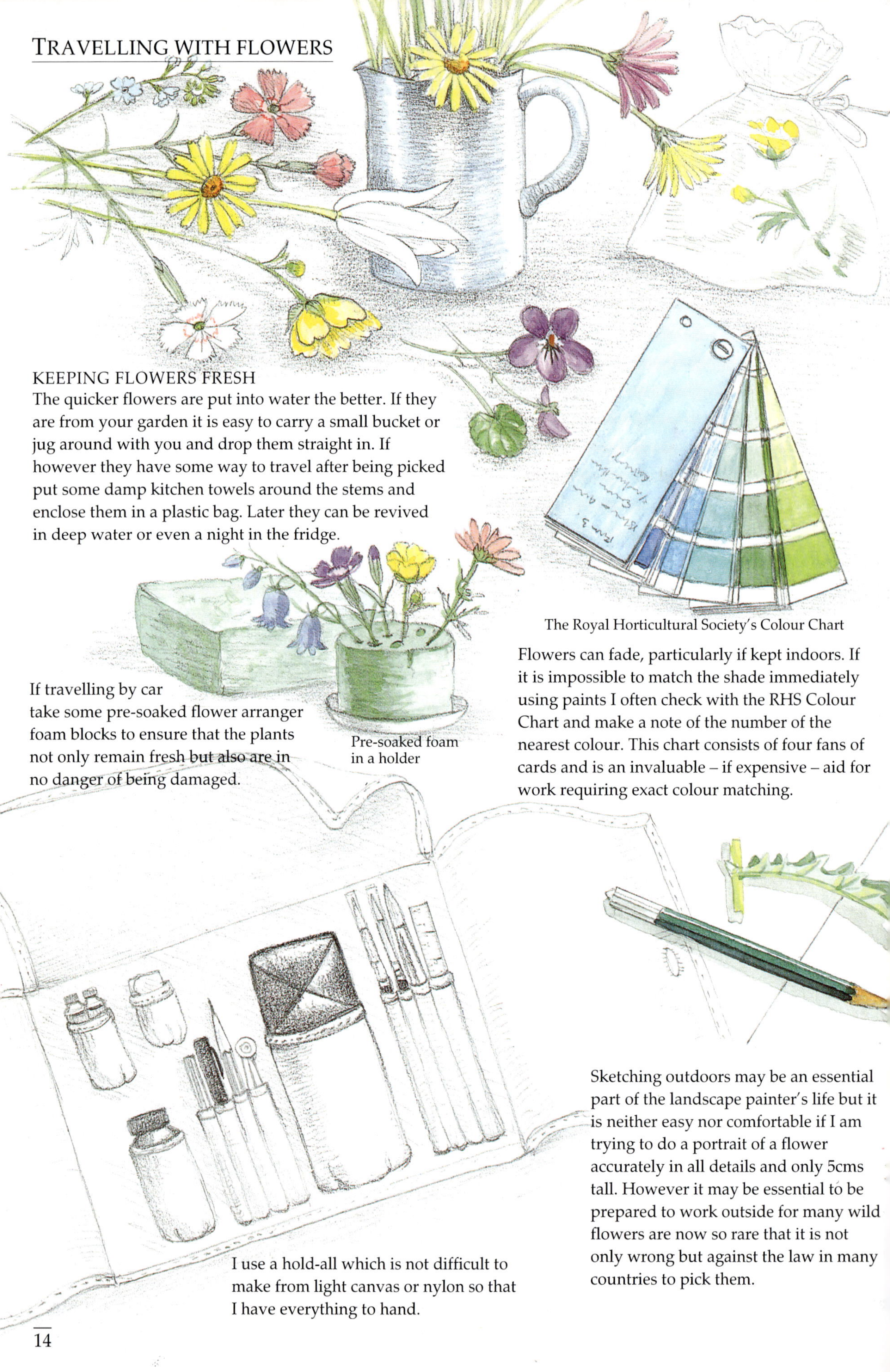

KEEPING FLOWERS FRESH

The quicker flowers are put into water the better. If they are from your garden it is easy to carry a small bucket or jug around with you and drop them straight in. If however they have some way to travel after being picked put some damp kitchen towels around the stems and enclose them in a plastic bag. Later they can be revived in deep water or even a night in the fridge.

The Royal Horticultural Society's Colour Chart

Flowers can fade, particularly if kept indoors. If it is impossible to match the shade immediately using paints I often check with the RHS Colour Chart and make a note of the number of the nearest colour. This chart consists of four fans of cards and is an invaluable – if expensive – aid for work requiring exact colour matching.

If travelling by car take some pre-soaked flower arranger foam blocks to ensure that the plants not only remain fresh but also are in no danger of being damaged.

Pre-soaked foam in a holder

Sketching outdoors may be an essential part of the landscape painter's life but it is neither easy nor comfortable if I am trying to do a portrait of a flower accurately in all details and only 5cms tall. However it may be essential to be prepared to work outside for many wild flowers are now so rare that it is not only wrong but against the law in many countries to pick them.

I use a hold-all which is not difficult to make from light canvas or nylon so that I have everything to hand.

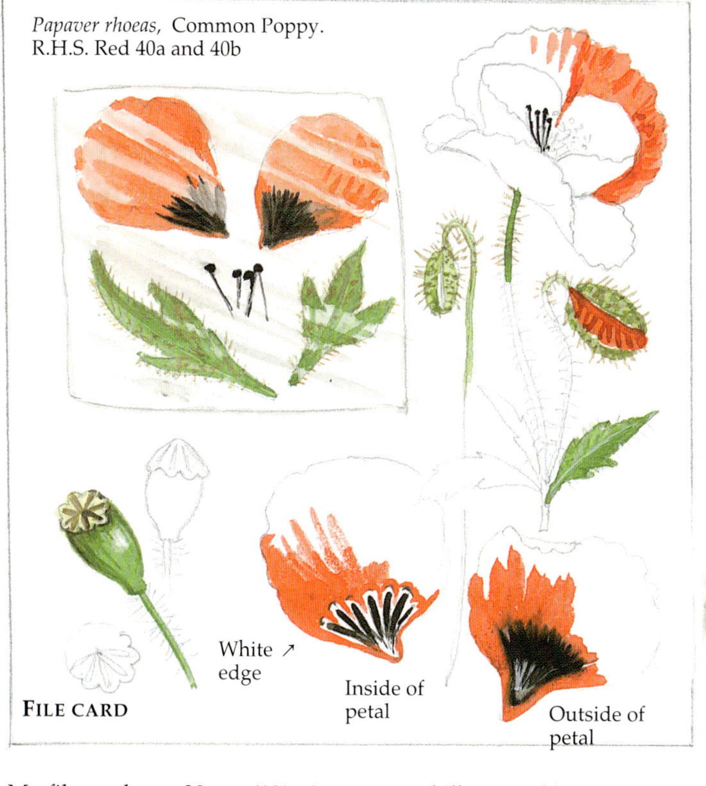

From the time I first started to illustrate books I decided it was essential to record on file cards every flower that was sent to me. I built up a comprehensive library over the years and it is a simple matter to extract the card I need if I want to paint a summer flowering plant in the depths of winter. I have a lasting record of each one and need not have another specimen sent to me – a good conservation point.

My file cards are 30cms (12ins) square and illustrated in as much detail as is possible at the time. Sketches are in pencil and paint although in my case colour may have to be restricted to one petal, one leaf and a section of stem if too many flowers arrive at the same time. After each sketch the plant, or part of it, is placed under clear adhesive plastic film, without pressing it and this usually results in very natural petal colours still retained after many years, especially the yellows. I add many notes regarding habit of growth, numbers of leaves and petals, whether matt or shiny and the number of the nearest matching colour in the RHS Colour Chart.

Self-adhesive film

R.H.S. Colour Chart No. 40

Strips of sticky paper

RESSING FLOWERS

Pressed flowers are one of the most important means of identifying plants available to botanists, and fill vast storage units in herbariums around the world – the most comprehensive being at Kew Gardens. For the average flower painter however, a pressed plant that has lost all its colour and resembles a few shoots of brittle and broken hay is not very inspiring or useful. Far better to sketch the wild species and leave them to grow and multiply. Press only garden flowers instead.

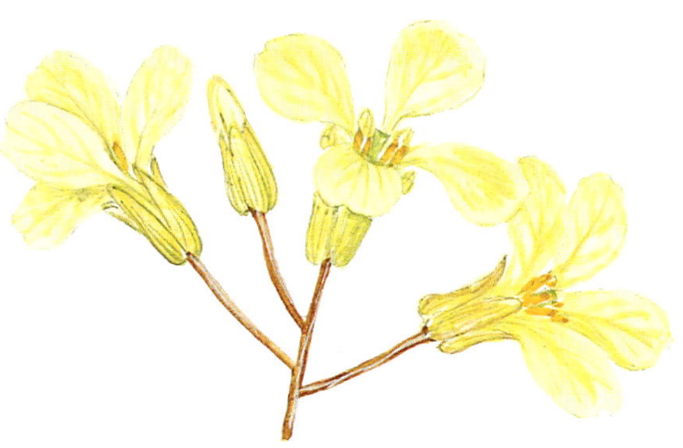

Typical flowers of the Cabbage family

Whichever type of flower painting you wish to adopt, from delicate loose-style impressions to detailed botanical studies, it will be worth spending time looking at the way flowers are formed and studying a few basic facts of botany which may add to your interest in plants and prevent simple mistakes such as thorns facing the wrong way up the stem which I once saw in an otherwise excellent drawing of a rose.

The diagrams, not to scale, show you the parts of a flower and a few simple rules to follow when drawing them at varying angles.

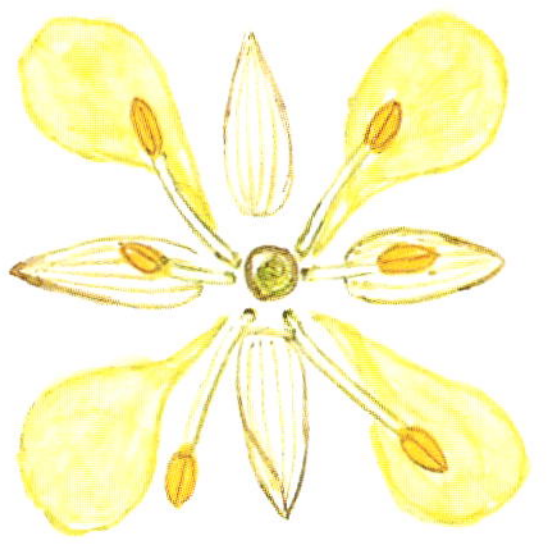

Take a flower apart and it consists of:

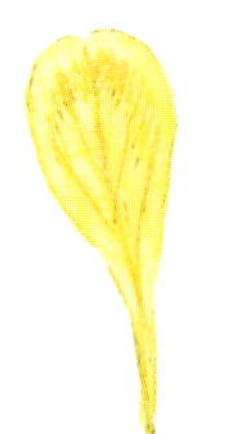

4 petals in the shape of a cross.

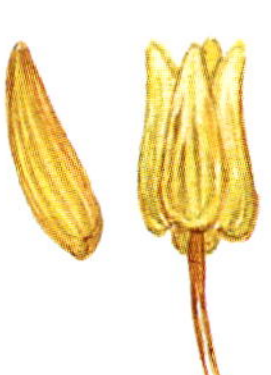

4 sepals which form the calyx.

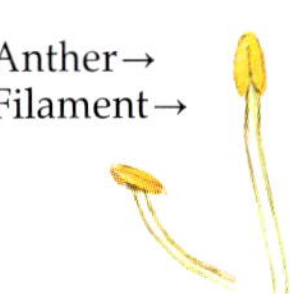

Male parts

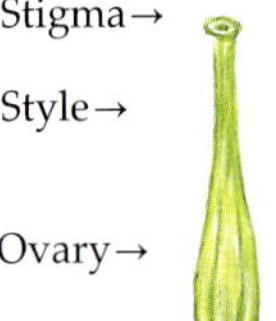

Female parts

6 stamens often 4 tall, 2 short.

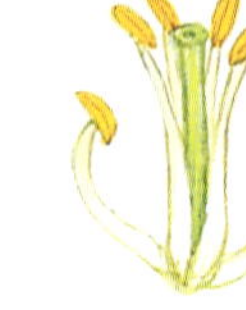

Typical arrangemen of stamens around t ovary.

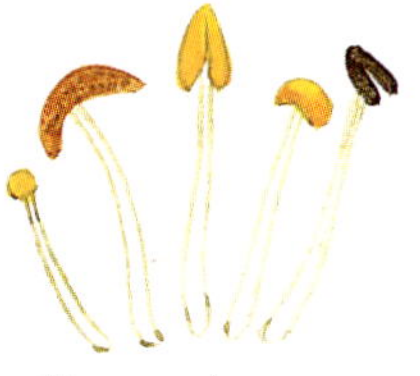

Stamens from various species.

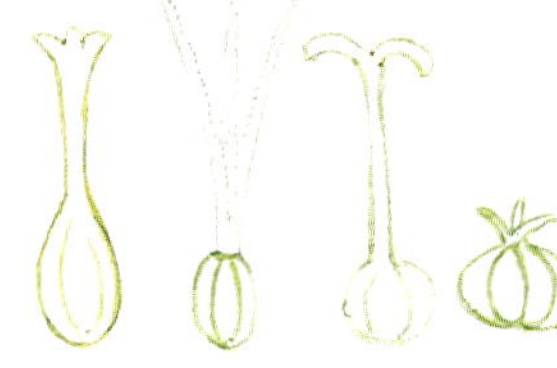

Ovaries from various species.

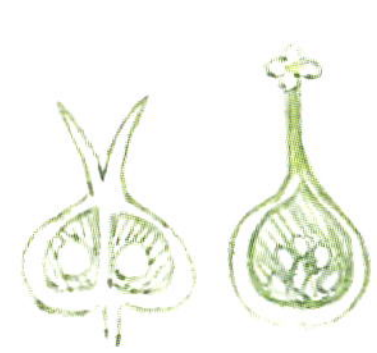

Sections of ovaries.

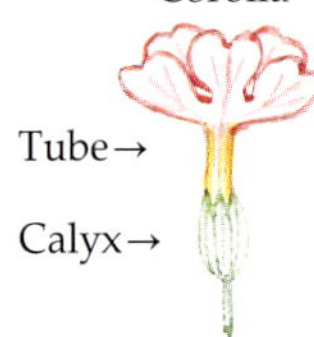

Flower with joined petals forming a tube.

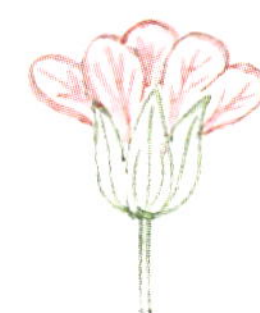

Flower with separate petals.

PERSPECTIVE AND OBSERVATION – PINK FAMILY

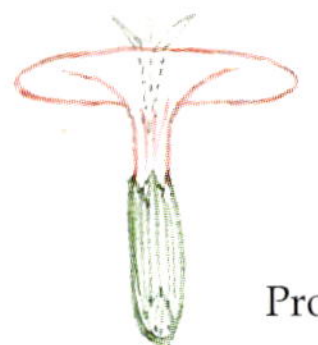

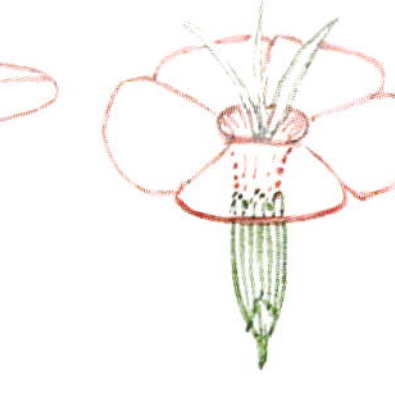

Pretend the flower is made of glass and look through it in order to correctly join the corolla to the tube and the calyx.

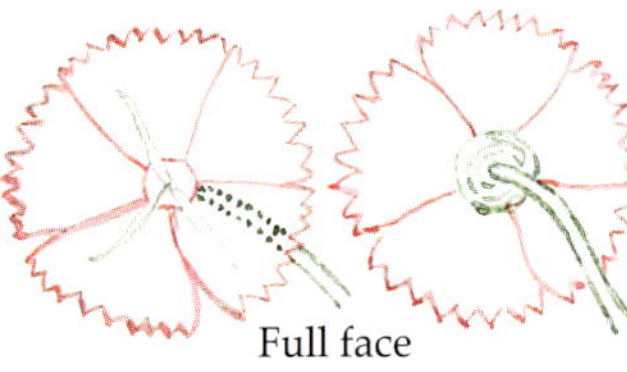

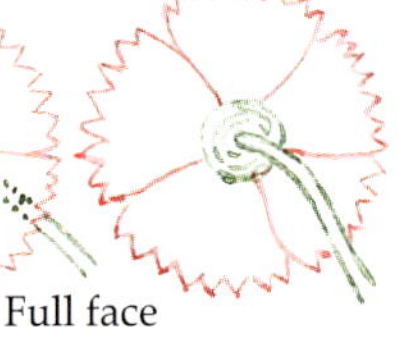

Front view: tube and calyx not visible from the front.

Back view: only calyx visible.

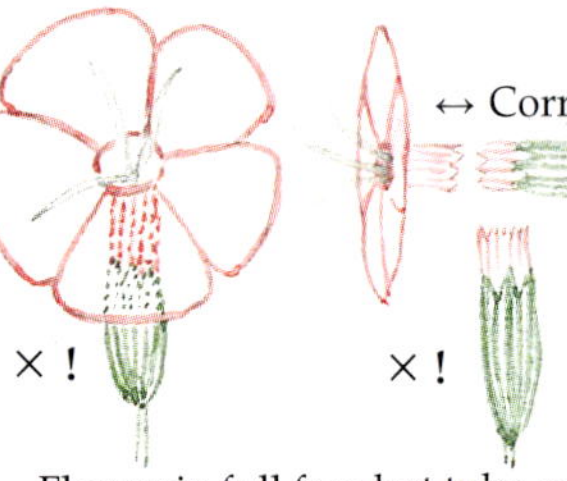

Flower in full face but tube an calyx incorrectly positioned a though in profile. Result – a broken neck!

POSITION AND TYPES OF CALYX

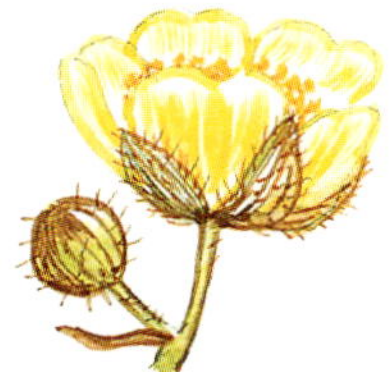

Meadow Buttercup with upright sepals.

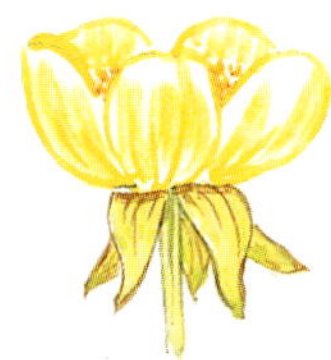

Bulbous Buttercup with turned down sepals.

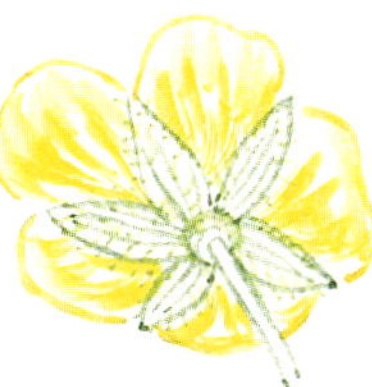

Typical position of sepals *between* the petals.

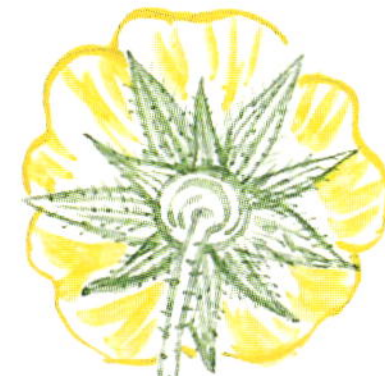

Calyx plus outer epicalyx with the sepals in the middle of the petals.

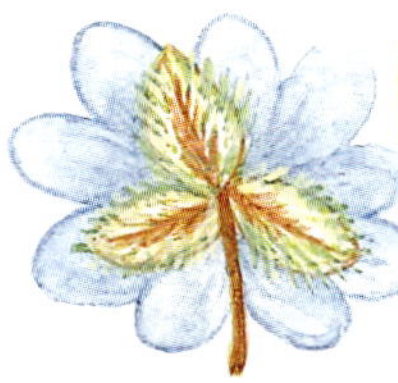

Hepaticas have many petals but only three sepals.

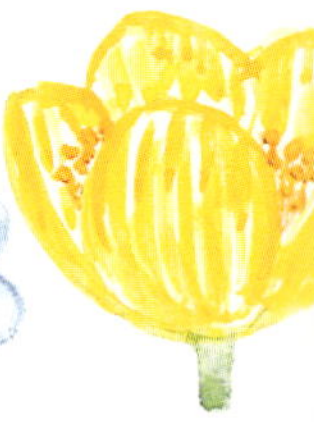

Marsh Marigold typical sepals b yellow petal-lik sepals. Petals ab

PETAL NUMBERS

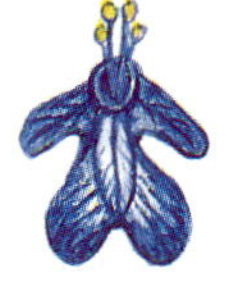

Germanders

1 LIP

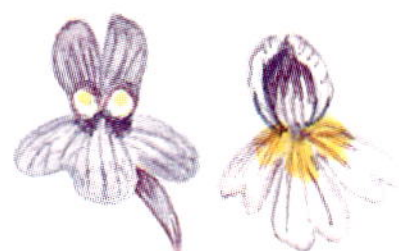

Toadflaxes and Eyebrights

2 LIPS

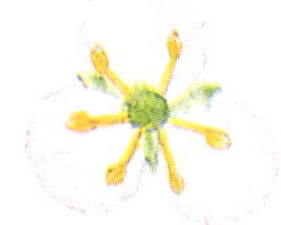

Water Plantains

3 PETALS

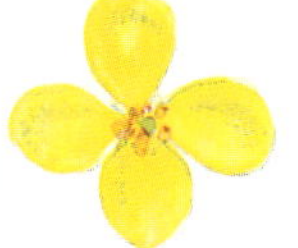

Cabbages

4 PETALS

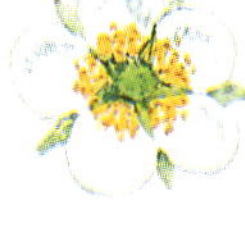

Buttercups

5 PETALS

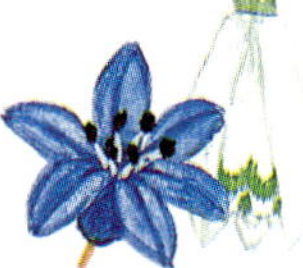

Lilies

6 PETALS

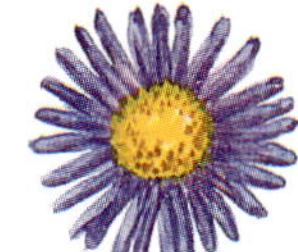

Daisies

MANY PETALS

PETAL SHAPES WITHIN A CIRCLE

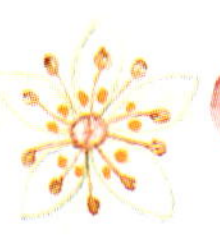

Oval separate

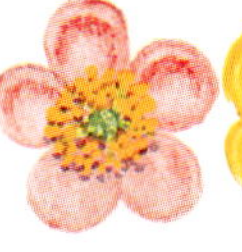

Oval to round touching

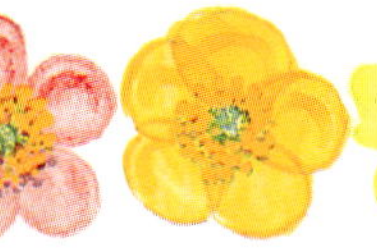

Overlapping

Notched

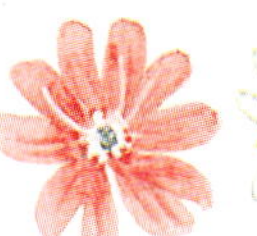

Cleft partway

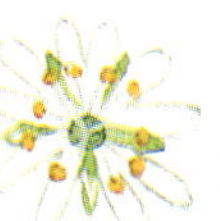

Deeply cleft

Petals joined partway

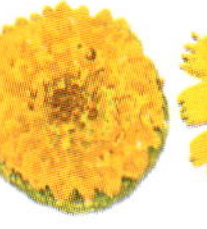

Disc florets

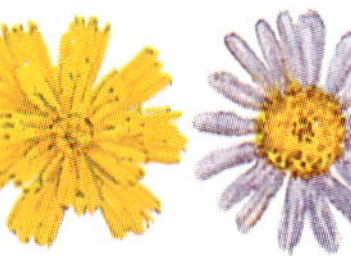

Ray florets

Disc and ray florets

IRREGULAR SHAPES WITHIN A CIRCLE

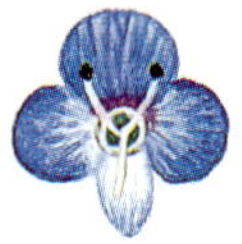

Speedwell

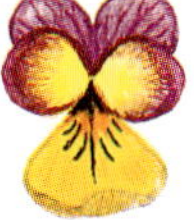

Pansy

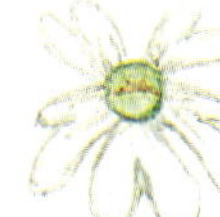

Hogweed

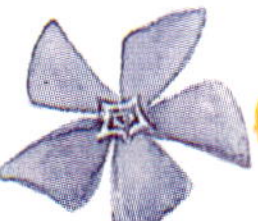

Periwinkle

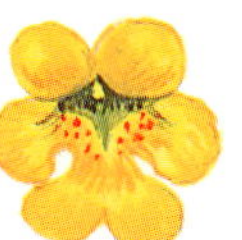

Monkey Flower

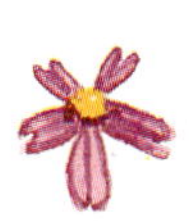

Fairy Foxglove

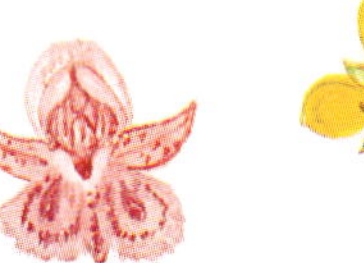

Orchid

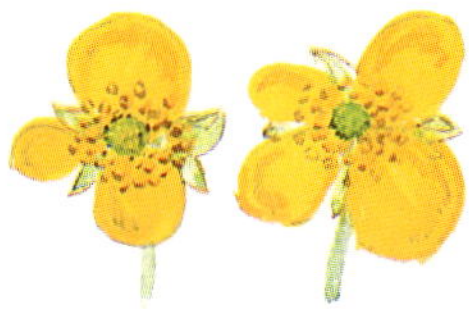

Goldilocks Buttercups hardly ever produce a perfect flower or even the full complement of 5 petals.

UNUSUAL SHAPES

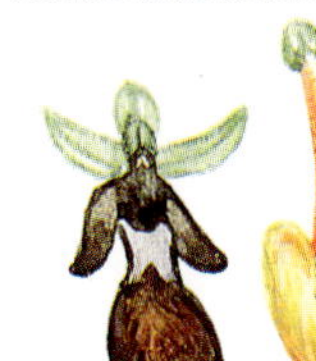

Fly Orchid

Honeysuckle

Foxglove

Monkshood

Corydalis

Pea Family

Touch-me-not

Cyclamen

Bluebell

Harebell

SHAPE OF FLOWERHEADS

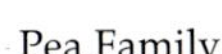

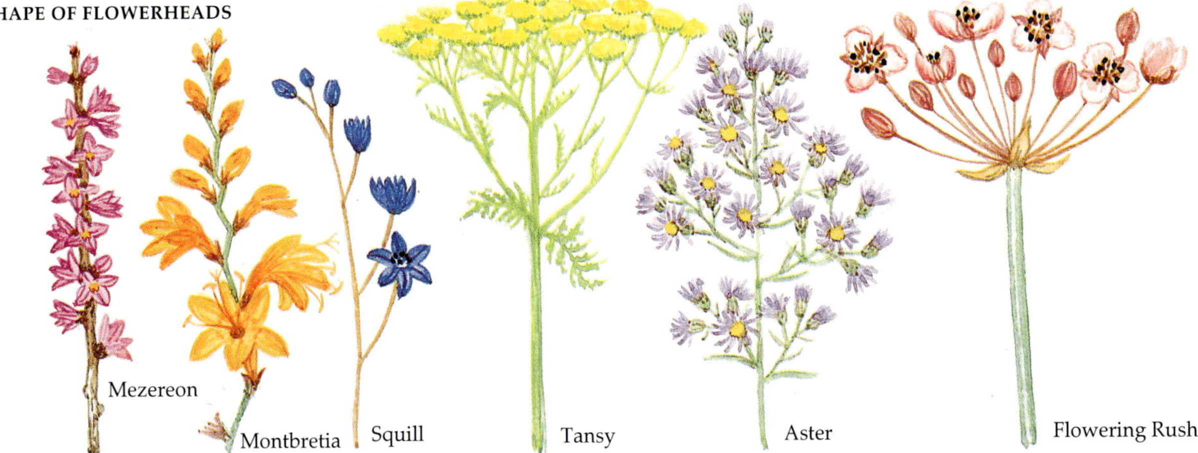

SPIKE — ZIG-ZAG SPIKE: All flowers unstalked.

RACEME: All flowers stalked.

CORYMB: Flowers at the same level.

PANICLE: Informal or loosely branched.

UMBEL: All spoke-like stalks radiate from central point.

THE SHAPE OF LEAVES

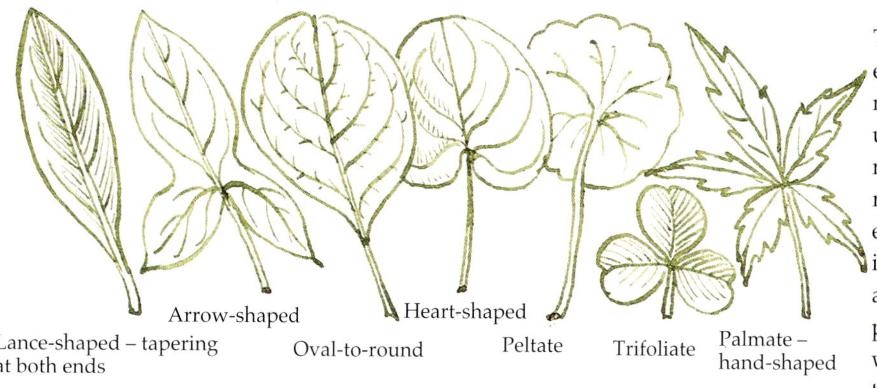

The basic shapes of leaves vary enormously from round to narrow grass-like ones. They are usually flat and thin so that the maximum amount of sunlight can reach the largest areas. To encourage this the plant arranges its leaves in different positions to assist photosynthesis and the production of chlorophyll upon which most plants depend for their existence.

EDGES

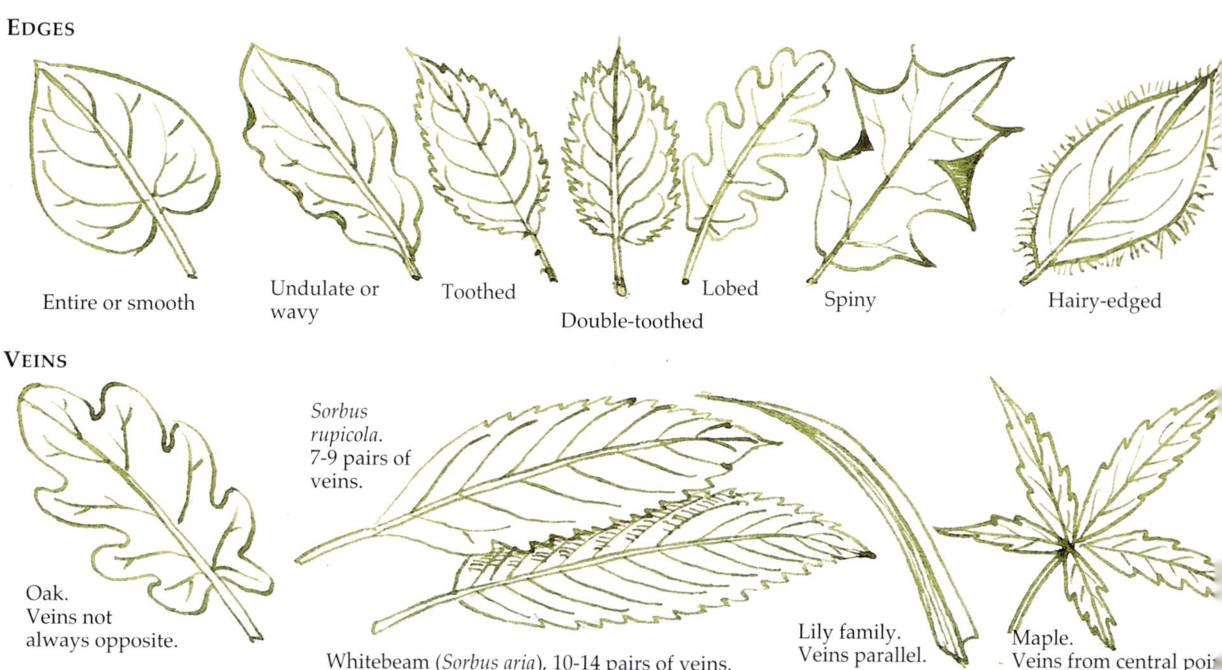

Note their positions and numbers. Some spread out from one point at the base while others spread out on each side of the mid-rib, though some are not opposite each other. It is often necessary to count the veins to help identify different species within one family such as the Sorbus group.

POSITION OF LEAVES

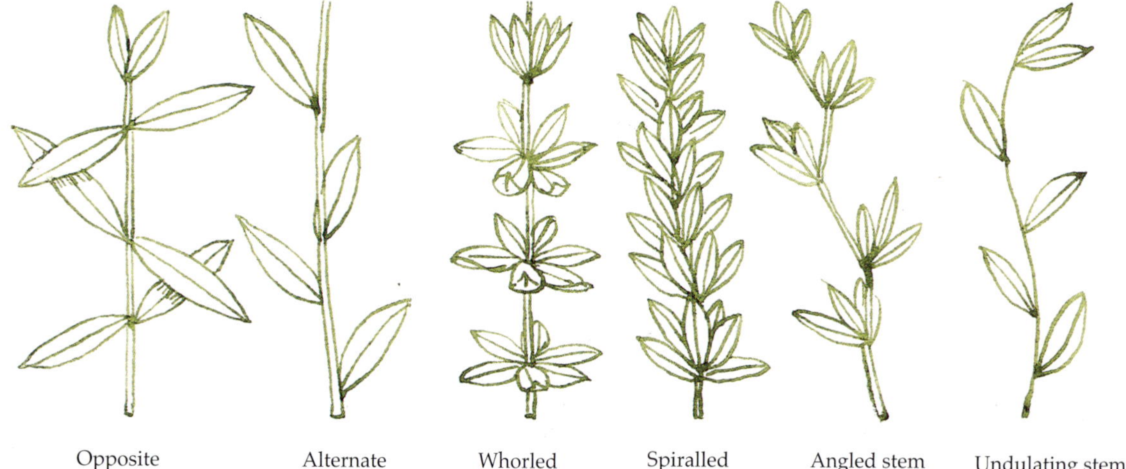

MID-RIBS IN CONTINUOUS CURVES

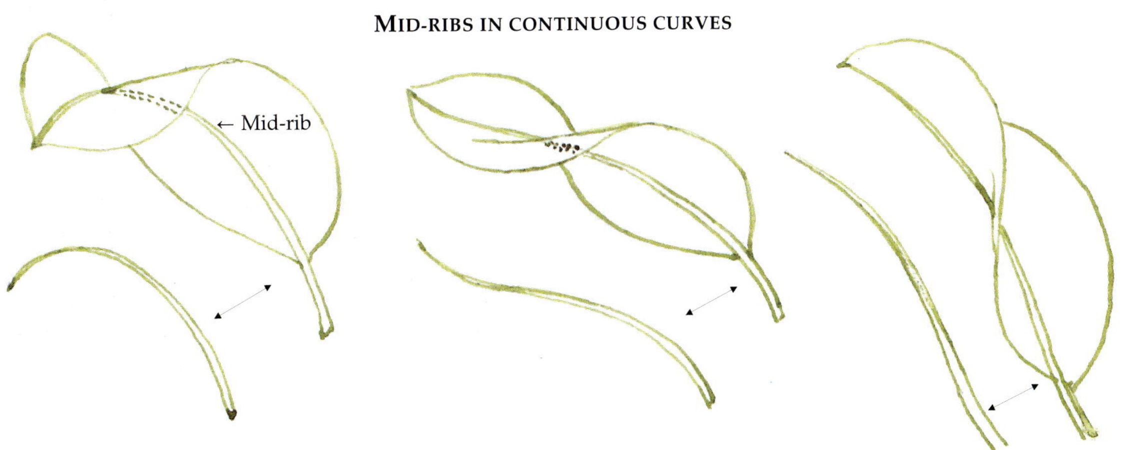

As I have already said about the shape of flowers, imagine that leaves too are made of glass. Look carefully at the curve of the edges and particularly of the mid-rib and check that they follow in one continuous unbroken line.

FRACTURED MID-RIBS

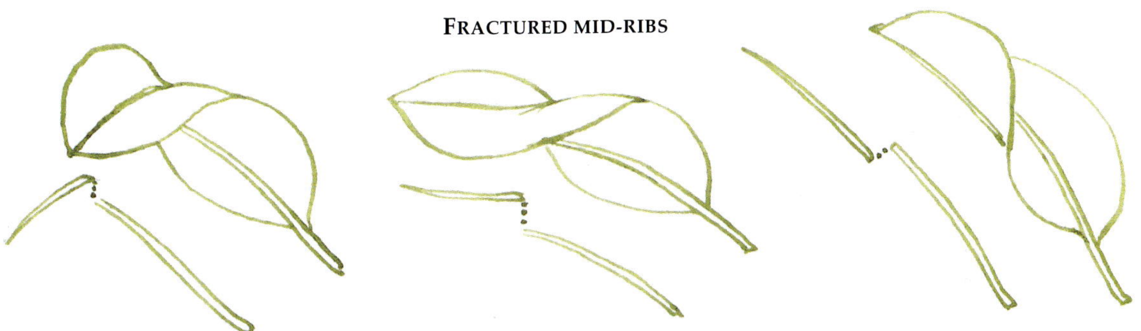

Examples of broken mid-ribs and incorrectly curved leaf edges which do not meet together, with some correctly curved ones to show the difference.

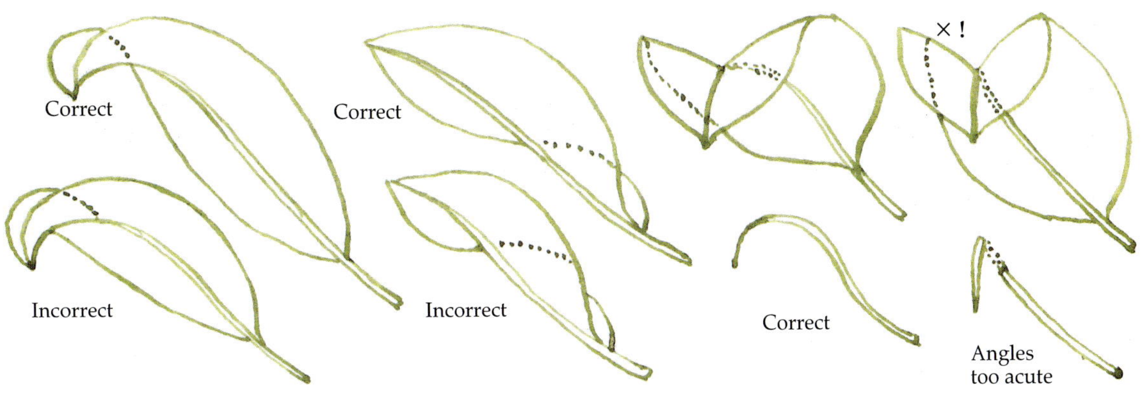

SHAPES AND COVERING OF STEMS

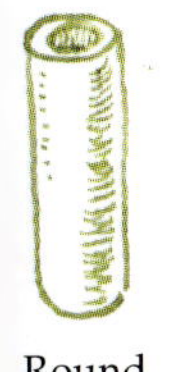
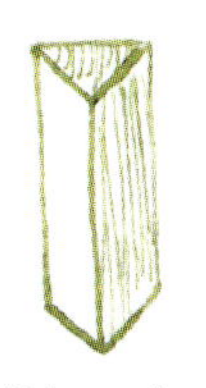
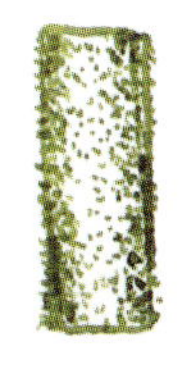
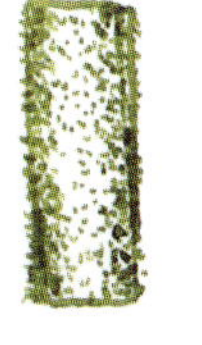
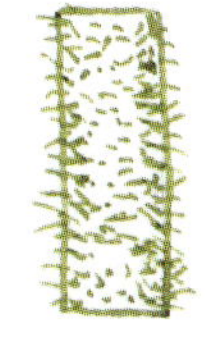
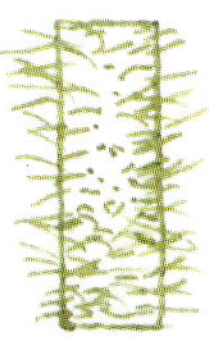
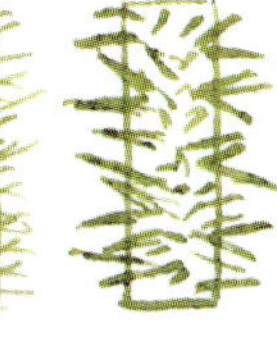
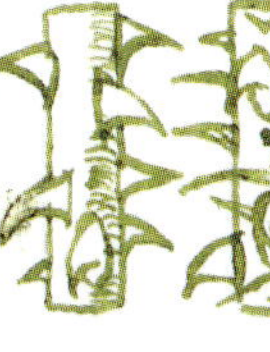
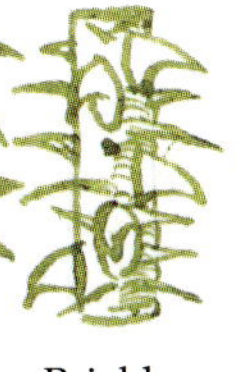
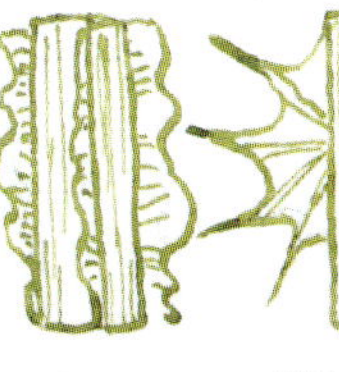

Round | Square and ridged | Triangular | Velvety | Short hairs | Long hairs | Prickles | Thorns | Prickles and thorns | Narrow wings | Wide wings and spines

Making a Start

Start to design a small picture keeping to the most simple pattern possible which can often turn out to be best as well as the easiest to follow. Further ideas on composition and design can be found on pp. 42-44.

Lightly pencil in the lines which will divide your rectangle into 4 small ones of uneven size to remind you not to place a flower exactly in the centre.

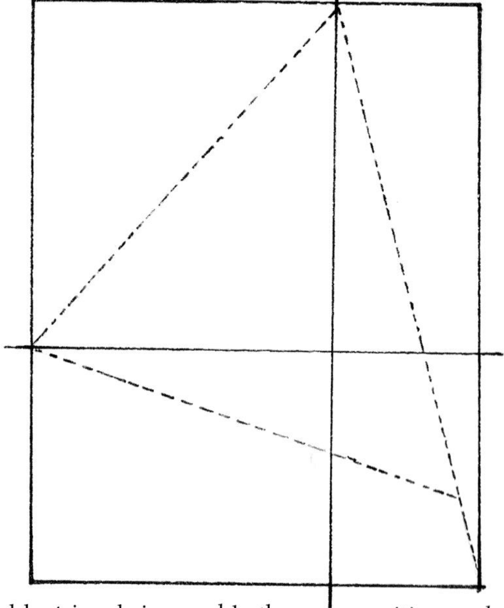

Add a triangle in roughly the same position as shown here – now you have a plan prepared.

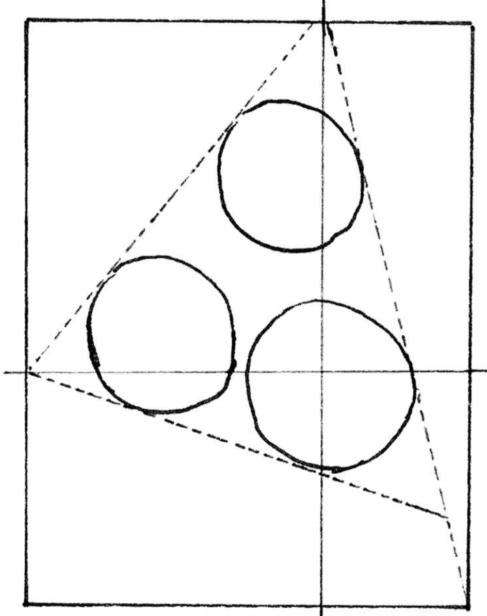

Choose three flowers such as primroses and place the first flower in the lowest corner of the triangle where the two main lines cross. If you have chosen flowers of different sizes put the largest one here to add weight to the base of the picture and the smallest at the top.

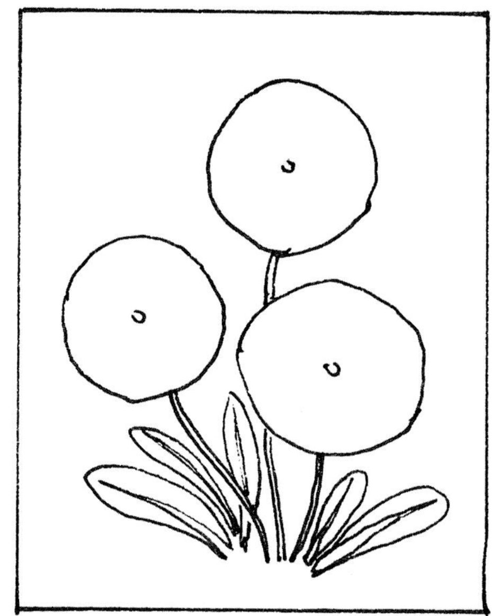

This is always a pleasing shape to look at, unadventurous and unoriginal but good to start with. Such an arrangement requires an odd number of flowers none of which will cut the picture in half or be quite in the middle. Add stems and leaves and again an odd number will fit in well.

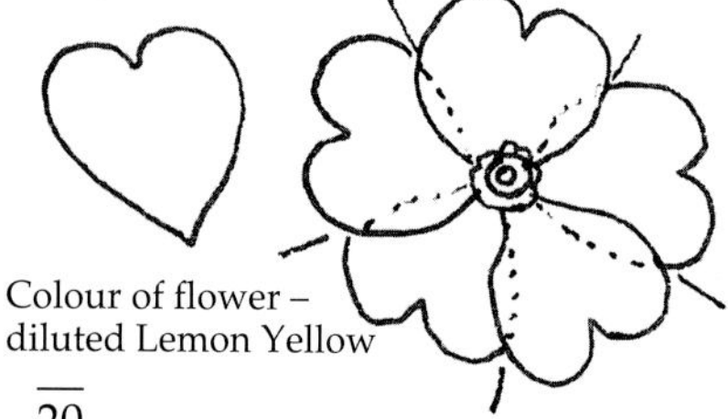

Colour of flower – diluted Lemon Yellow

Lightly mark in the position and shape of the petals within the circles remembering that even in nature they may not be exactly the same and that some may overlap the others.

Regard these examples as one-off exercises and in future dispense with patterns and guide lines and draw freehand for a more natural effect.

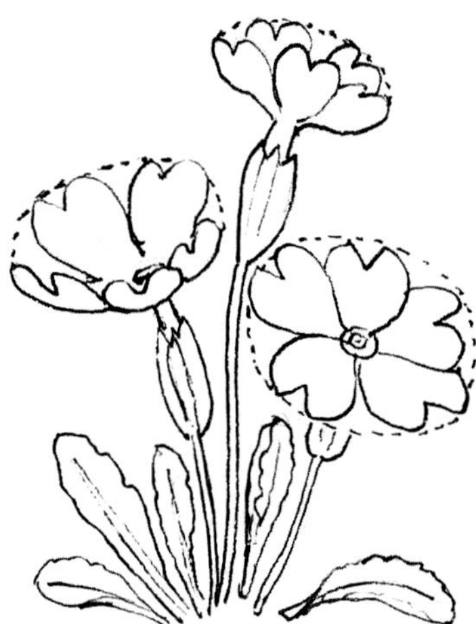

Follow the same design but draw the flowers from different angles remembering to join them to the calyx without breaking their necks (p. 16). A simple rule that must be followed.

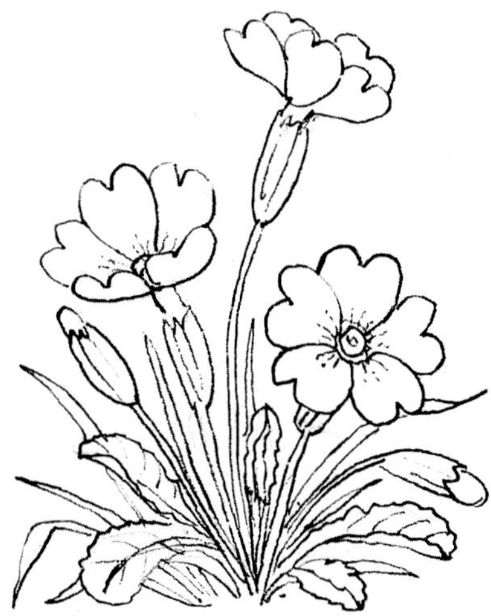

Now gather the stems and leaves together to form a single plant rather than separated parts from one. Add some buds and grasses and it immediately looks more alive.

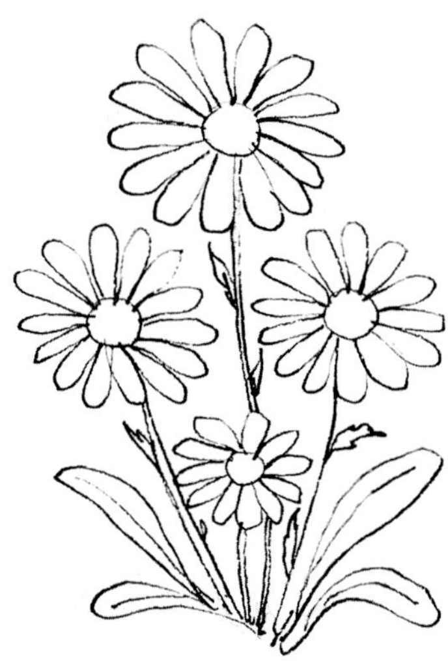

However carefully you arrange an even number of flowers I never think they look satisfactory. Two flowers are even worse than four. This is a bad top-heavy arrangement as I have deliberately put the largest flower in the wrong position. However all rules regarding shape and numbers of flowers can be changed so experiment and choose any design that suits you.

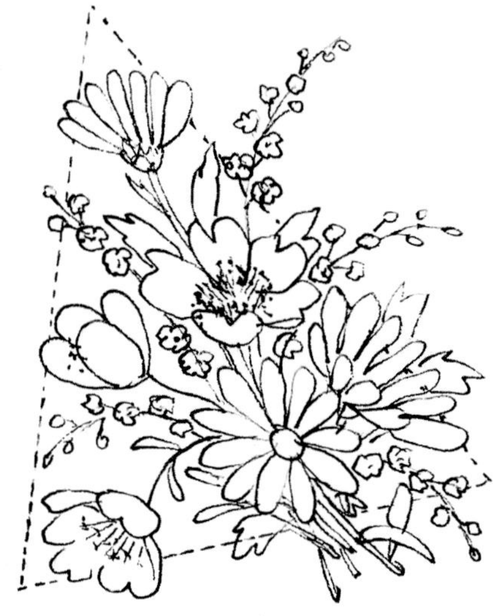

A collection of mixed flowers to paint arranged in a loose flowing way but still within a triangle allowing a few small spikes to wander outside. Where there are many flowers the odd number need not apply but place some of the largest near the base to balance the whole – and to cover up some of the stems which are often too numerous and stiff to arrange satisfactorily.

You can follow the progress of primroses in this book from pencil drawings on p. 25 to the first painting on p. 48 and finally a completed painting of a plant with flowers and buds facing in all directions on p. 54.

TRACING FLOWERS

THE EASY WAY TO START

Many beginners tell me they cannot draw from living plants because they are not sure how to start and find it easier to copy illustrations from books. Although I always stress that this should not become a habit I quite understand their fear of committing their first efforts to paper. If you still feel like this I suggest you trace these simple outlines I have drawn and look on the exercise as a bridge to assist you to cross from copying to original sketches which you will find far more rewarding.

First draw the outlines on tracing paper then scribble on the back with a soft pencil. Using a hard pencil transfer the image to your sketch pad by redrawing the lines. Draw the outlines many times arranging and rearranging their positions until you are familiar with them and are happy with the design and shape of your picture. Finally try drawing some of them freehand and if you want to paint your flowers see p. 44 for easy stages to colour work.

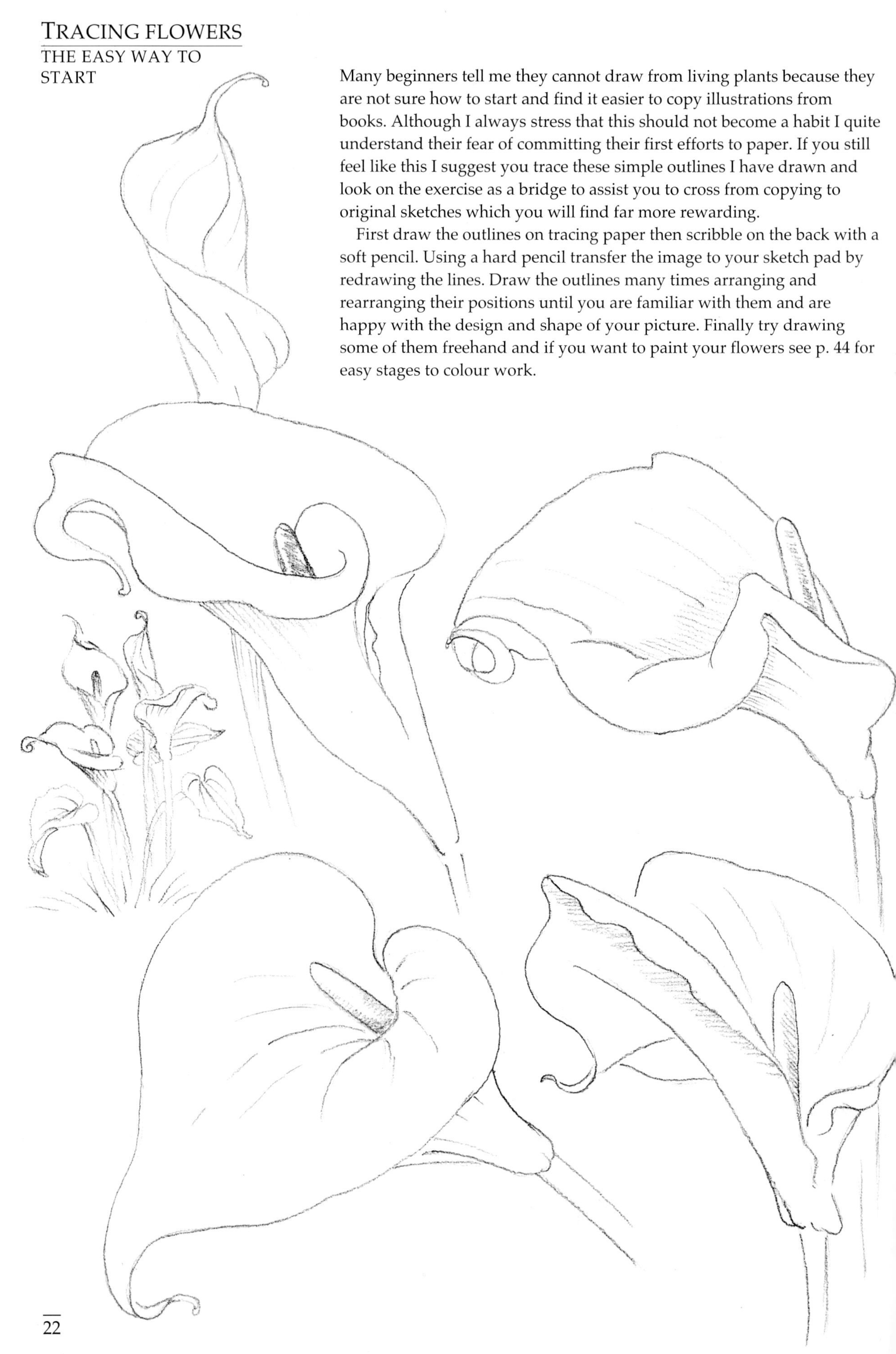

A quick sketch often looks far more natural than a slow carefully executed study of a too-perfect flower which resembles a pressed specimen with no life in it. Don't be in too much of a hurry to move on to painting, you may find that the much neglected art of pencil sketching as fascinating as I do, as well as being quick and easy when working outdoors. Turn flowers in all direction sketching as you do so and at the same time observe all the essential points such as the calyx and the buds. When you decide to paint an Ox-eye Daisy see p. 44.

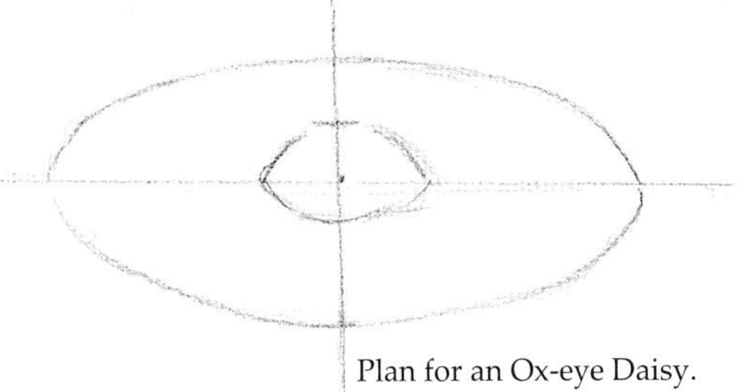

Plan for an Ox-eye Daisy.

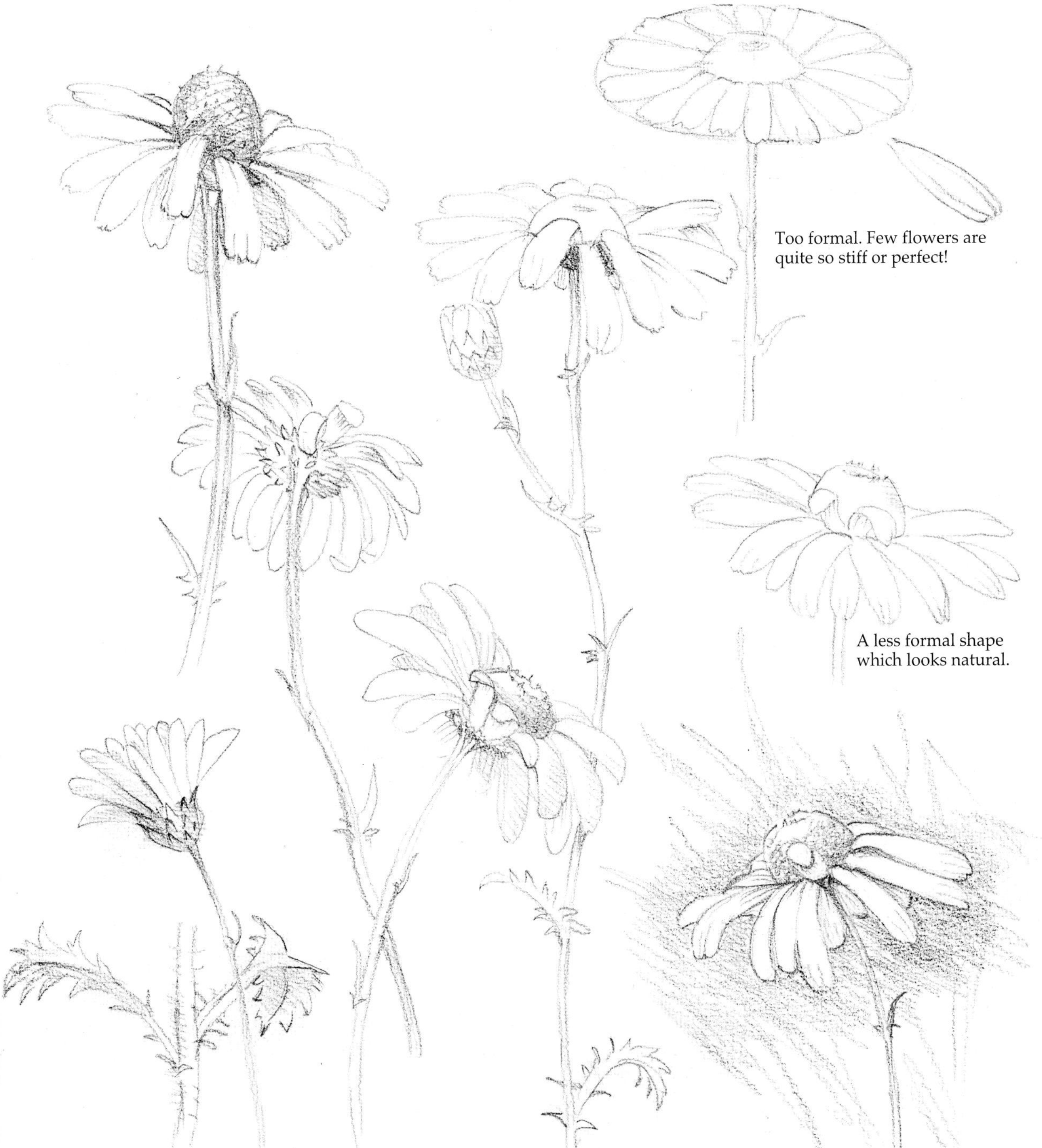

Too formal. Few flowers are quite so stiff or perfect!

A less formal shape which looks natural.

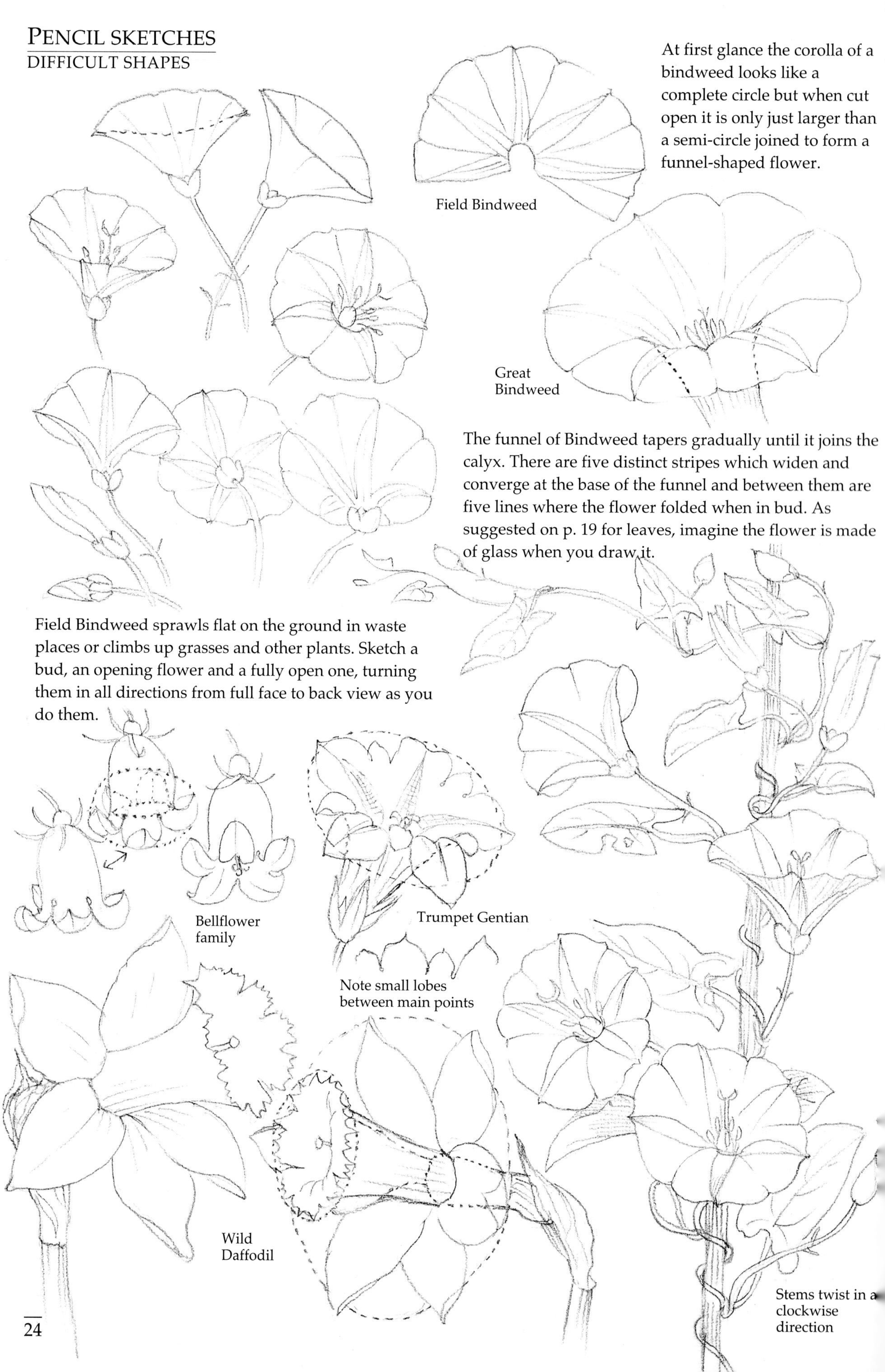

At first glance the corolla of a bindweed looks like a complete circle but when cut open it is only just larger than a semi-circle joined to form a funnel-shaped flower.
Field Bindweed
Great Bindweed
The funnel of Bindweed tapers gradually until it joins the calyx. There are five distinct stripes which widen and converge at the base of the funnel and between them are five lines where the flower folded when in bud. As suggested on p. 19 for leaves, imagine the flower is made of glass when you draw it.
Field Bindweed sprawls flat on the ground in waste places or climbs up grasses and other plants. Sketch a bud, an opening flower and a fully open one, turning them in all directions from full face to back view as you do them.
Bellflower family
Trumpet Gentian
Note small lobes between main points
Wild Daffodil
Stems twist in a clockwise direction

Still continue to sketch as many flowers as you can find – mainly in outline to begin with, which often looks most attractive in an uncluttered way, with nothing to distract the eye from seeing the essential shape of the flowers, all of which have their own personality.

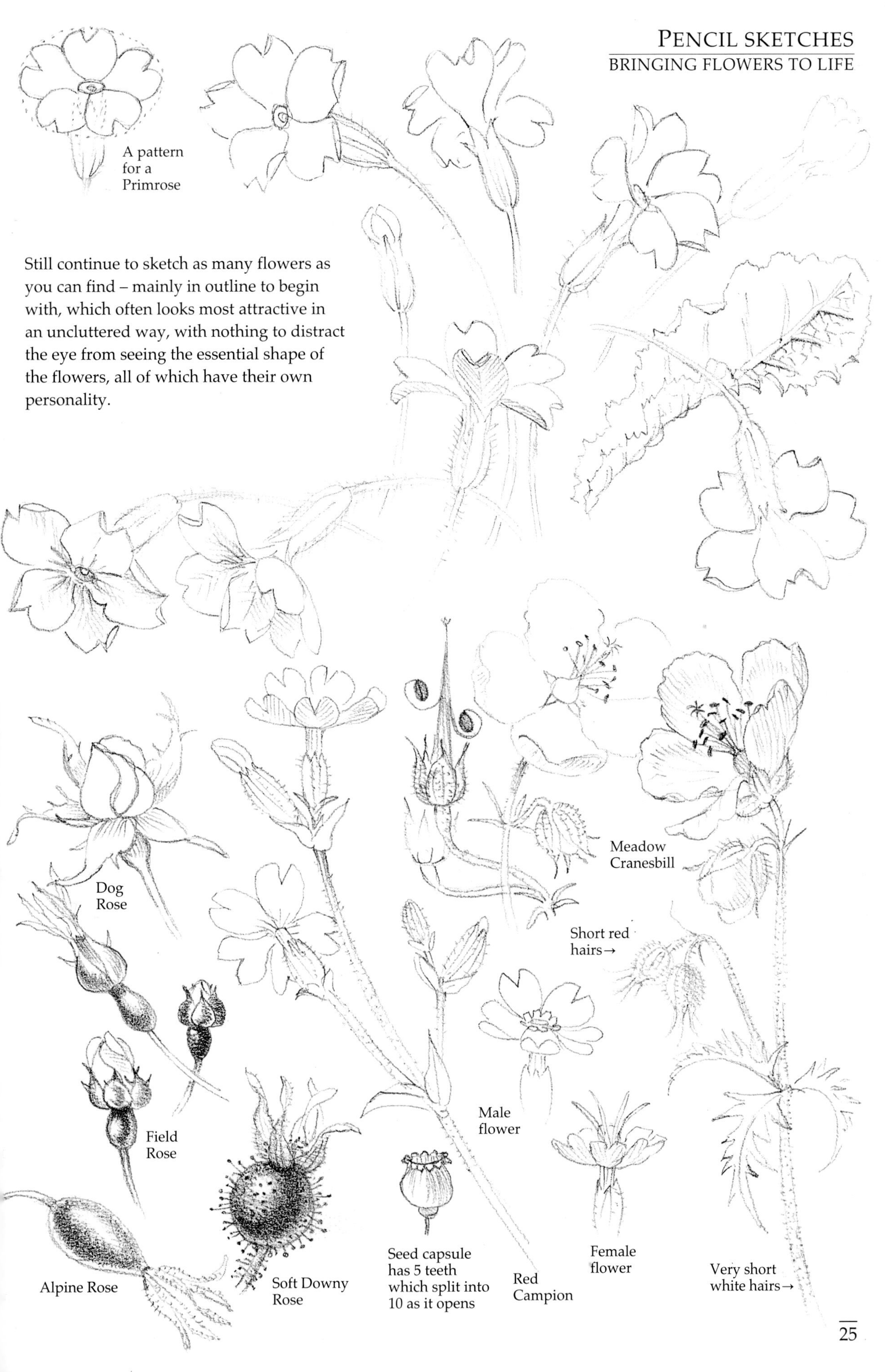

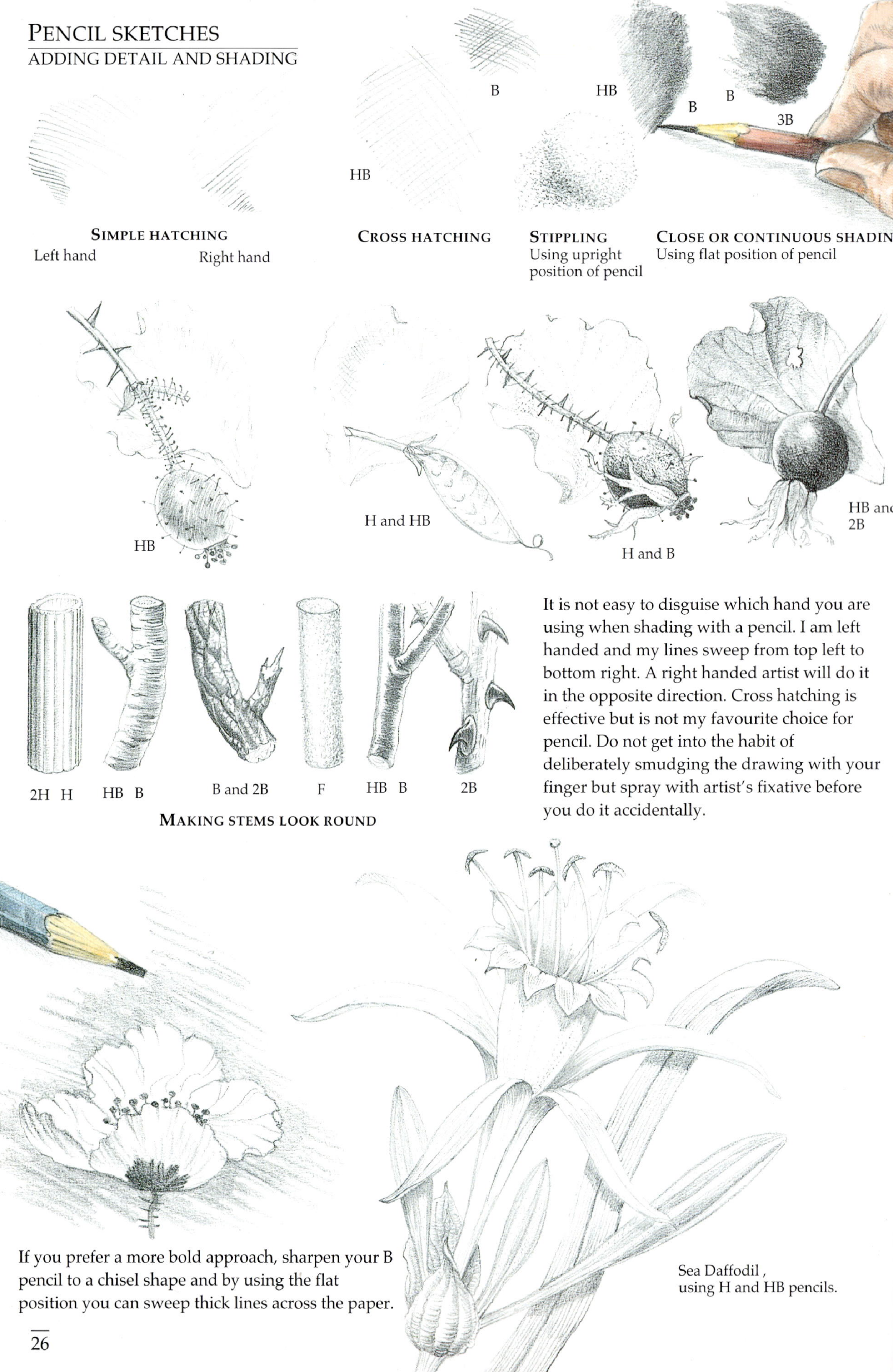

It is not easy to disguise which hand you are using when shading with a pencil. I am left handed and my lines sweep from top left to bottom right. A right handed artist will do it in the opposite direction. Cross hatching is effective but is not my favourite choice for pencil. Do not get into the habit of deliberately smudging the drawing with your finger but spray with artist's fixative before you do it accidentally.

If you prefer a more bold approach, sharpen your B pencil to a chisel shape and by using the flat position you can sweep thick lines across the paper.

Sea Daffodil ,
using H and HB pencils.

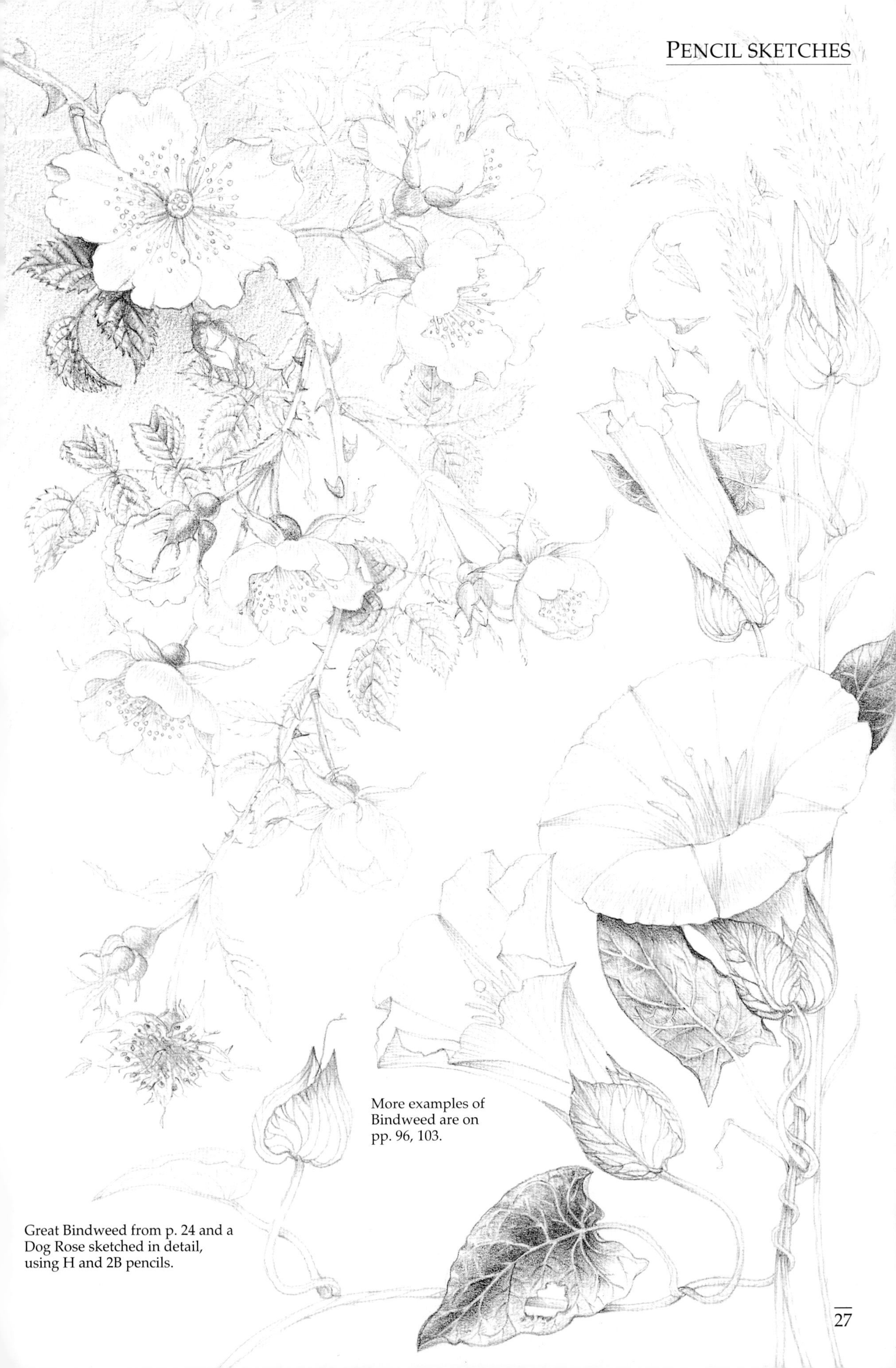

More examples of Bindweed are on pp. 96, 103.

Great Bindweed from p. 24 and a Dog Rose sketched in detail, using H and 2B pencils.

Pencil sketches – leaves

Adding detail and shading

The same techniques for shading flowers can be applied to leaves but in a less delicate manner and with even more variety which for me gives great satisfaction because not only can you add deeper tones of 'colour' but also show highlights from the merest sheen to the high gloss of Camellia leaves without the use of paint which I find most exciting. Whereas with paint you can apply a few quick washes and only a suggestion of veins and shadows and still show the character of the leaf by its very shape and colour, with pencil a 'wash' of grey is not usually sufficient and more detail is required.

Hazel

Stage 1 Stage 2 Stage 3

This type of leaf gives you the chance to use soft B pencils which are too dark for most flowers. Some people may say the final result is like a black and white photograph which has taken a long time to produce but you can stop at any stage so how much detail is applied is up to you. I like to do leaves in the foreground in full detail but allow those in the background to recede by using less and less shading until they are just a pale outline almost out of focus.

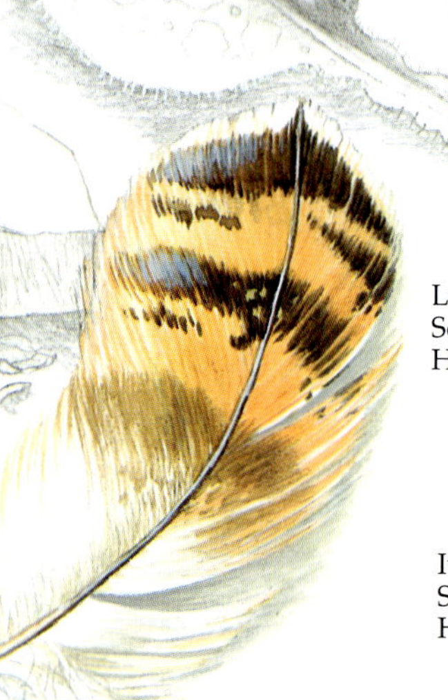

Lungwort.
Soft and hairy
HB and B.

Camellia.
Glossy
HB to 2B.

Ivy.
Slightly shiny
HB to 5B.

Bugloss.
Bristly
HB and H.

Holly.
Very shiny
B and 5B.

Soft plastic-type erasers can be cut to a point or wedge with a knife. If you get bits of rubber on your drawing a feather is good for brushing them away without smudging the picture. Duck or pigeon wing feathers are ideal or softer ones like my beautifully coloured Great Bustard feather. Wash your feather regularly. Remember that the softer the pencil the more easily it will smudge.

Spear
Thistle.
Hairy and spiny
H and HB.

Wood
Sage

Meadow
Clary

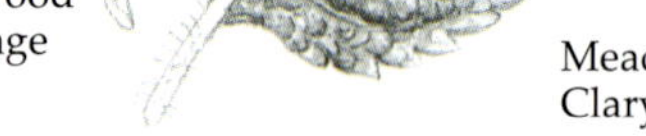

Wrinkled HB to 2B

The underside of some leaves show the veins in high relief and when drawing plants such as Hazel, Blackberry or Lime it adds interest to show some leaves from the back. Lungworts and Camellias have all the interesting parts on the top and are merely pale green underneath with hardly any veins showing, more interesting to do in paint than in pencil.

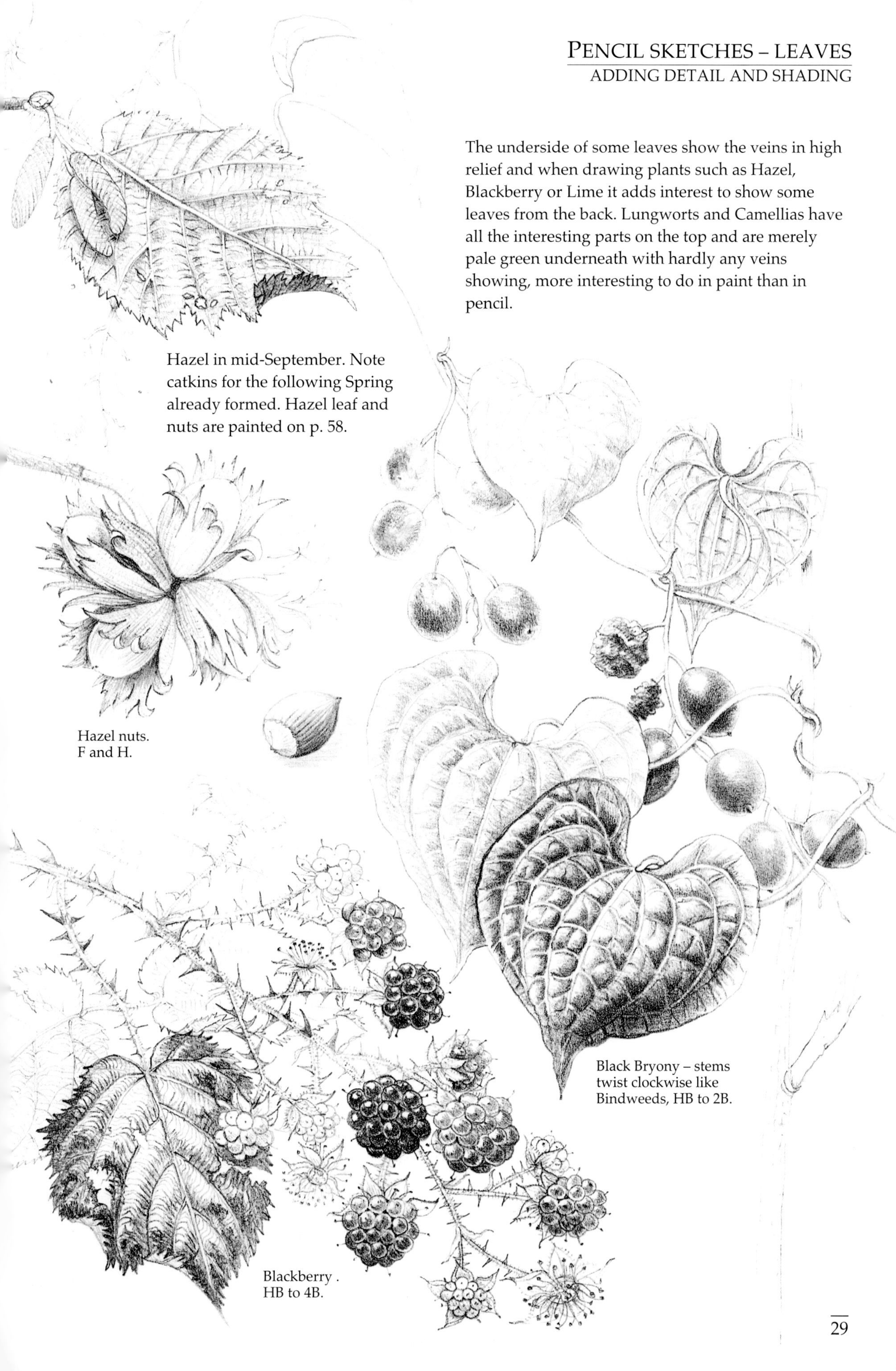

Hazel in mid-September. Note catkins for the following Spring already formed. Hazel leaf and nuts are painted on p. 58.

Hazel nuts.
F and H.

Black Bryony – stems twist clockwise like Bindweeds, HB to 2B.

Blackberry .
HB to 4B.

PEN AND INKS

BLACK INK

Much the same techniques for pencil drawing can be applied to pen and ink, varying from simple outlines to more detailed sketches.

Bearing in mind that unlike pencil you only have two choices, black or white, with no intermediate shades of grey it is often more effective when doing flowers to understate the shading, as too much detail can look heavy or fussy.

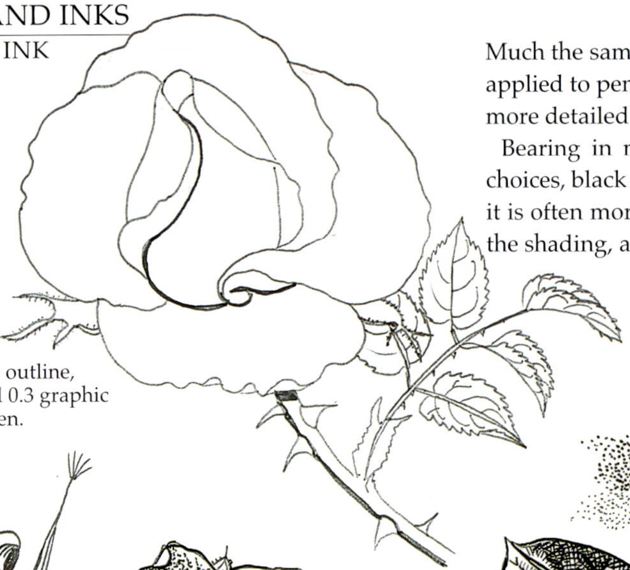

Simple outline, 0.1 and 0.3 graphic liner pen.

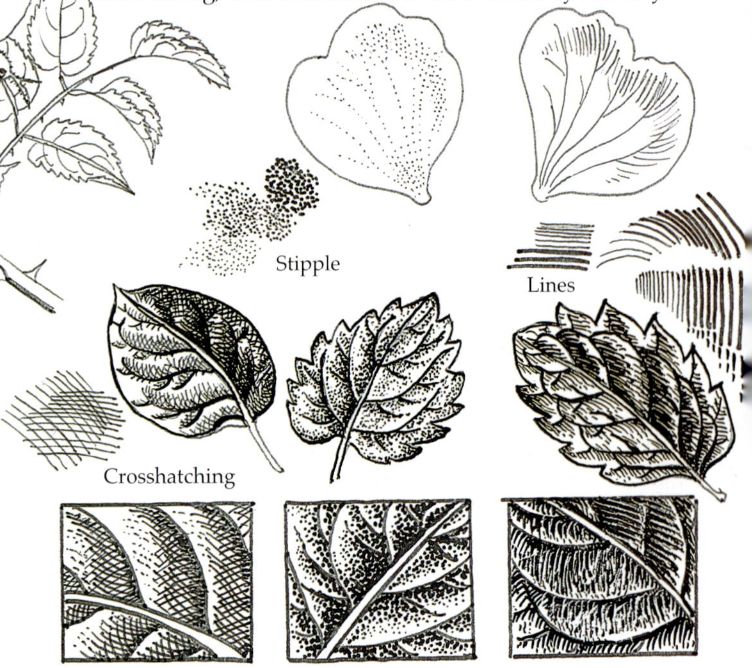

Stipple

Lines

Crosshatching

Details enlarged. If your drawing is to be published, it is best to work 1½ times larger than is required so that when reduced the lines and shading become very fine which improves the overall effect.

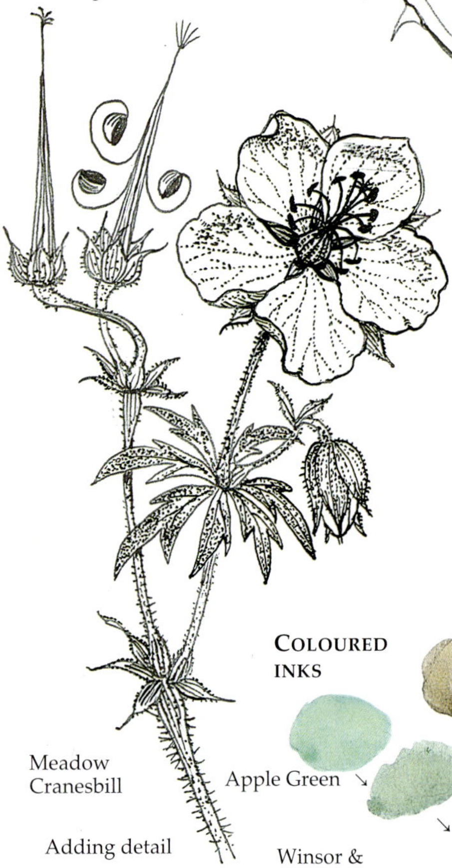

Meadow Cranesbill

Adding detail

COLOURED INKS

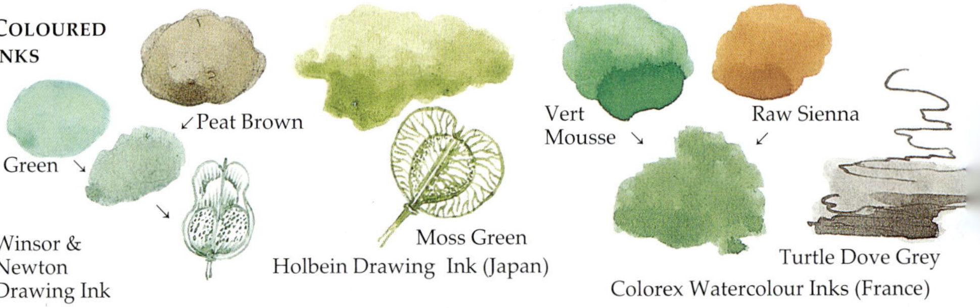

Apple Green

Peat Brown

Winsor & Newton Drawing Ink

Moss Green

Holbein Drawing Ink (Japan)

Vert Mousse

Raw Sienna

Turtle Dove Grey

Colorex Watercolour Inks (France)

Choose the type of pen that suits you, from fine to broad and start by outlining your sketch using a 2H pencil which will not smudge and can be easily erased after the ink is completely dry.

There are a great variety of coloured inks, all of which can be mixed or diluted with water, though remember that permanence is not claimed by the various makers. Some greens are rather too brightly coloured to be used for leaves but can be improved by adding brown. A complete drawing in either green, brown or grey can look very attractive as an alternative to black. Other colours are manufactured to 'dazzle' the eye and are more suitable for posters than delicate flower studies but all can be diluted and painted in washes using a brush and will take successive layers of colour.

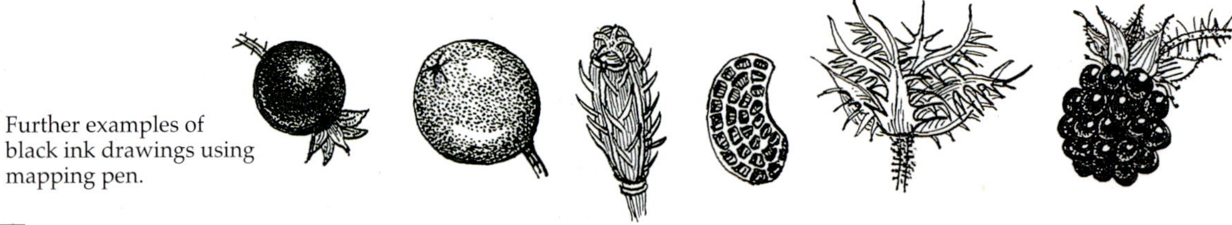

Further examples of black ink drawings using mapping pen.

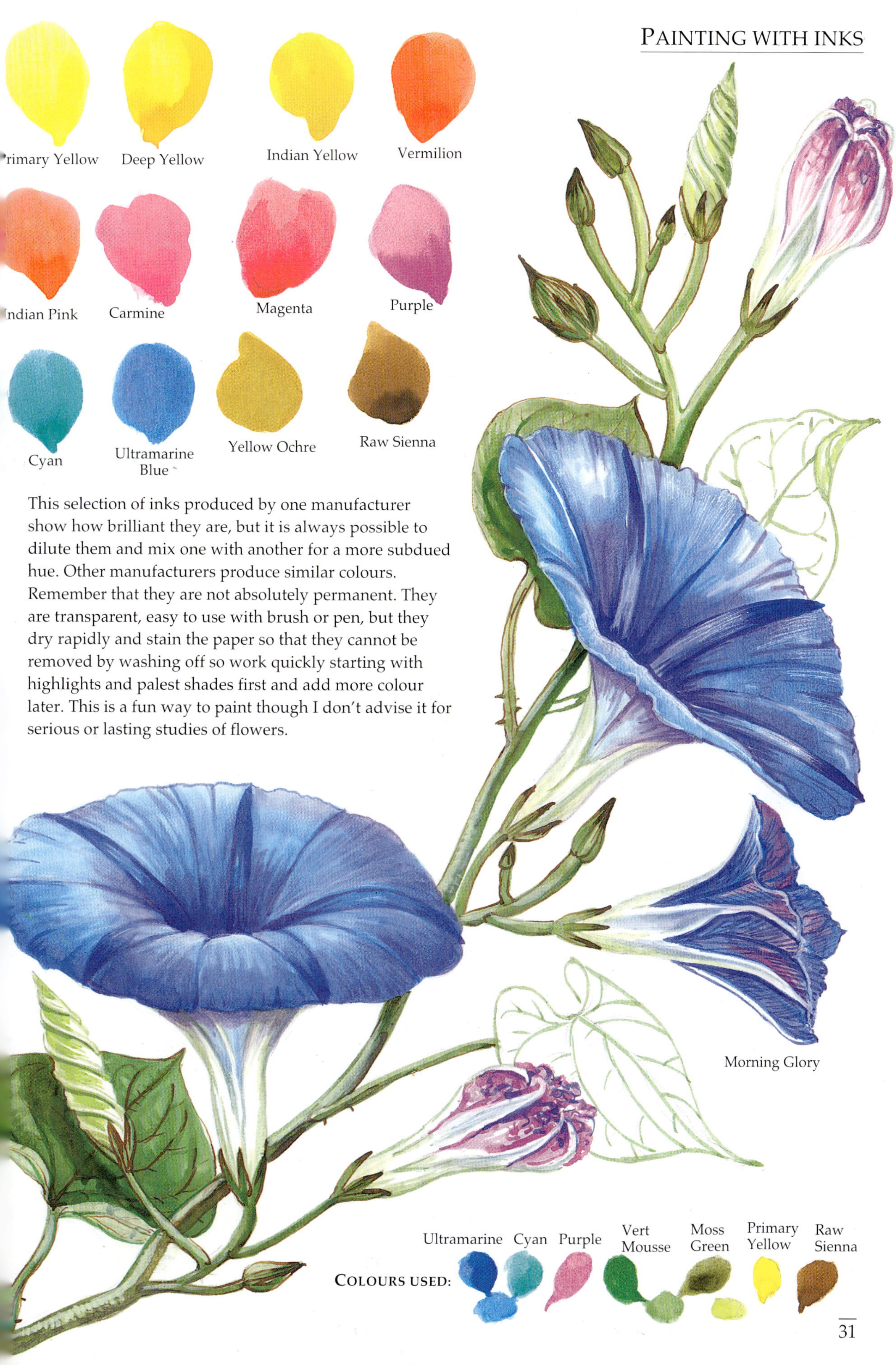

This selection of inks produced by one manufacturer show how brilliant they are, but it is always possible to dilute them and mix one with another for a more subdued hue. Other manufacturers produce similar colours. Remember that they are not absolutely permanent. They are transparent, easy to use with brush or pen, but they dry rapidly and stain the paper so that they cannot be removed by washing off so work quickly starting with highlights and palest shades first and add more colour later. This is a fun way to paint though I don't advise it for serious or lasting studies of flowers.

Morning Glory

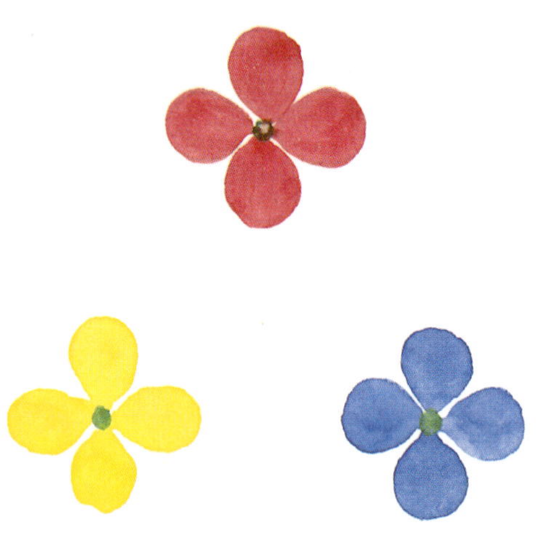

The three primary colours, so called because they cannot be mixed from any other colour.

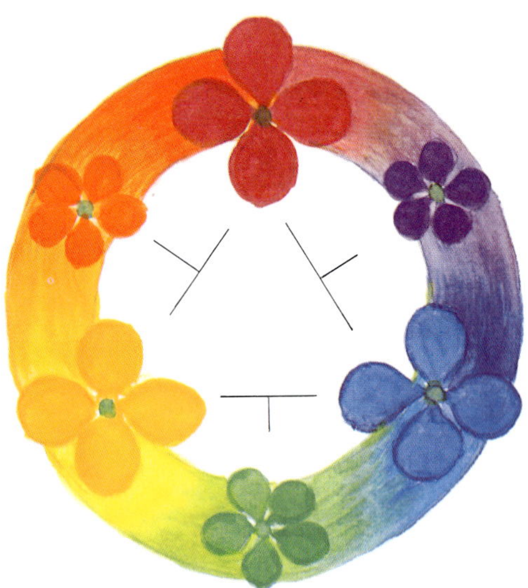

A rainbow of colours showing how a mixture of the primary ones produces secondary colours.

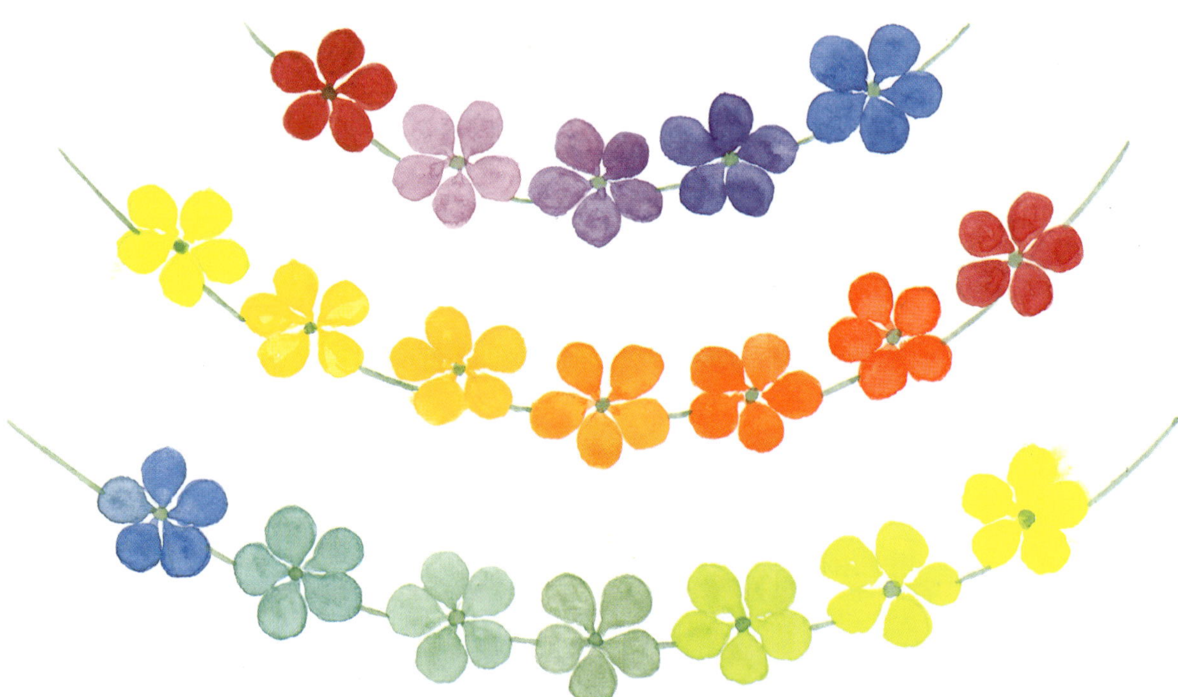

EASY MIXES

Three necklaces of flowers showing the primary colours graded from pale to deep tones and changing in the middle as a second primary colour is introduced and mixes in. These are easy colours to mix and produce clean clear shades and so choose them in preference to any others when you first start to practise mixing your own paints.

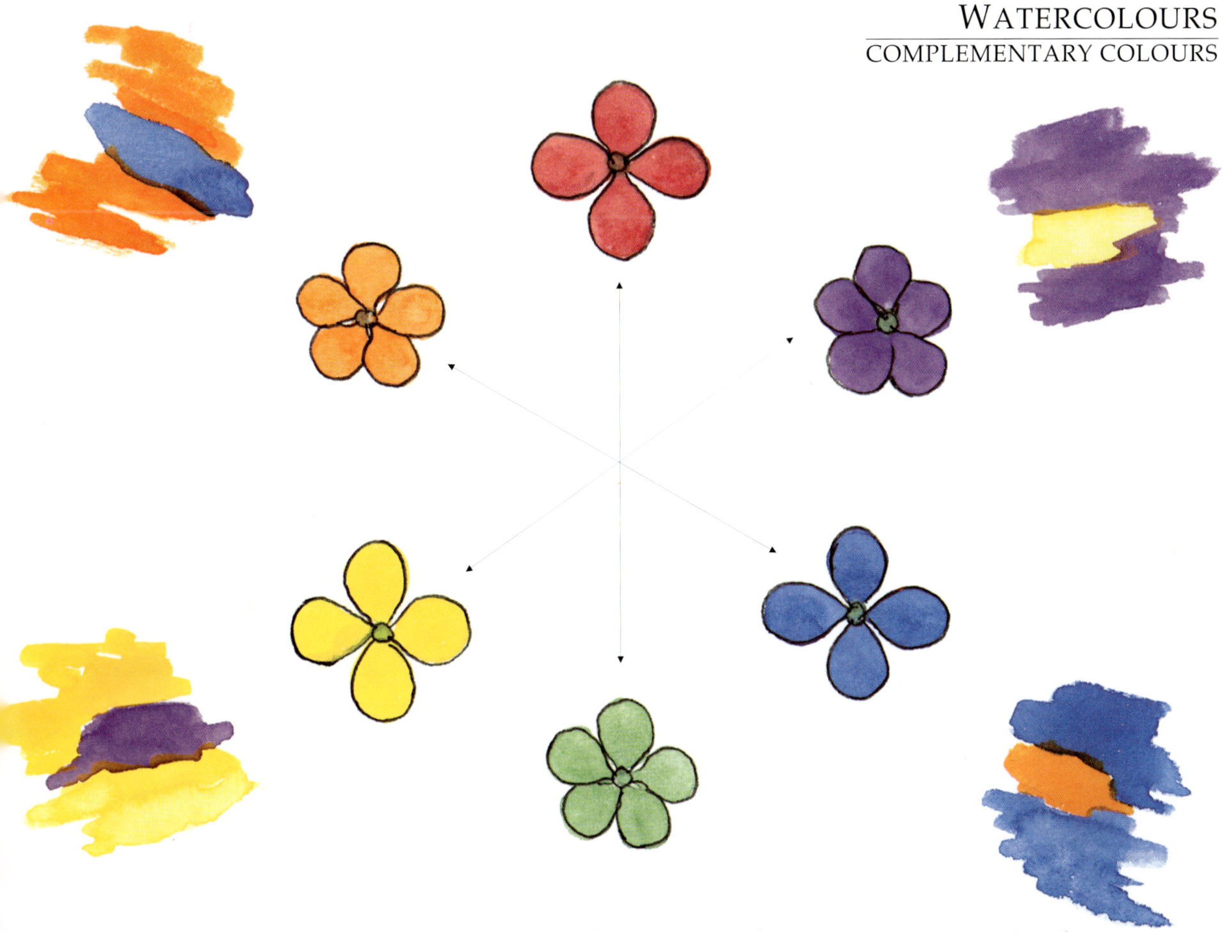

Pick out the primary and secondary colours from the rainbow on the opposite page and look at them in isolation. You will find that the standard complementary colours are opposite each other. These pairs of colours cannot be mixed together or the result will be mud – unless that is the shade you want! If placed side by side however each will improve the impact of the other whether you are thinking of neighbouring plants in a garden or curtains next to a wall. Red is the complementary colour to green, a hot colour next to a cool. Red can be overpowering next to pastel shades, but if leaves separate them it is acceptable.

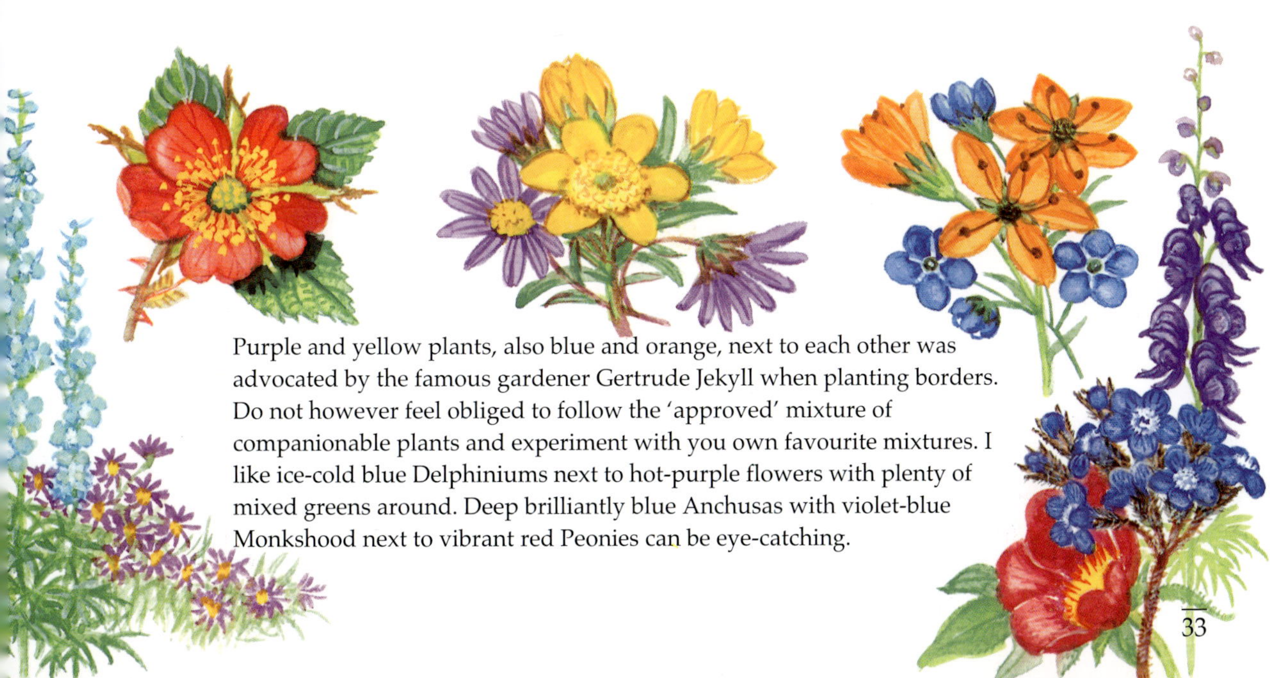

Purple and yellow plants, also blue and orange, next to each other was advocated by the famous gardener Gertrude Jekyll when planting borders. Do not however feel obliged to follow the 'approved' mixture of companionable plants and experiment with you own favourite mixtures. I like ice-cold blue Delphiniums next to hot-purple flowers with plenty of mixed greens around. Deep brilliantly blue Anchusas with violet-blue Monkshood next to vibrant red Peonies can be eye-catching.

WATERCOLOURS FOR THE FLOWER PAINTER

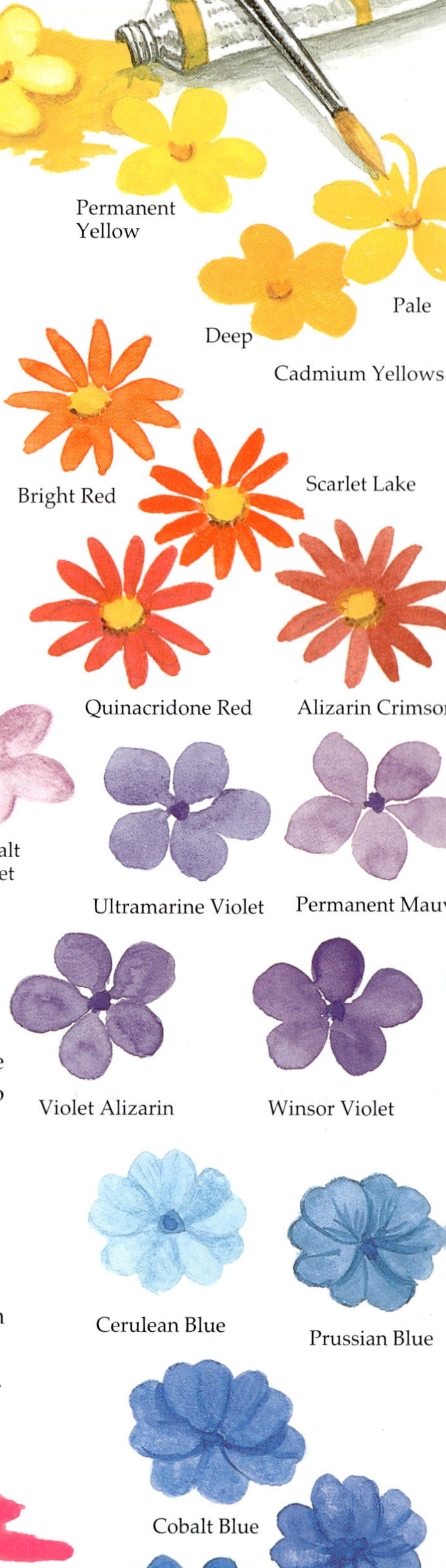

Watercolour is the most beautiful medium invented for portraying delicate and small flowers, transparent, clean and easy to use. Well known manufacturers market around 100 colours. The names may vary but the colours are much the same and there are far more than the average artist requires. In spite of the number you will get great satisfaction when you learn to mix your own paints. If possible buy Artist's quality and then you will discover the sheer pleasure of being able to spread a transparent swirl of scarlet over the paper and find that you have before you the petal of a poppy as thin and glowing as silk. Buy only a limited number of colours to begin with, either in half pans which are usually large enough, or in tubes which may hold too much and eventually go dry. If they do it is a simple matter to slit the soft metal down the length of the tube and turn back the edges and use it as a pan and then roll them back!

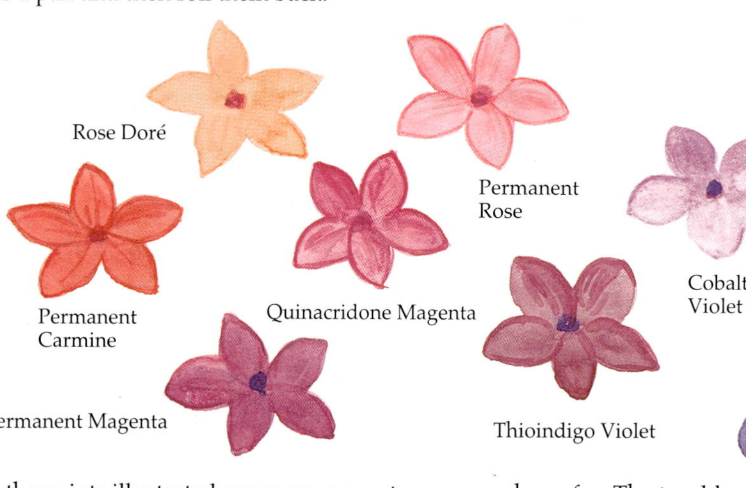

All the paints illustrated are as permanent as one can hope for. The trouble arises if the artist wants to use what I call 'problem pinks', from carmine to magenta. Nature favours these shades more than most and until recently man could not match these pinks in brilliance or permanence. The latest pinks which Winsor and Newton market have been produced with the flower painter in mind. They are shown above but a pure carmine is still elusive. Perhaps it is more acceptable in a painting to aim for a softer shade for these over-bright flowers. If it is essential to achieve the exact colour when illustrating a book for instance, there are fugitive paints, often in the gouache range or in inks which can be used. The original art work will fade in time but the illustration in the book will be fixed for far longer.

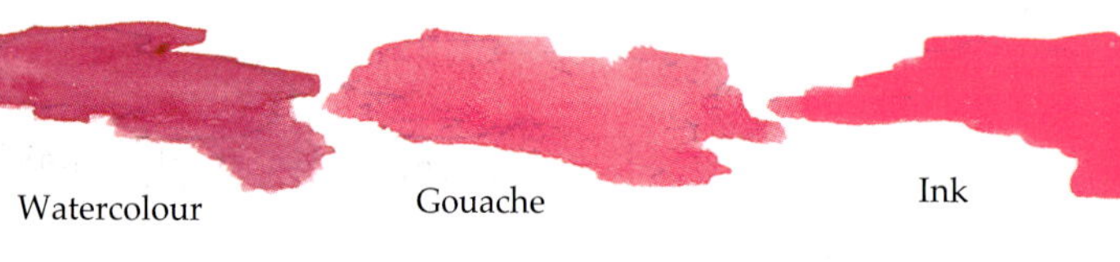

Three different media showing how difficult it is to achieve the correct colours within the 'problem pink' range. Carmine and magenta watercolours look good while wet but dry a little dull. Inks and some pink gouache (see chart of colours on p. 126) are perfect but somewhat brash and are not permanent.

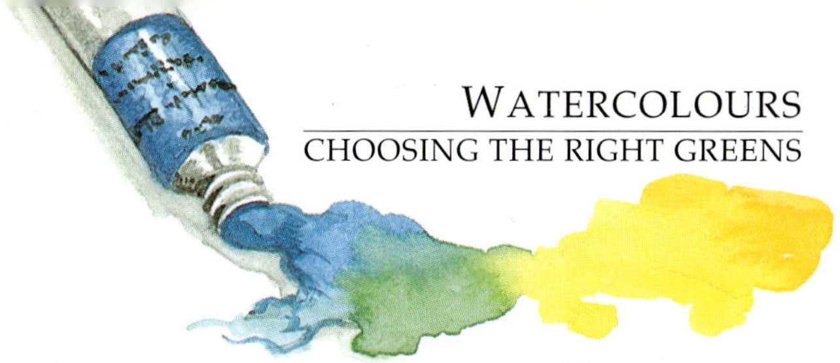

Some manufactured greens are suitable for leaves as they are, others are rather too bright and need subduing by mixing with yellow, greys and earth colours.

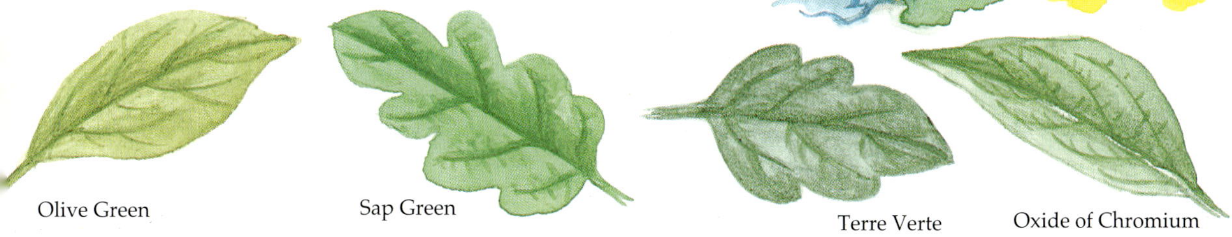

Olive Green

Sap Green

Terre Verte

Oxide of Chromium

Manufactured and permanent colours suitable for leaves.

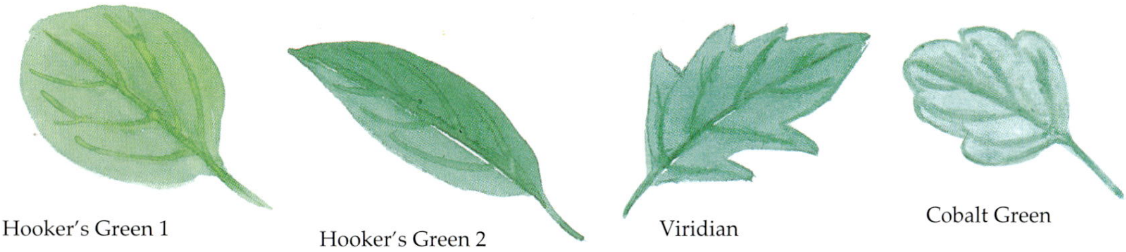

Hooker's Green 1

Hooker's Green 2

Viridian

Cobalt Green

Manufactured and permanent colours not suitable for leaves, unless mixed with other colours such as the Siennas, or yellows.

MIXING YOUR OWN GREENS

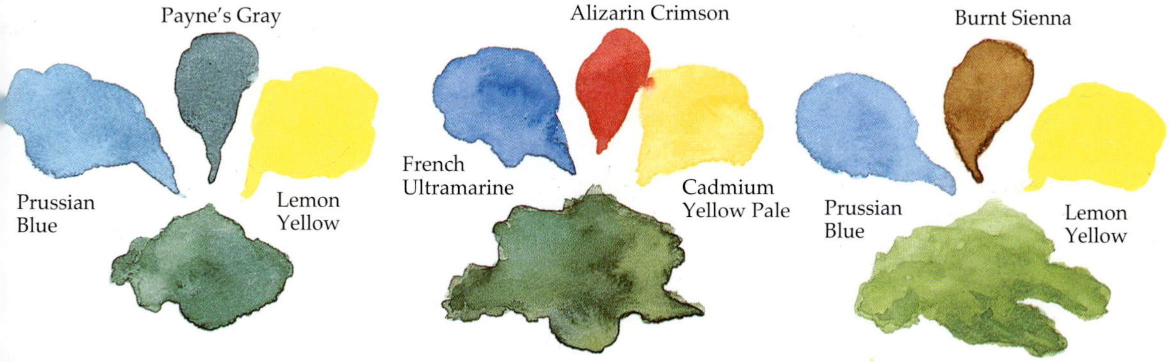

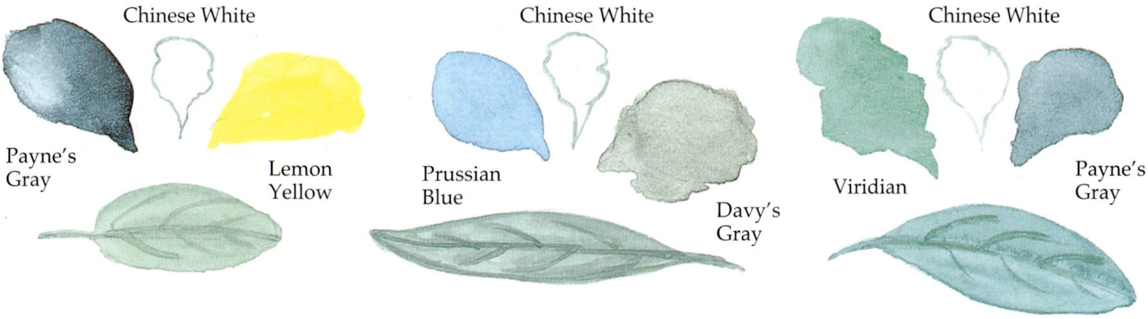

Payne's Gray

Prussian Blue

Lemon Yellow

Alizarin Crimson

French Ultramarine

Cadmium Yellow Pale

Burnt Sienna

Prussian Blue

Lemon Yellow

Chinese White

Payne's Gray

Lemon Yellow

Chinese White

Prussian Blue

Davy's Gray

Chinese White

Viridian

Payne's Gray

Mixing any blue pigment with any yellow will produce green with varying results and with practice you will find which colour mix you prefer. Add other colours such as a hint of crimson, Payne's Gray or Burnt Sienna to change the shade. Silvery leaves vary from blue-grey to yellow-grey and often almost white if covered with hairs.

WATERCOLOURS
THE 'EARTH' SHADES

As well as the colours required for flowers and leaves you will also need the lovely 'earth' colours, the Umbers, Siennas, Naples Yellow and browns for seed pods, stems and dead leaves. I also like to have various greys and Chinese White.

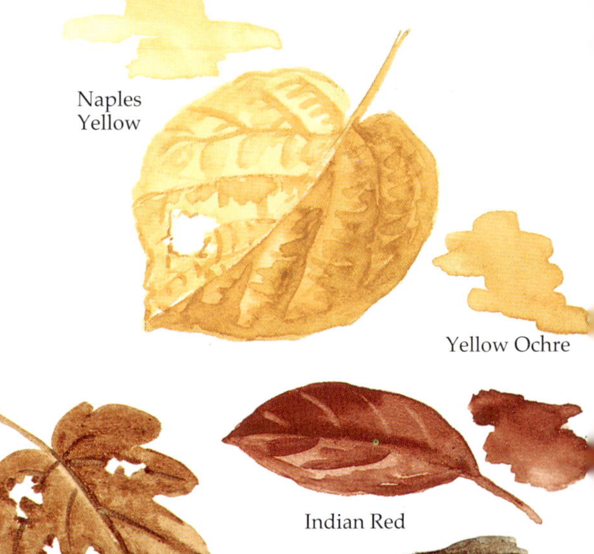

Raw Sienna

Raw Umber

Indian Red

Sepia

Burnt Sienna

Burnt Umber

All the 'earth' colours are permanent and can be mixed with each other and with Yellows and Reds to match the subtle changes of colour through autumn and into winter. There are several more colours within this range but I prefer to mix my own.

BLACKS AND NEARLY-BLACKS

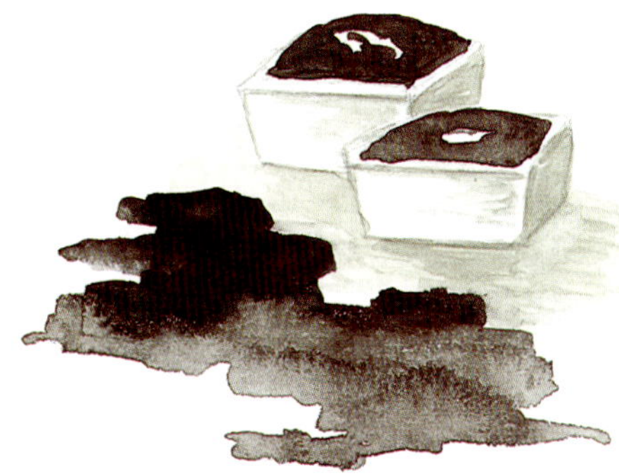

Black is only occasionally required by the flower painter. Lamp Black is a colder shade than Ivory Black but dries more evenly. However there is not a lot to choose between them. Even a blackberry is not really a true black, it has tones of red or purple in it. Mix equal parts of deep blue and crimson, add a hint of yellow and you will have a black which is more 'alive' than a manufactured one. Add more red for a warm grape colour or more yellow for a brown-black. Experiment with other colours too as illustrated below. Neutral tint can be classed as almost Black, Payne's Gray is a deep blue-grey and Davy's Gray is cool and pale and useful for delicate shadows. Note that Chinese White water colour, or Zinc White gouache should be used as other whites react on various other colours and tend to cause them to fade in time.

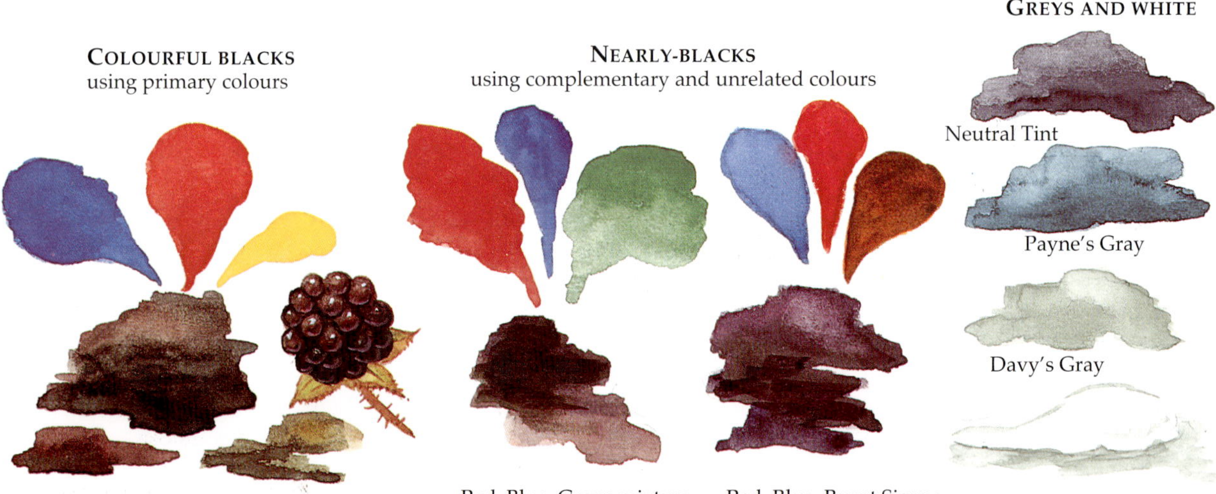

As I have already warned, mixing some colours together can be disastrous unless the paints chosen are closely related ones, or Primary colours such as red and yellow to make orange. The result in this case will be clean and easily varied according to the amount of one colour compared with the other. It is when complementary or unrelated ones are mixed together that the result is disappointing to say the least.

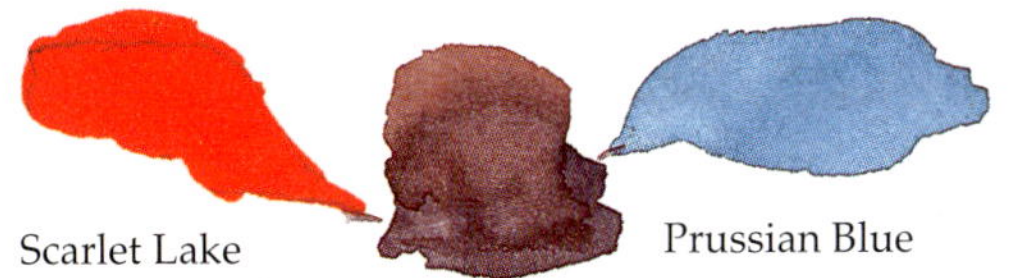

Making a really good clear mauve or purple is not easy even though red and blue are primary colours. The final result is often dull. The chosen red must be as far from scarlet as possible – a bluish-red – and the blue must have a hint of red in it, certainly not a green-blue. The colours shown above are totally wrong.

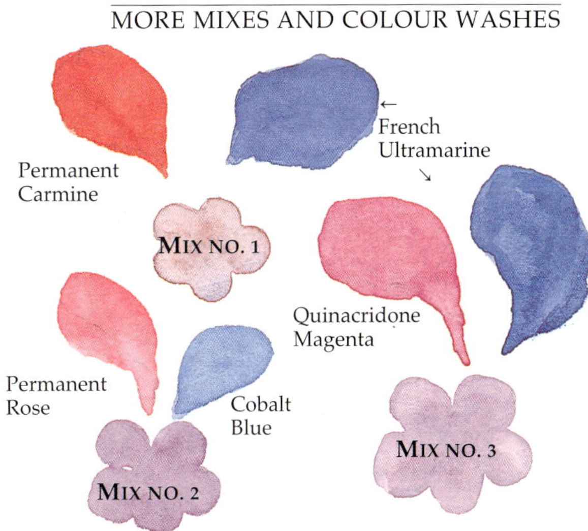

Mix no 1 is the least satisfactory and No 3 the best, but there are now several good permanent paints in the mauve-purple range which are very acceptable as shown on p. 34.

COLOUR WASHES

1st wash

2nd wash added after 1st wash has dried.

Graduated wash

COLOUR WASHES

It is a hand-shaking moment when you attempt your first wash of colour.

Mix a little paint and a lot of water in a china dish or any suitable container. Using a large brush load it with the diluted paint and starting at the top sweep right across the paper fairly quickly. If you find it easier you can damp your paper first and the paint will flow and merge more easily. Load the brush again and do a second row running it just over the edge of the first stroke and continue like this. Do not worry if it does not look absolutely even in colour, skies and fields and walls are never exactly the same shade all over. I find the slight slope on my desk is a help when doing washes. Where the sky finishes a misty background of trees or hills can be added while the paper is still damp so that they merge into a mottled 'out of focus' effect. You can use a damp sponge on a plain blue sky before it dries and 'lift out' clouds where you like.

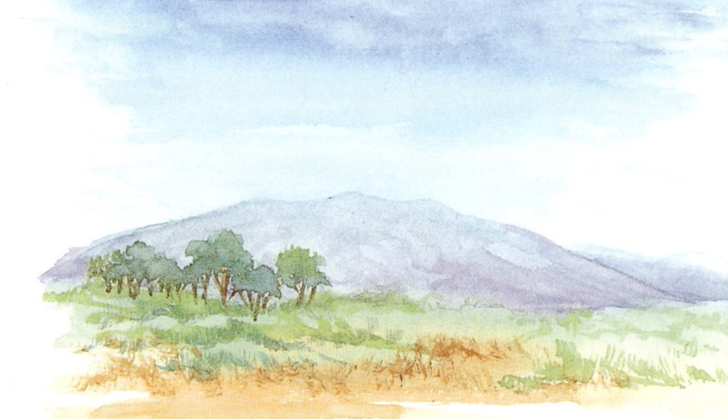

GRADUATED WASHES

A useful technique to master, whether you are painting a petal which pales from dark to light or a blue sky behind a landscape. Start at the top with the deepest shade of blue you require and dilute with more water as you descend to the paler horizon, finishing with a mere hint of blue. Try mixing a little Cerulean blue with your original Cobalt or Ultramarine to cool the colour in the lower part of the sky.

White flowers in a landscape

Using masking fluid

The use of masking fluid is regarded as a gimmick by many artists but some flower painters find it is very useful.

If you want to do the sky or a background scene as shown on the previous page and also include a field of white or pale coloured flowers in the foreground it is often difficult to paint between and around every flower, particularly if they are merely pale dots in the distance.

The fluid either colourless or pale yellow is a rather sticky rubbery solution which will ruin a brush unless you rinse it regularly and finally wash it in warm soapy water.

Stage 1
Masking fluid painted on. Background added when dry.

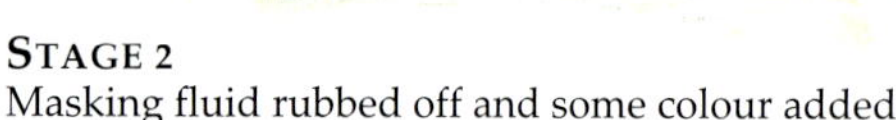

Stage 2
Masking fluid rubbed off and some colour added.

Apply with an old or inexpensive brush or a mapping pen, as though you are painting the flowers and allow to completely dry. The yellow tinted fluid shows up best on white paper. Then paint your background all over and again allow time to dry. Nothing will penetrate the rubber Finally gently rub away the solution with a finger or a soft rag and it will roll off easily. You can then paint your white flowers as you wish.

Stage 3

After the initial wash of background colour you can add more masking fluid, perhaps to accentuate some grasses or leaves. Follow the same procedure and paint more background washes where you want it to look darker and finally rub away the second application of fluid to reveal the paler grass.

Finally spattering the fluid by drawing a thumb down the length of an old toothbrush can add interest to backgrounds. Again you can spatter the fluid several times, varying your background washes as you progress. Note – you can spatter paint very effectively too if you like, or use a small sponge instead of a brush for 'out of focus' types of background. Soaked in paint and then squeezed out well it can be dabbed lightly over the paper and will leave interesting textures and tones when used over masking fluid.

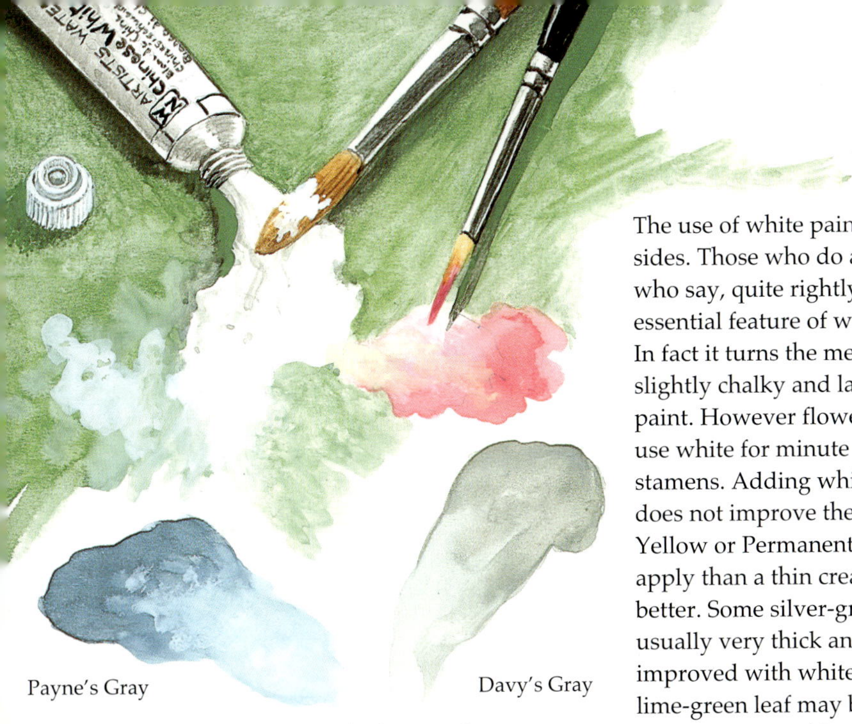

Payne's Gray

Davy's Gray

Mixed with Chinese White

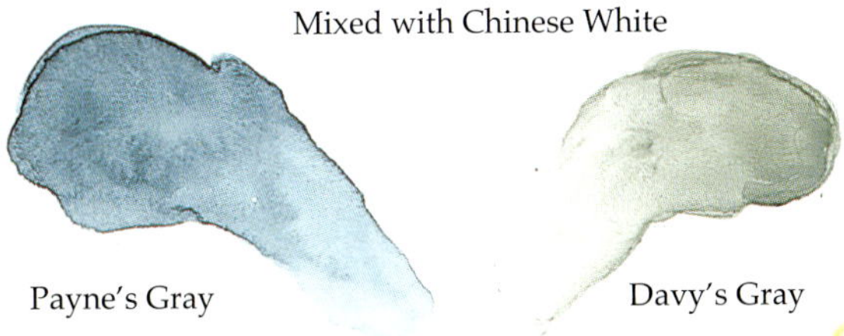

Payne's Gray

Davy's Gray

Diluted with water

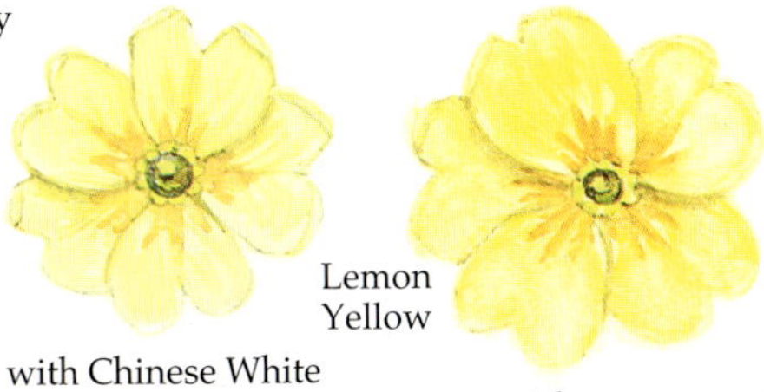

The use of white paint divides artists into two opposing sides. Those who do and the purists who do not and who say, quite rightly, that to add white destroys the essential feature of water colours – their transparency. In fact it turns the medium into a gouache, opaque, slightly chalky and lacking the 'glow' of the original paint. However flower painters on either side seem to use white for minute details such as fine hairs and stamens. Adding white to lighten many colours I feel does not improve them, a thin dilute layer of Lemon Yellow or Permanent Rose is far more pleasurable to apply than a thin cream of gouache-like paint and looks better. Some silver-grey or silver-green leaves are usually very thick and hairy or velvety and can be improved with white. A touch of white to a very pale lime-green leaf may be beneficial but there is rarely an improvement in blues, mauves etc.

Remember it is essential to use Chinese White (or Zinc White Gouache) because Permanent White will cause fading of many of the colours with which it has been mixed.

Lemon Yellow

with Chinese White

with water

Permanent Rose

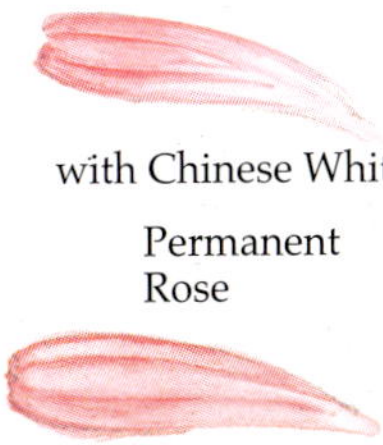

with Chinese White

with water

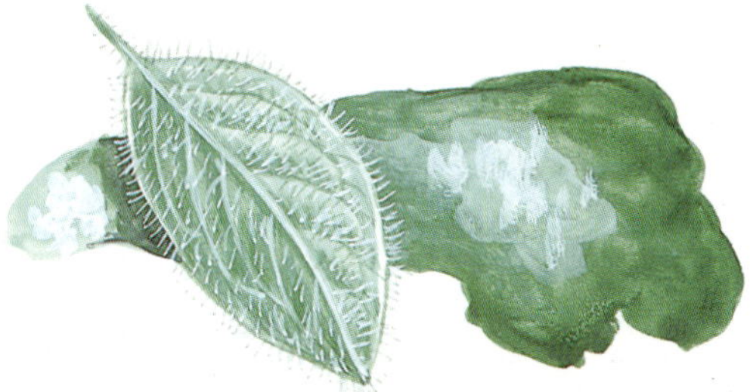

Terre Verte with white paint

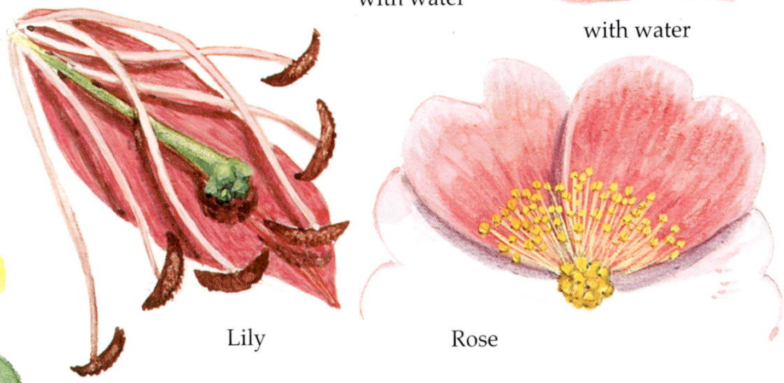

Lily

Rose

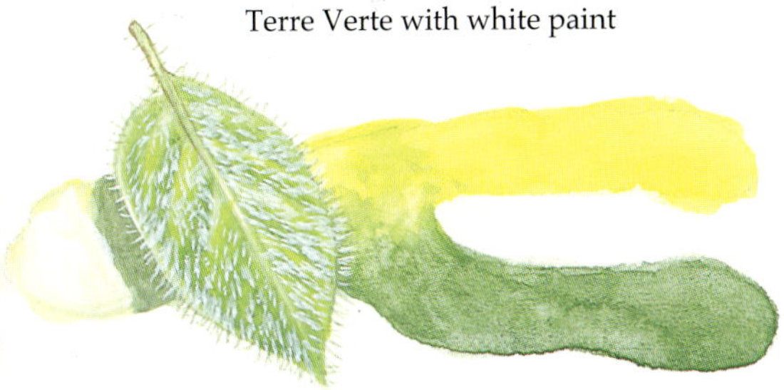

Lemon Yellow, Oxide of Chromium and white paint

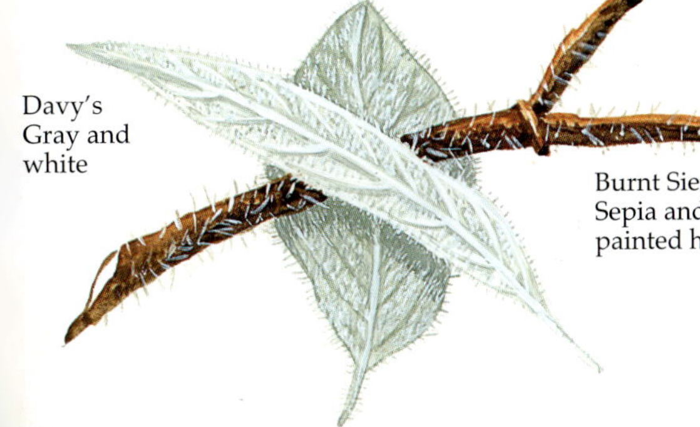

Davy's Gray and white

Burnt Sienna, Sepia and white painted hairs.

It is not difficult to paint between the large stamens of the Lily but when you have a Rose with its boss of creamy stamens tipped with yellow pollen which you want to paint in detail then white paint tinted yellow will be a much easier and more accurate way of doing them. Use a small brush, though the size is of less importance than its perfect tip, and paint the stamens when the petals are quite dry. Stems and leaves covered in silvery-grey hairs are equally easy to do using grey paint on white backgrounds but white paint where they show up against a dark ground.

Adding colour to pencil or ink sketches is not only a quick and easy first step from black and white to all colour work but can also be most attractive in its own right. It is a method I still frequently use to show the parts of a plant I wish to include but do not want to illustrate in full detail because they are either too large or of less importance botanically and merely need to be indicated.

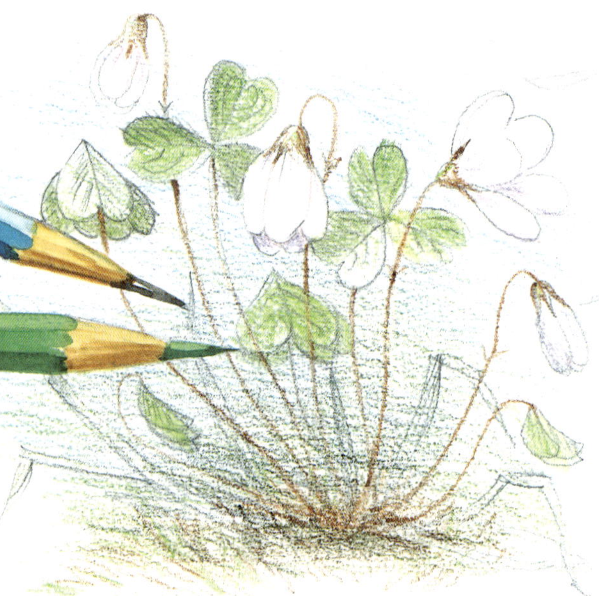

Marker pens are produced in many shades and are just the quickest way I know of adding colour to a pencil or pen sketch. They flow very smoothly and dry immediately. Here I have only used Cool Grey to show grasses behind a plant of Wood Sorrel.

Water soluble coloured pencils do not easily smudge and so are very useful to take away with you and use in the field to indicate rather than totally colour a plant. Later a wet brush can be used to smooth out the medium and turn it into a water paint.

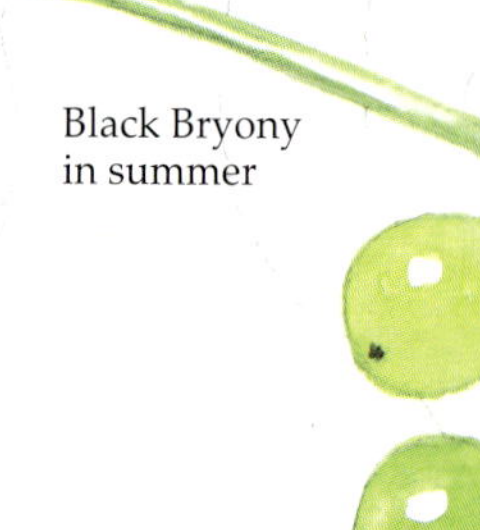

Black Bryony in summer

Bryony berries in winter

As I often have to include large leaves or roots in my botanical paintings, I use outline only for these so that they do not overpower the spike of fully painted but perhaps small and delicate flowers. I like this effect and frequently use it with pencil, paint or inks – usually brown or green. Black is too dominant and destroys the three-dimensional look of the picture.

Again I have used grey marker pens to indicate grasses and limestone rocks on a downland where the White Rockrose grows in SW England. It is so rare you must not pick it. I wanted to keep to a cool grey and white overall effect with only touches of colour on the upper parts of the leaves and the tufts of golden stamens.

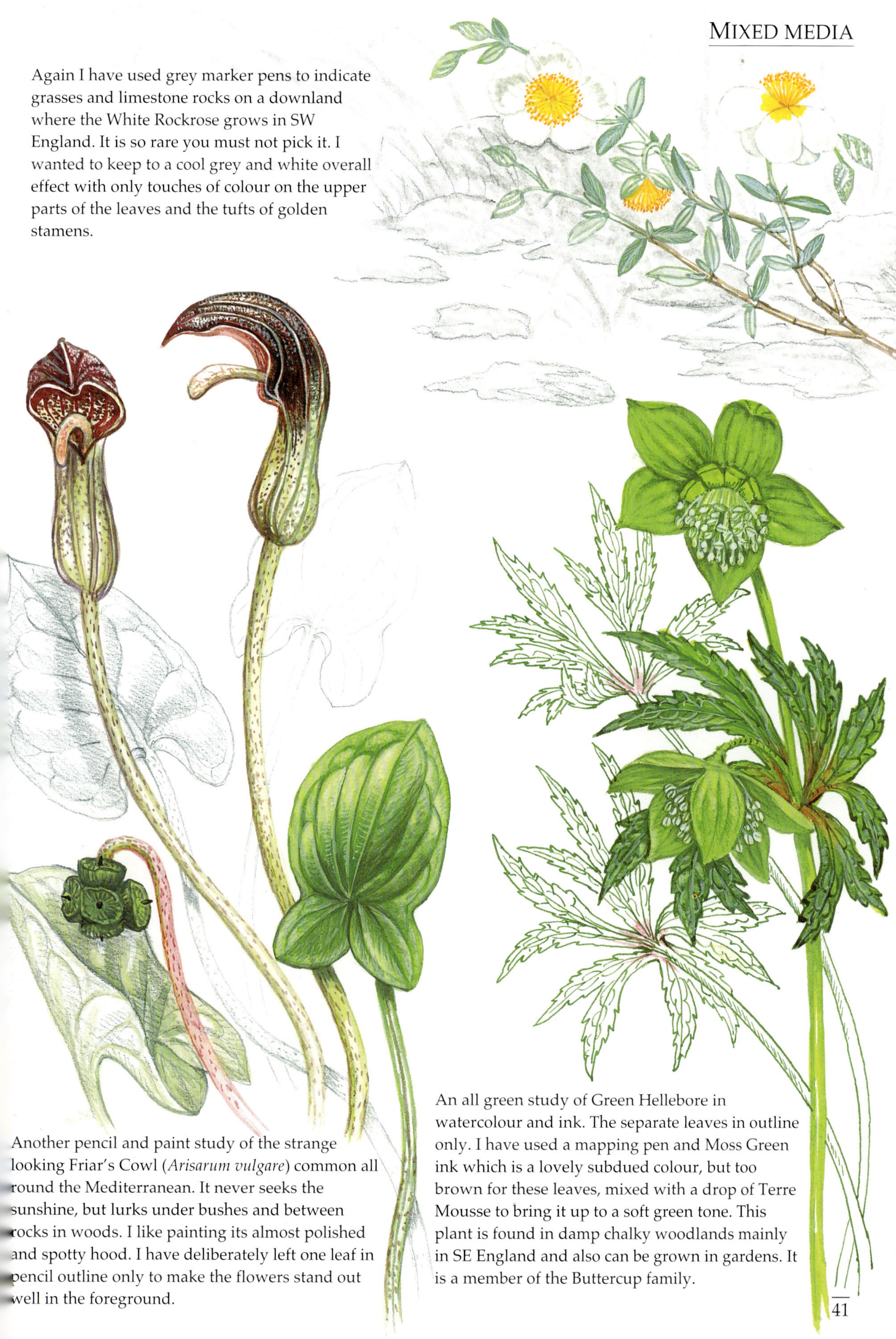

Another pencil and paint study of the strange looking Friar's Cowl (*Arisarum vulgare*) common all round the Mediterranean. It never seeks the sunshine, but lurks under bushes and between rocks in woods. I like painting its almost polished and spotty hood. I have deliberately left one leaf in pencil outline only to make the flowers stand out well in the foreground.

An all green study of Green Hellebore in watercolour and ink. The separate leaves in outline only. I have used a mapping pen and Moss Green ink which is a lovely subdued colour, but too brown for these leaves, mixed with a drop of Terre Mousse to bring it up to a soft green tone. This plant is found in damp chalky woodlands mainly in SE England and also can be grown in gardens. It is a member of the Buttercup family.

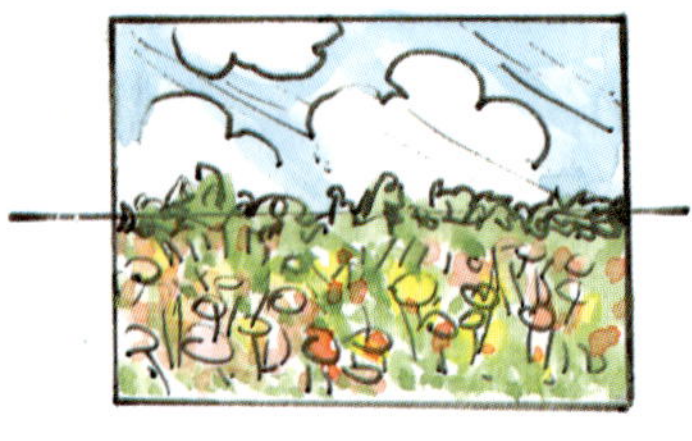

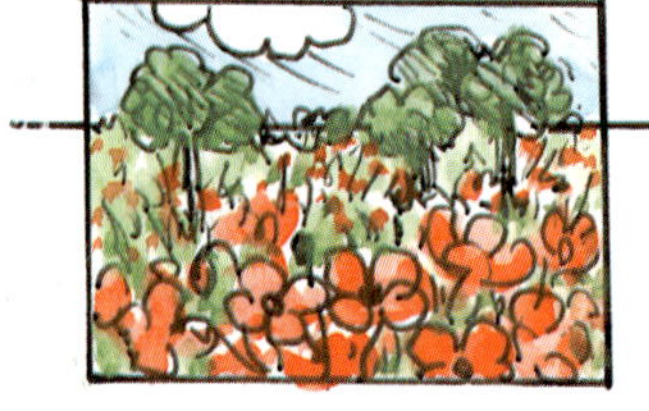

On p. 20 I suggested a few simple rules for a pleasing design using three flowers and here are a few further remarks.

There are no hard and fast rules regarding composition and even if there were most could be broken from time to time with interesting results. However there are a few basic ones which help to make a picture look 'easy on the eye' and one that you could 'live with' – if that is the effect you wish to achieve. If it isn't then by all means break rules, be original and enjoy experimenting, for there is no need to slavishly follow any well-trodden path that is said to lead to an harmonious design.

Landscapes – and this includes garden scenes – usually look better if the line where the sky joins land is not exactly in the middle.

Similarly the picture should not have a tree or a church steeple, for instance, in the centre neatly dividing the painting into two scenes. Move your viewpoint slightly, or mentally uproot your tree and replant it slightly to one side. The same rule applies to a vase of flowers, a little off-centre is preferable and perhaps a more attractive shaped vase will enhance the effect.

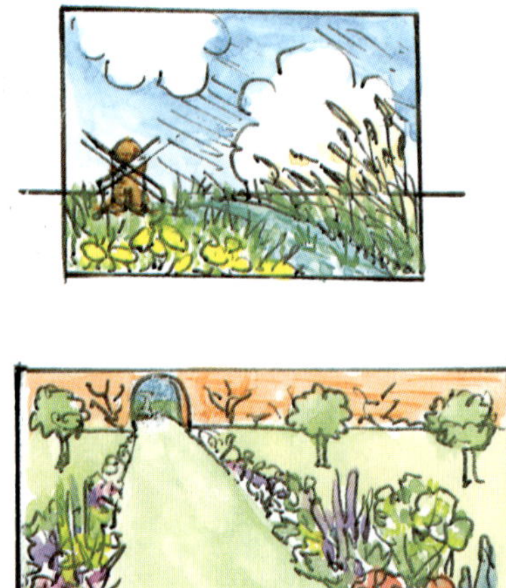

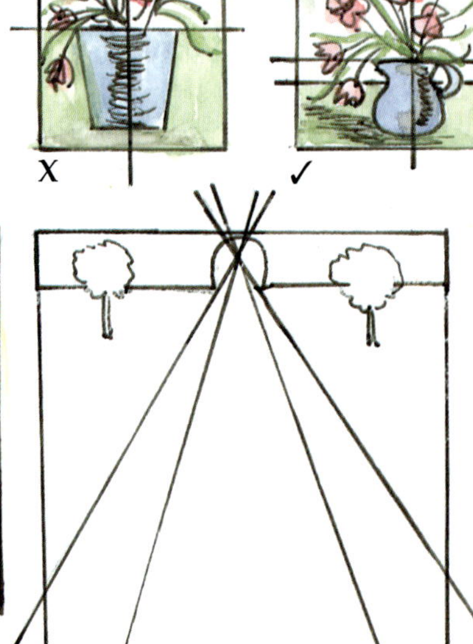

Shadows on the tree and vase look better if placed on the side which is *nearest to the edge of the picture* rather than a heavy mass of dark colour in the middle, because this too seems to cut a picture in half and is inclined to dominate it.

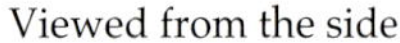

Viewed from the side

Viewed from the centre

Disregarding all the previous advice there is no reason why a formal garden should not look really impressive if treated in an equally formal manner with the main features exactly in the middle rather than to one side. After all, many such gardens were designed to fit into geometric patterns in the first place. Follow a few simple rules of perspective with your vanishing point in the centre near the top and draw your guide lines to each corner at the bottom making the flower beds and the grass path as wide or as narrow as you like.

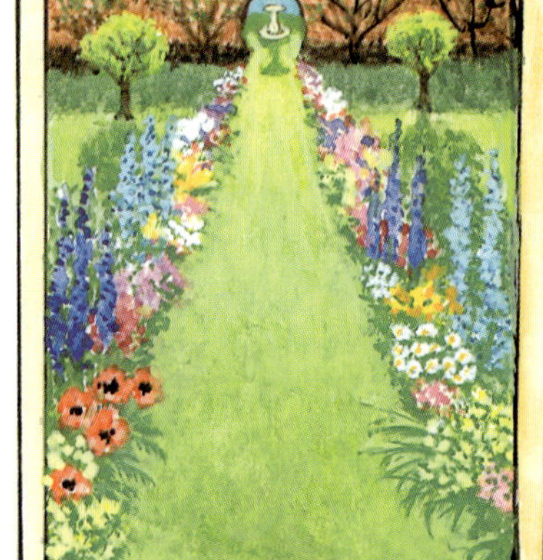

Remember that flowers in the borders must gradually reduce in size as they too must vanish into the distance.

There is one basic design rule to which I usually adhere when planning a page of flower 'portraits' or a picture. I learnt when I was a photographer, in the days when black and white was the only choice, that the correct placing of significant objects was even more critical and important than when colour took over and added another dominating dimension to the picture. This seemingly unimportant design point is what I call 'looking in to the picture'. Whether it is a branch, a flower, bird or butterfly I think it is imperative that it leads the eye *in* and not *out* of the picture. There is nothing wrong with the top picture on the right but with the flowers facing outwards there is a 'hole' in the middle.

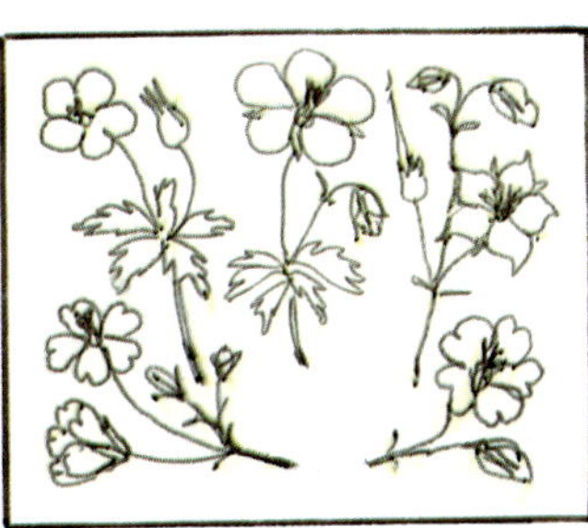

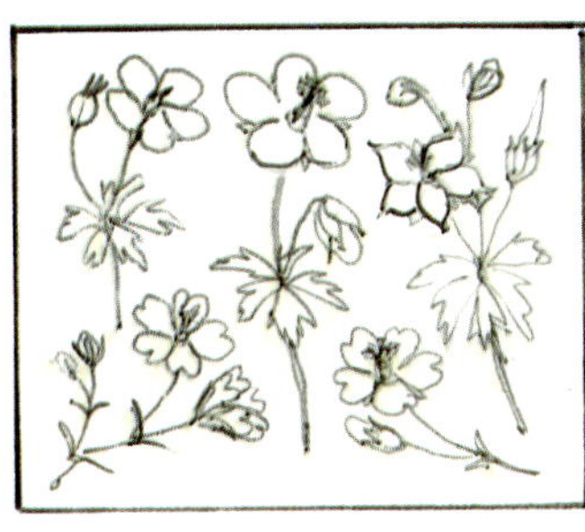

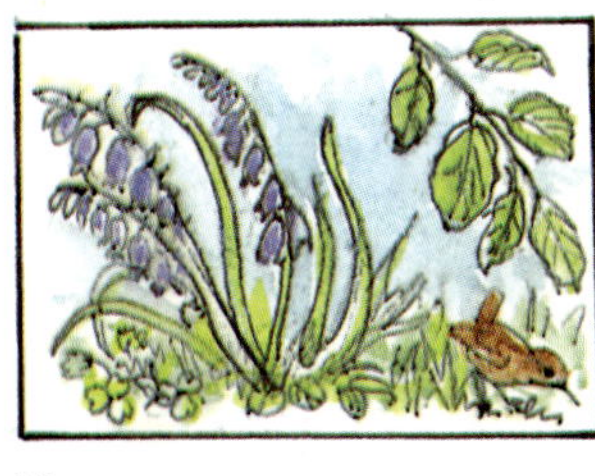

X

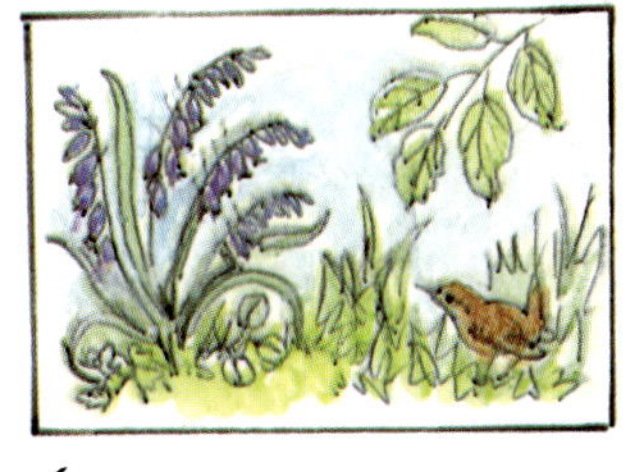

✓

When you plan to paint your picture, perhaps your first one, the choice of mount is very important. Don't fall back on a 'safe' white or cream one when grey, blue, green or sand could be far better. Many people tend to shy away from a mount that is dark regardless of the fact that it may suit their picture admirably. A double mount made from two colours that are compatible can add a wonderful lift and richness to a painting. Cut out mounts can be made at home if you have the equipment to do bevelled edges or bought ready made from art shops, either single or double and in a great variety of colours and sizes. Finally there are professional picture framers in most towns.

Even a bad painting will improve when well framed and a really good one will improve beyond words!

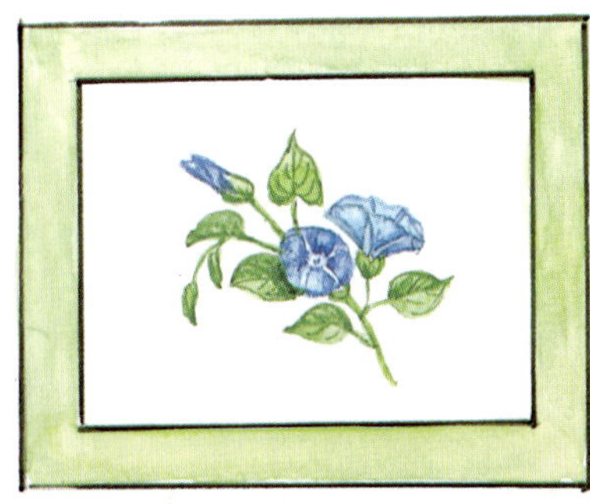

Mount too narrow

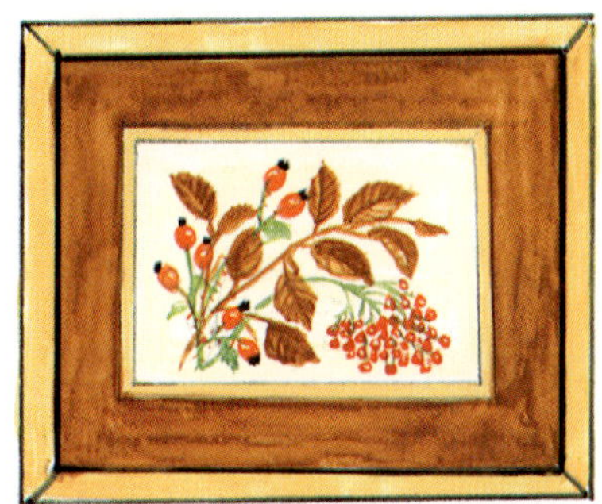

Colour scheme for 'Autumn'

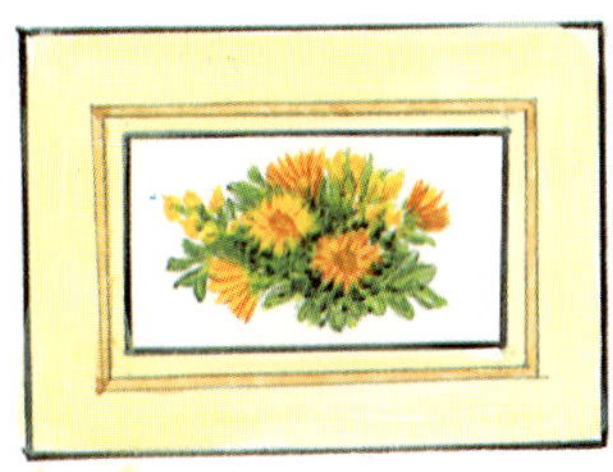

Single mount with drawn lines and colour wash

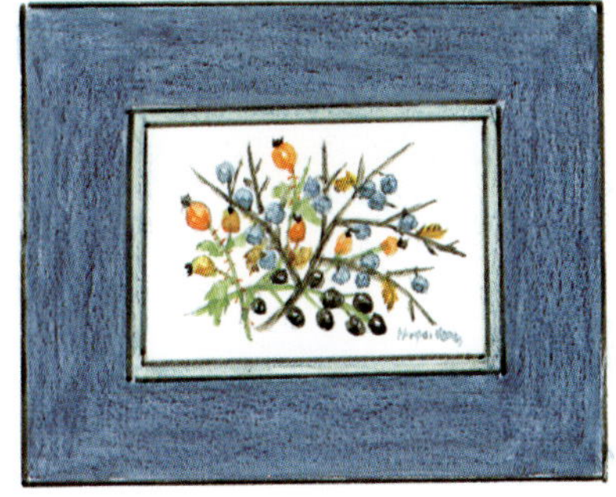

Double mount

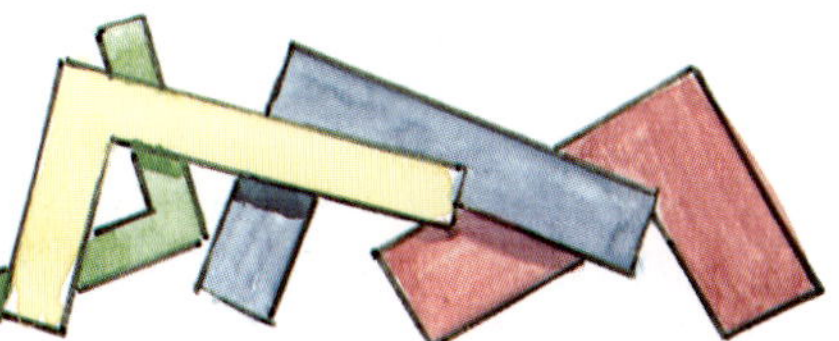

Pieces of mounting board cut into various sizes so that you can choose the best size for your picture.

DO'S AND DONT'S – MOSTLY DONT'S.

Don't have too narrow a mount, it will look mean.

Don't have a frame that looks too heavy or wide for a small delicate painting. Experiment though – it might work well.

Don't have a frame that is too bright – for me that includes over-shiny gold ones – it will detract from the main feature – your painting.

Do choose mounts and frames which 'set off' your picture and complement it rather than providing competition.

PAINTING BY STAGES

Here is one of the Lilies which, on p. 22, I suggested you traced, shown in 3 simple stages for you to practise in watercolour. Very few colours are required as I've used Davy's Gray as a basis instead of mixing a grey from primary colours. It has been well diluted and tinted with Lemon Yellow or Sap Green. Take care to keep the highlights bright and clean by leaving some areas unpainted.

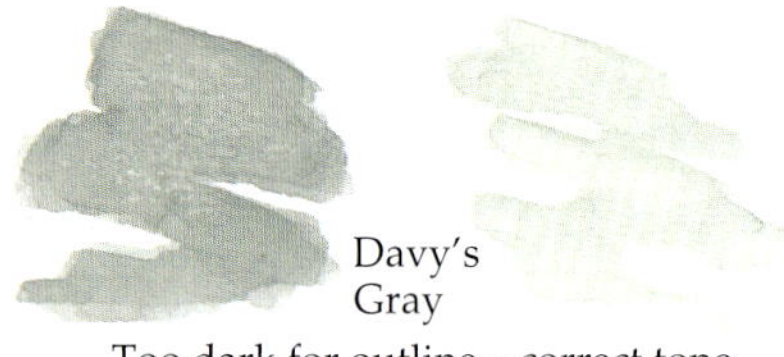

Davy's Gray

with Lemon Yellow

with Sap Green

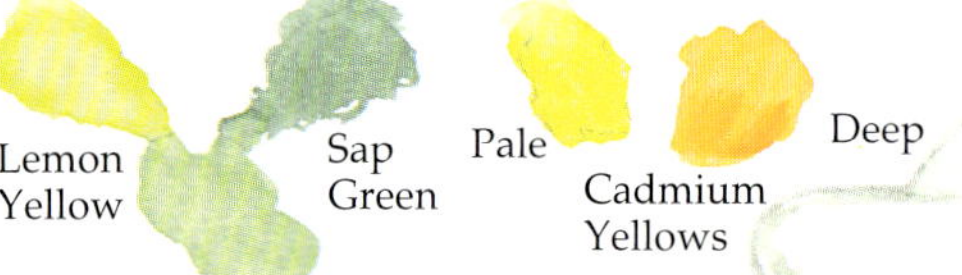

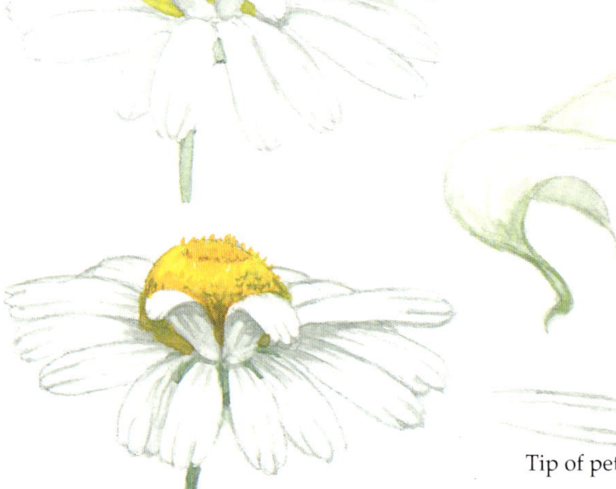

Tip of petal

The Ox-eye Daisy (from p. 23) uses the same colours as the Lily but this time the grey has not been mixed with other shades, only well diluted. Note the shape of the petal tip. This flower, which I love painting, appears in other parts of the book and you will find further examples in different styles on p. 38 and a landscape dominated by Daisies on p. 70.

You can be far more bold in your approach to painting large and colourful flowers like Clematis, which often has a mixture of shades in its petals. It is a good subject on which to practise putting a wash of one colour and before it is quite dry floating on another, allowing them to mix together. This is fun to do; cover a sheet of paper with Clematis petals in various colours until you become proficient at it.

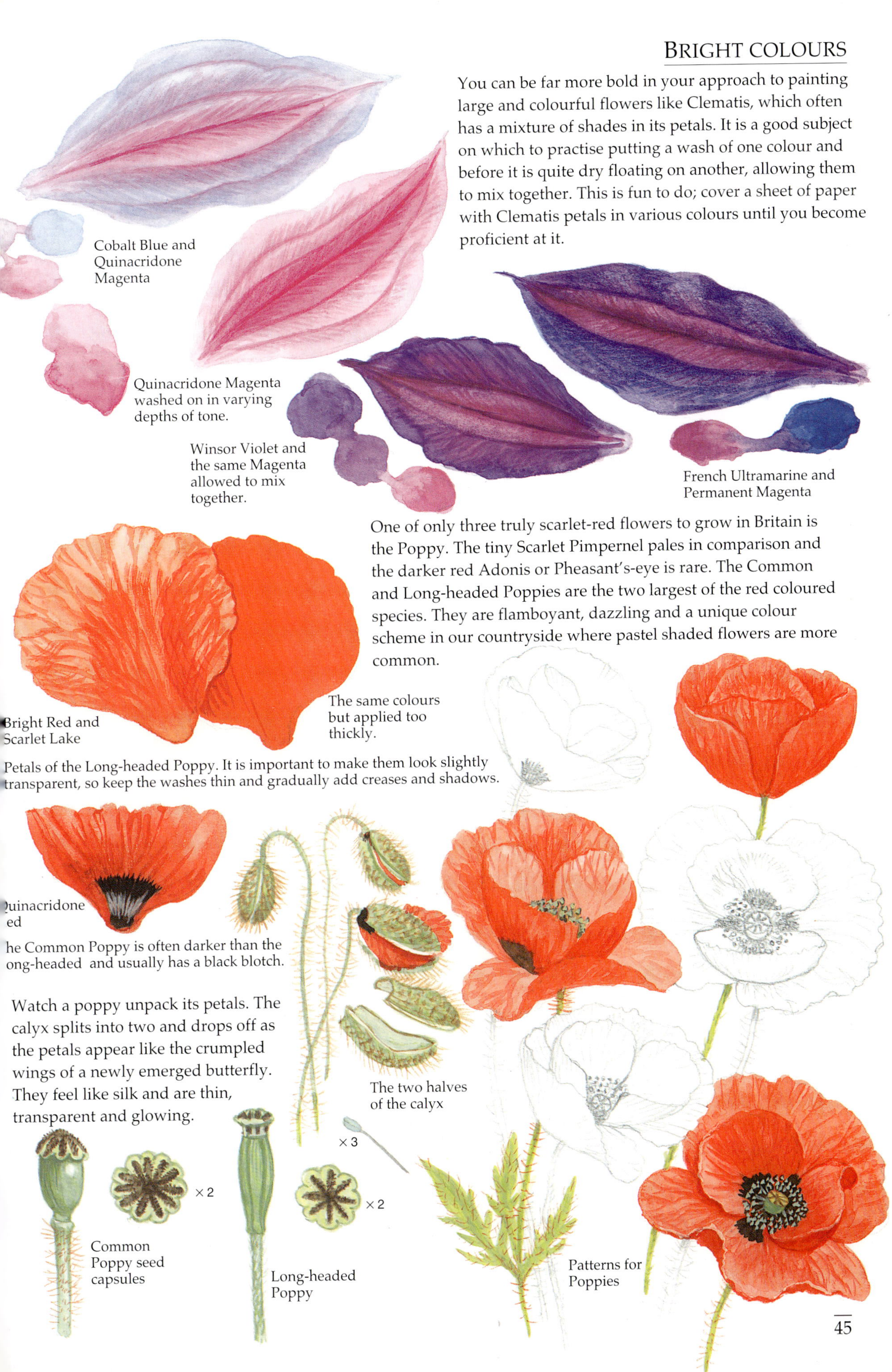

Cobalt Blue and Quinacridone Magenta

Quinacridone Magenta washed on in varying depths of tone.

Winsor Violet and the same Magenta allowed to mix together.

French Ultramarine and Permanent Magenta

One of only three truly scarlet-red flowers to grow in Britain is the Poppy. The tiny Scarlet Pimpernel pales in comparison and the darker red Adonis or Pheasant's-eye is rare. The Common and Long-headed Poppies are the two largest of the red coloured species. They are flamboyant, dazzling and a unique colour scheme in our countryside where pastel shaded flowers are more common.

Bright Red and Scarlet Lake

The same colours but applied too thickly.

Petals of the Long-headed Poppy. It is important to make them look slightly transparent, so keep the washes thin and gradually add creases and shadows.

uinacridone ed

he Common Poppy is often darker than the ong-headed and usually has a black blotch.

Watch a poppy unpack its petals. The calyx splits into two and drops off as the petals appear like the crumpled wings of a newly emerged butterfly. They feel like silk and are thin, transparent and glowing.

The two halves of the calyx

×3

×2

Common Poppy seed capsules

×2

Long-headed Poppy

Patterns for Poppies

HIGHLIGHTS

ADDING AND SUBTRACTING

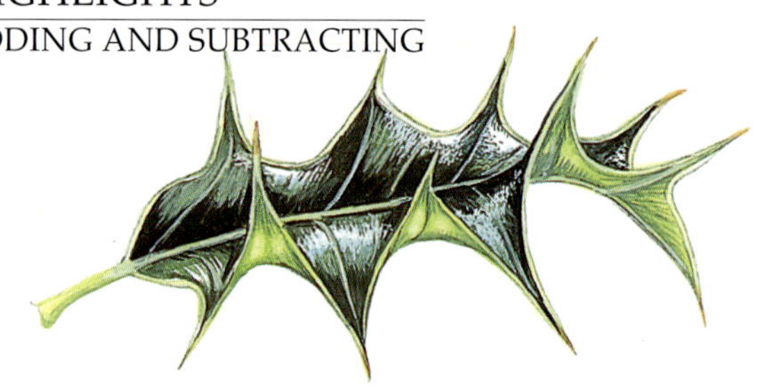

Leaves are far more likely to show highlights than any other part of the plant and there are various methods one can use to obtain the really bright, almost white, highlights on a Holly leaf and the softer sheen on others. These lights add modelling and form to a leaf and can clearly convey just what type of leaf we are painting. Again using the Holly as an example we must show that it is a hard leaf, stiff, smooth surfaced and polished to a high gloss and very dark in the shadows.

The Holly is a rather extreme case as it is more highly polished than the majority of leaves and requires at least the centre of the highlight left unpainted, for no amount of 'lifting' will remove every vestige of pigment, nor is this necessary in most cases. A faint blue wash, or stipple, can be added at the edge of the highlight to soften it leaving some pure white spots.

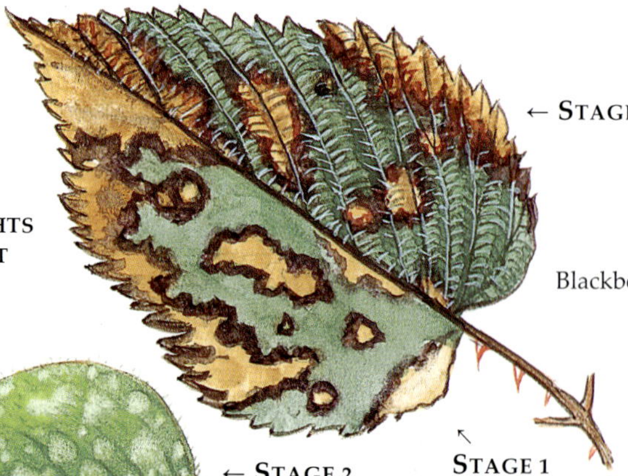

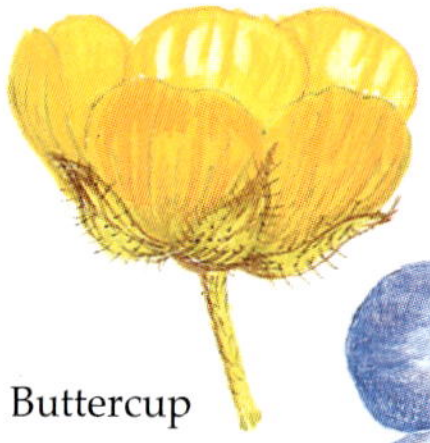

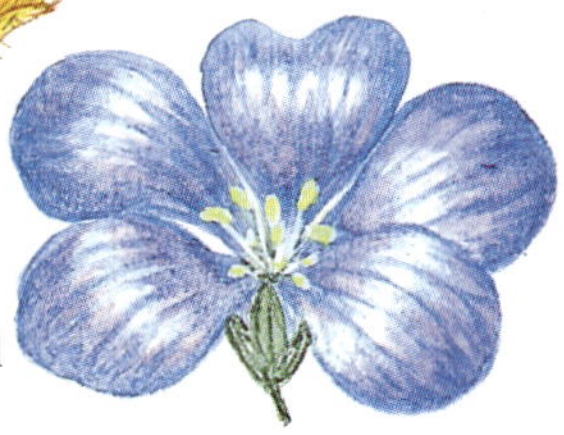

← STAGE 2

Blackberry

STAGE 1

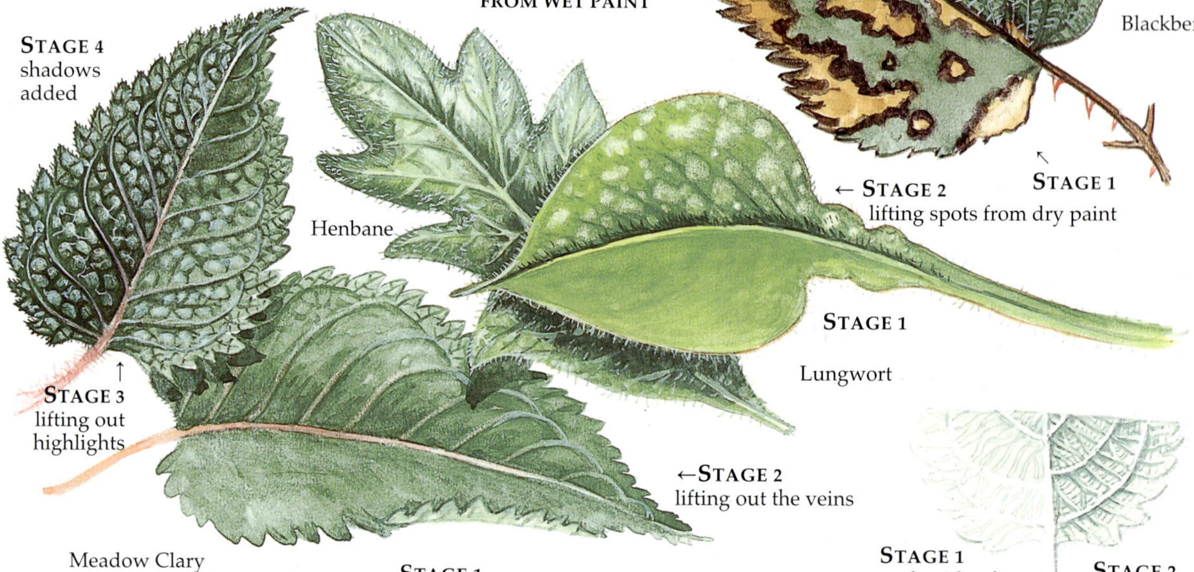

← STAGE 2
lifting spots from dry paint

LIFTING HIGHLIGHTS
FROM WET PAINT

STAGE 4
shadows
added

Henbane

STAGE 1

Lungwort

↑
STAGE 3
lifting out
highlights

←STAGE 2
lifting out the veins

Meadow Clary
wrinkled and closely
net-veined.

STAGE 1
colour wash of a shade mid-way
between highlights and shadows.

STAGE 1
underside of a
prominently
veined leaf.

STAGE 2
adding the
shading to m[ake]
the veins star[t]
out.

'LIFTING OUT'

Other leaves with wrinkled or closely net-veined surfaces may not be shiny but it is still necessary to lighten the high peaks of the wrinkles and darken the valleys in order to convey the texture of the leaf. An easy method is by a little 'lifting out' of the paint. You can do this either while the paint is still wet using a clean almost dry brush or after the first washes are dry with a much wetter brush, then dab the areas with a clean rag, tissue or cotton bud.

I used the second method for the Lungwort leaf as I wanted the spots to stay small and not spread too much.

You can of course do every wrinkle and vein separately from the start but it takes a lot of time and although perhaps necessary for a botanical study such precise detail is not needed for a freer style of flower painting. If the main leaf rib is very pale or a different colour it is best to leave it unpainted until the end.

Buttercup

Perennial
Flax

Some flowers have very shiny petals, Buttercups glisten in bright sunshine but a white highlight looks too extreme and I soften this with a wash of a pale Lemon Yellow. Other flowers which open wide have a marked 'halo' around the centre of the corolla.

Even on a sunless day leaves cast shadows over the ones below them and also down part of the stem. Adding these prevents the picture from looking flat and lifeless. They literally 'lift' the leaf up and away from other parts of the plant, but they are not easy to do and many painters do not attempt to add them. Just which mix of colours makes a 'shadow' is almost impossible to say for every one seems to be different depending on the presence, strength or absence of sunlight, the colour and the composition of the leaf. Some are solid and totally opaque casting darker shadows than other leaves which are thin and translucent allowing light to filter through them.

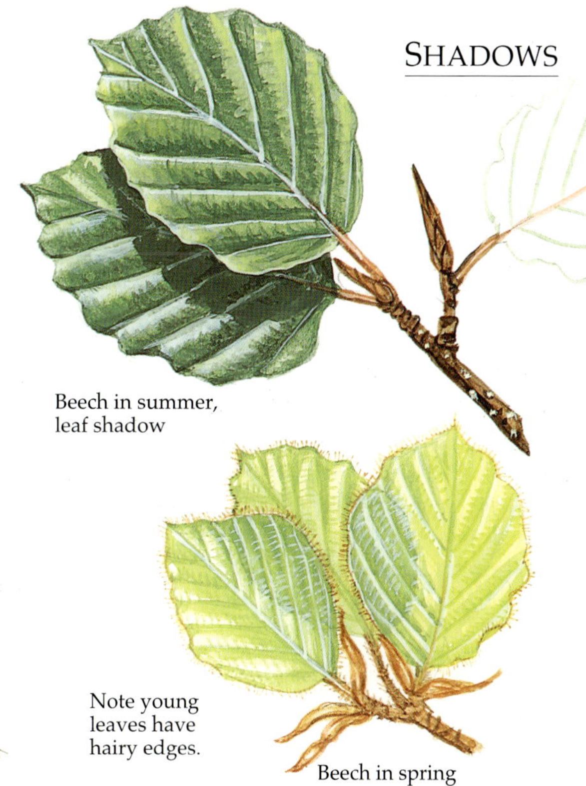

Beech in summer, leaf shadow

Note young leaves have hairy edges.

Beech in spring

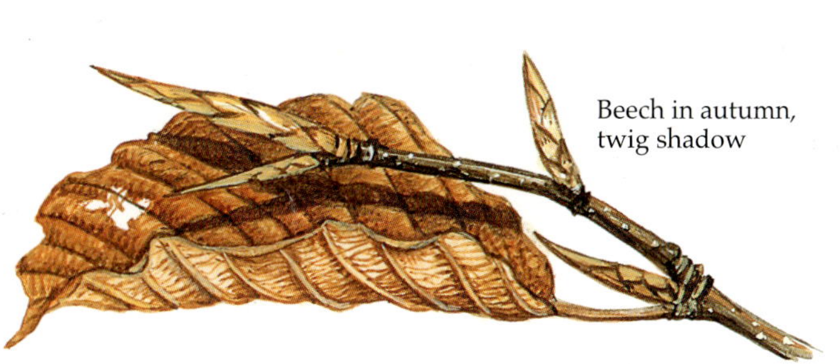

Beech in autumn, twig shadow

Never put black shadows for leaves but make a mixture of darker green and its complementary colour of red. Add Payne's Gray for deep leaf shadows and more yellow for the pale shadows. Autumn tinted leaves will need warmer shadows with added red to make them look more brown than black. Lift out veins etc. very slightly leaving just a hint that they are there so that the shadow is not too solid and dead. The brighter the sunshine the deeper the shadows. This is very noticeable in the tropics but do not over do them. In this and many other countries shade is less dense and softer.

Look up through the leaves of a newly opened Beech and you will realise how transparent they are in their first few weeks for you will be able to see the 'shadows' of the upper leaves through the lower ones.

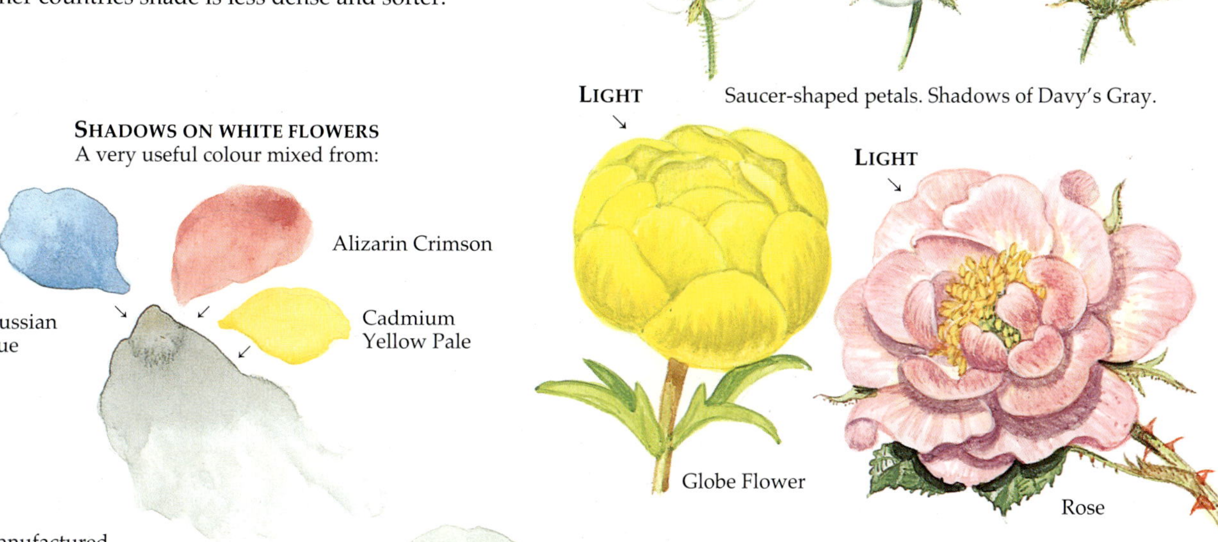

Saucer-shaped petals. Shadows of Davy's Gray.

SHADOWS ON WHITE FLOWERS
A very useful colour mixed from:

Globe Flower

Rose

Manufactured colours

Payne's Gray

Neutral Tint

Davy's Gray

Flowers too cast shadows but these must not be too heavy. Yellow flowers often take on a green or Raw Sienna hue and pink flowers may be mauve-grey but care must be taken not to make them look a dirty colour. For an orange flower try its complementary colour of blue.

MORE PAINTING BY STAGES

Having followed the guide lines on how to draw your first Primrose plant on p. 21, it is now time to paint it. Where do you begin?

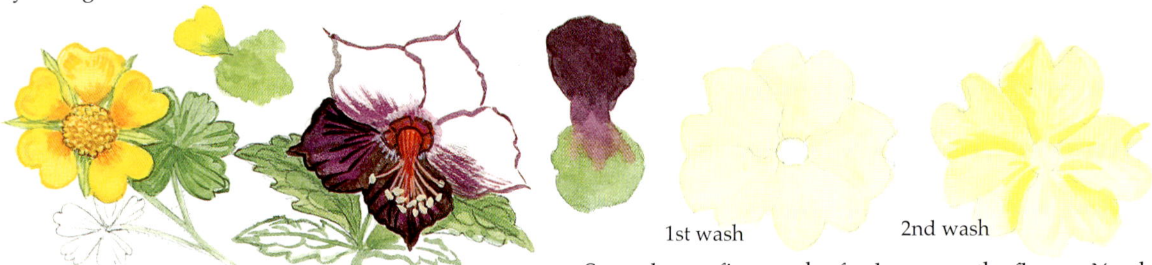

As a general rule I start with the flower *if it is paler* than the surrounding leaves. The opposite happens if the pale leaves are touching a dark flower in case the deeper pigment leaks into the paler one which can easily occur if the paints are not absolutely dry.

Spread your first wash of colour over the flower. You have probably held your breath while doing it! Now relax. Add a second wash to part of the petal so the flower does not look too flat.

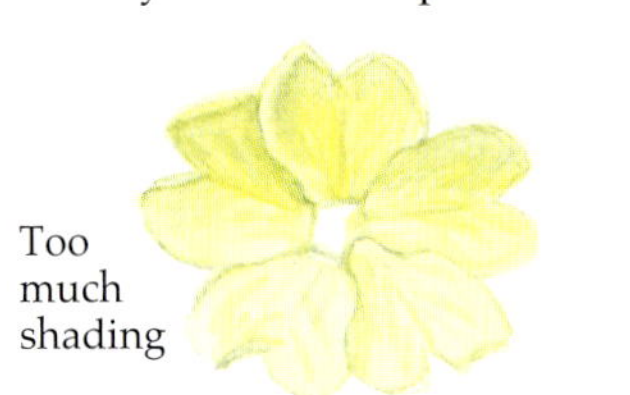

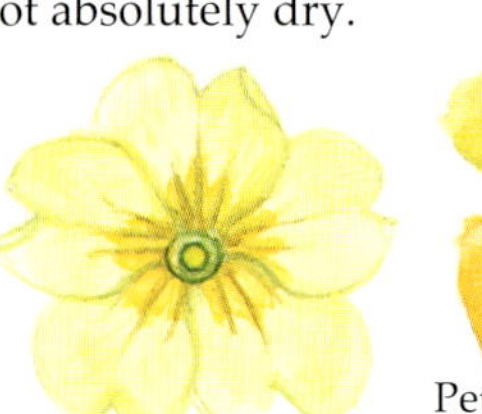

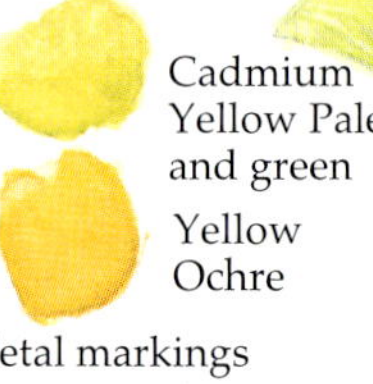

Light source

↖ Shadows ↗

Paint in some shadows. Primroses are cool coloured so keep the shadows cool too. Add a little Prussian Blue to your yellow – or Davy's Gray. Don't overdo it – or the flower will look dirty. Paint the centre of the flower, either thrum or pin-eyed forms, which are quite different. See where the light is shining on your side-facing flower and paint quite deep shading away from the light, keeping the part facing it pale and clean.

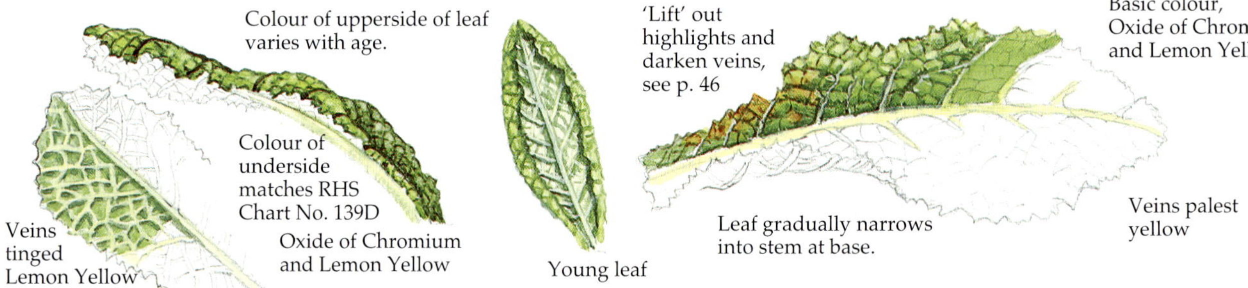

Primrose leaves are not easy. Care and patience are required. There is no need to attempt all the veins and wrinkles, a mere suggestion is quite acceptable. Wash over the top of the leaf, varying the colour from light yellow-green to darker green. The veins on the underside are very raised as shown on the 'map'. An overall wash of the pale vein colour is first applied and when dry the small squares between the 'roads' are painted a little darker, finally an even darker tone is added here and there to make the hollows deeper and particularly emphasise the mid-rib.

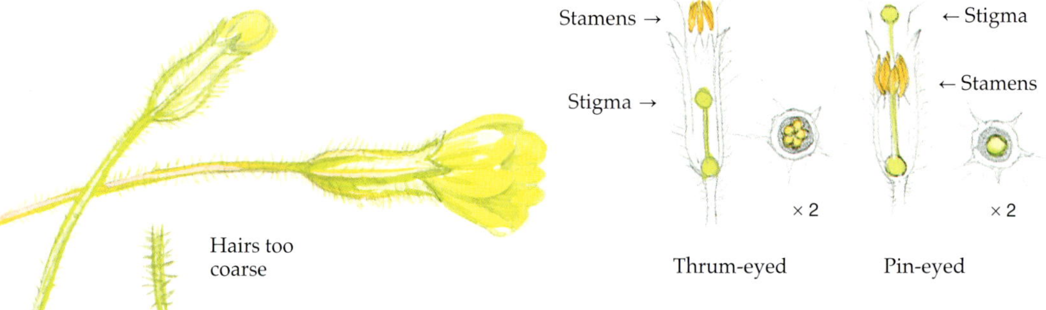

Colour the very pale stems, which are sometimes green tinged with pink and with a small brush, size 0 or less, very lightly 'stroke' on the hairs as thinly as possible. I have carried on the theme of my favourite Primroses, starting with pp. 20 and 21, then p. 25 and the final painting of a whole plant on p. 54.

THE MINIATURES OF THE FLORAL WORLD

These flowers may well be among the last ones a flower painter would choose to do, usually preferring the larger and more flamboyant members of the plant world. Perhaps there will be occasions when the need – or the urge – arises to cope with such minute flowers as these when recording the wild flowers of a village or a field or a wild patch in the garden. These miniature flowers need fine brushes and much patience.

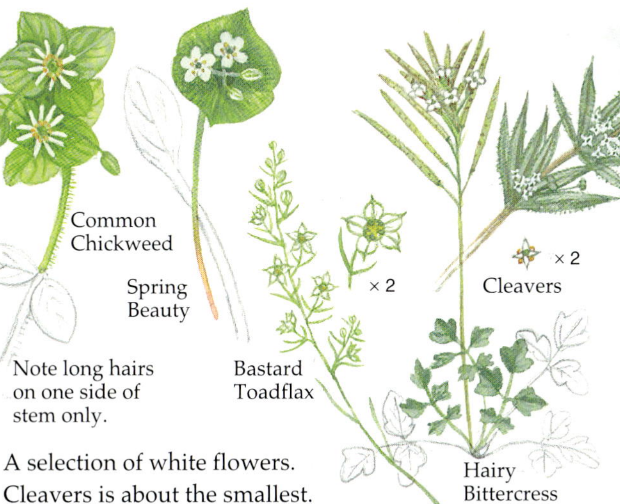

A selection of white flowers. Cleavers is about the smallest. Any gardener who has suffered from Hairy Bittercress may prefer to remove rather than paint this tiresome weed. Bastard Toadflax is a rare plant of southern England. The remaining two flowers are quite easy to do as they are surrounded by leaves.

Cow Parsley

Different approaches. You can paint any plant of the Carrot family as a froth of lace, very appropriate for this one, also called Queen Anne's Lace. I used masking fluid and a wash of colours for one style, but for the other there are no short cuts. I often use a magnifying glass for such fine work so that I can really look into the tiny flowers.

Green Field Speedwell →
Grey Field Speedwell
Blue Woodruff
× 5
Common Corn Salad
Early Forget-me-not

There are very few really small blue flowers. Common Corn Salad is one of the tiniest and very pale compared with Forget-me-nots and Speedwells.

× 2
Fennel
London Rocket
Oxalis exilis
Slender Trefoil
Sand Spurrey
Danish Scurvy Grass
Squinancywort →
← Sea Milkwort

There are almost as many small flowered yellow plants as white but they are not difficult so do not need outlining first. Fennel is a tall culinary herb to grow in the garden. The petals roll inwards. London Rocket is one of many plants of the Cabbage family naturalised but rare in England. Following the Great Fire of London it became well established on the ruined walls of the city. The small Oxalis, known as the Least Yellow Sorrel, is also a naturalised plant in southern England and sometimes becomes a tiresome weed. Slender Trefoil with up to 6 tiny 2-3mm flowers is easily overlooked.

There are many tiny pink and mauve flowers in tightly packed heads such as Clovers but not many with few or solitary flowers under 5mm. The first three shown here can be found by coasts but Squinancywort is more widespread.

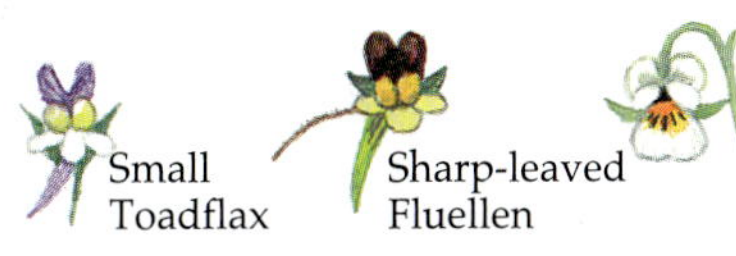

Small favourites of mine and one that has no right to be included but which I couldn't resist. A Common Poppy found growing on a sun-baked farm track in Majorca and painted actual size. It obviously gave up the struggle at an early age.

A CLOSER LOOK AT FAVOURITE WILD FLOWERS

Meadow Crane's-bill is one of the loveliest wild flowers I know. It is fairly widespread in Britain, wanders through Europe into Asia and even reaches Japan. It is drawn on p. 25 but it should be painted in order to appreciate the almost ethereal blue of its flowers.

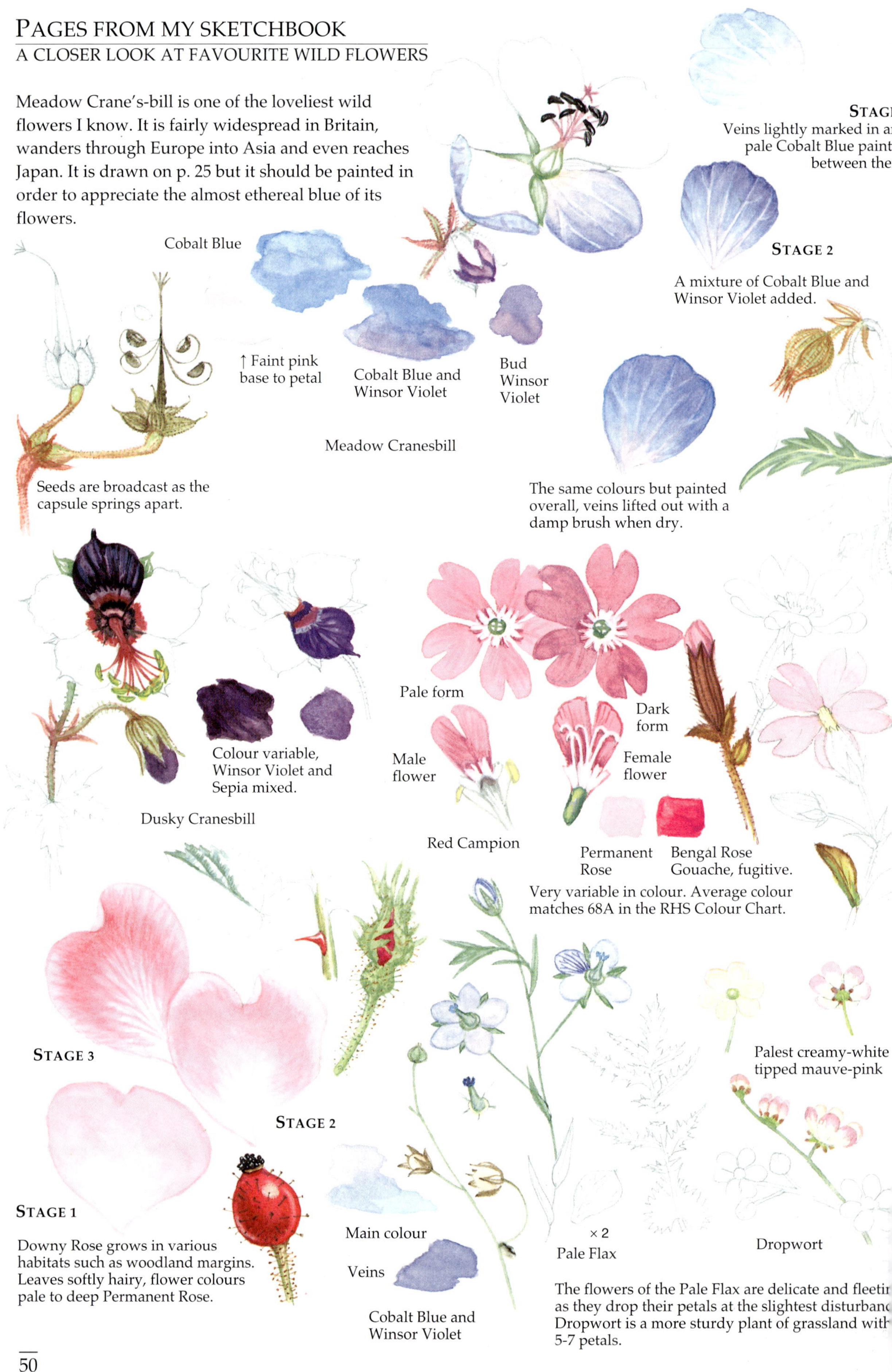

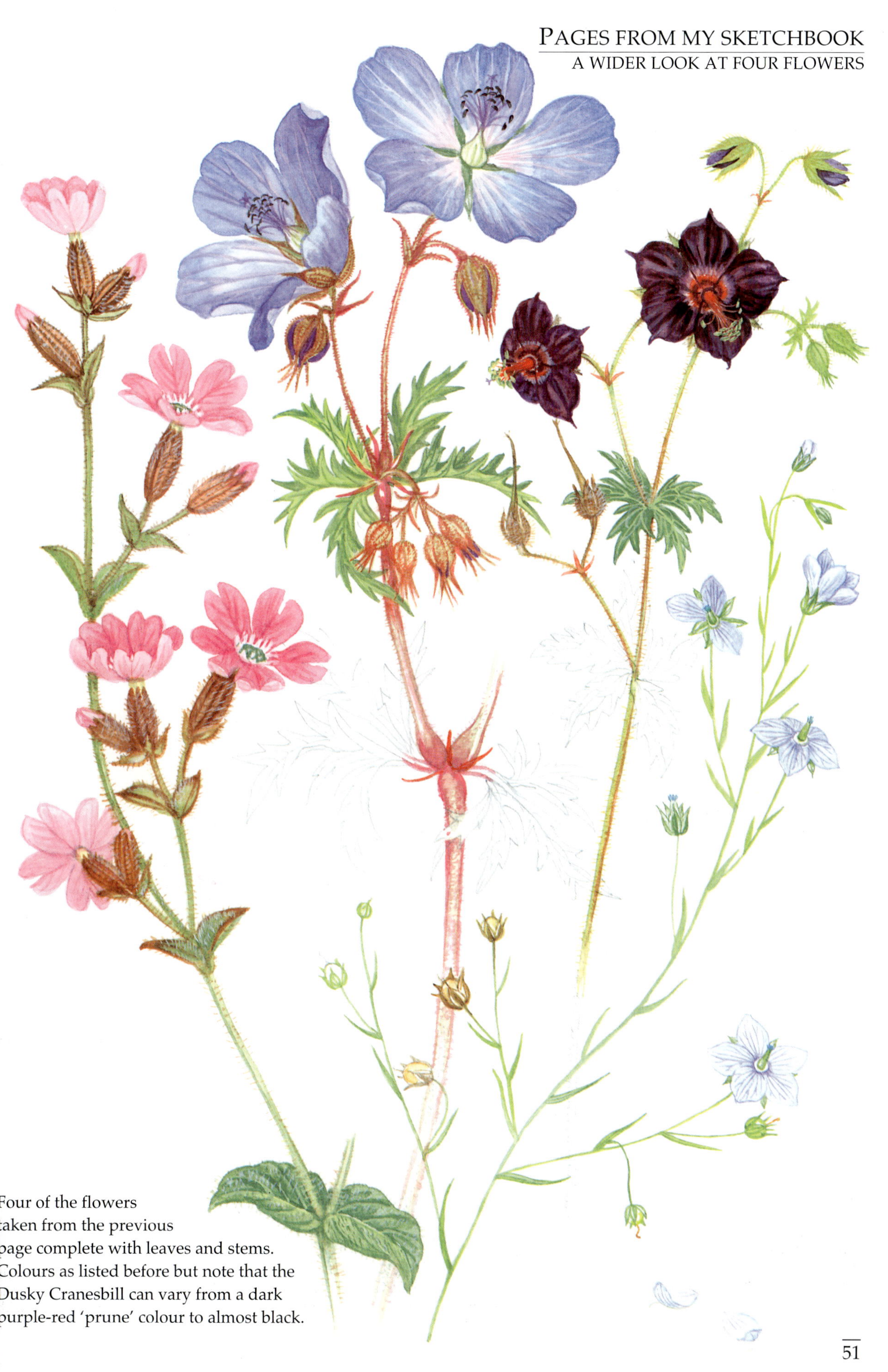

Four of the flowers taken from the previous page complete with leaves and stems. Colours as listed before but note that the Dusky Cranesbill can vary from a dark purple-red 'prune' colour to almost black.

THROUGH THE MAGNIFYING GLASS

FRINGES, FLUFF AND FINE HAIRS

Many leaves and stems are very hairy as are some flowers, particularly the Mint Family – Motherwort is one of the prettiest and most fluffy. Another favourite is the Bearded Bellflower, found mainly in France and Germany, but it can be bought in Britain occasionally. The main colour is Cobalt Blue. All the white hairs have been added to the flowers using Chinese White and a 00 brush.

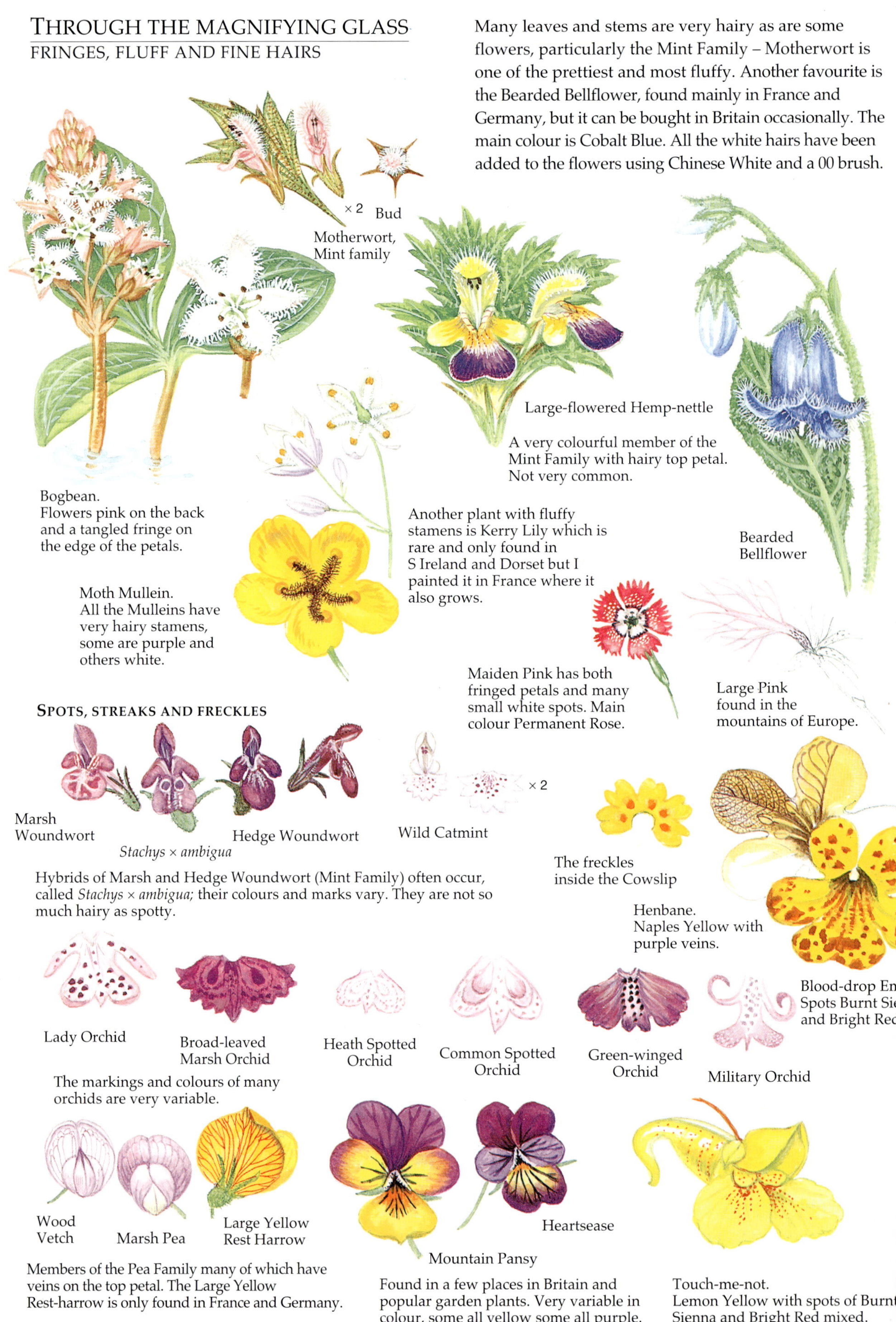

×2 Bud

Motherwort, Mint family

Large-flowered Hemp-nettle

A very colourful member of the Mint Family with hairy top petal. Not very common.

Bogbean.
Flowers pink on the back and a tangled fringe on the edge of the petals.

Another plant with fluffy stamens is Kerry Lily which is rare and only found in S Ireland and Dorset but I painted it in France where it also grows.

Bearded Bellflower

Moth Mullein.
All the Mulleins have very hairy stamens, some are purple and others white.

Maiden Pink has both fringed petals and many small white spots. Main colour Permanent Rose.

Large Pink found in the mountains of Europe.

Spots, streaks and freckles

Marsh Woundwort

Stachys × ambigua

Hedge Woundwort

Wild Catmint ×2

Hybrids of Marsh and Hedge Woundwort (Mint Family) often occur, called *Stachys × ambigua*; their colours and marks vary. They are not so much hairy as spotty.

The freckles inside the Cowslip

Henbane.
Naples Yellow with purple veins.

Blood-drop Em
Spots Burnt Sie
and Bright Red

Lady Orchid

Broad-leaved Marsh Orchid

Heath Spotted Orchid

Common Spotted Orchid

Green-winged Orchid

Military Orchid

The markings and colours of many orchids are very variable.

Wood Vetch

Marsh Pea

Large Yellow Rest Harrow

Heartsease

Mountain Pansy

Members of the Pea Family many of which have veins on the top petal. The Large Yellow Rest-harrow is only found in France and Germany.

Found in a few places in Britain and popular garden plants. Very variable in colour, some all yellow some all purple.

Touch-me-not.
Lemon Yellow with spots of Burnt
Sienna and Bright Red mixed.

Through the Magnifying Glass

A Close Look at Seed Dispersal

Seeds and their containers are fascinating to paint as they are so varied. An achene for example is a single dry seed which does not split. In the Daisy family many of these are wafted great distances under their silky parachutes, or pappus, which may be white or golden coloured and the hairs either simple or feathered. Use a 0 or 000 brush and Davy's Gray and white for Dandelions.

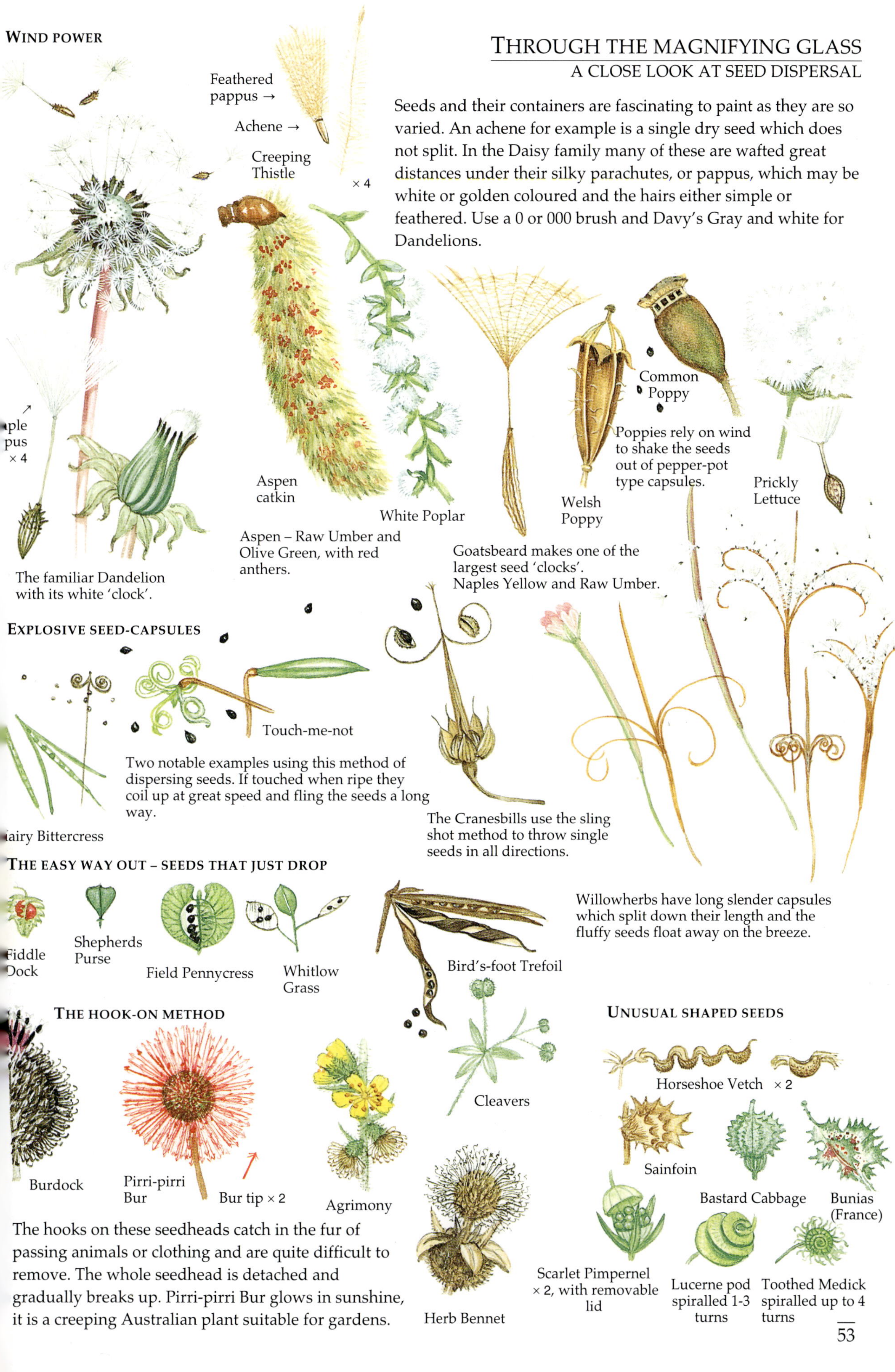

The hooks on these seedheads catch in the fur of passing animals or clothing and are quite difficult to remove. The whole seedhead is detached and gradually breaks up. Pirri-pirri Bur glows in sunshine, it is a creeping Australian plant suitable for gardens.

A SKETCHBOOK IN SPRING WOODS

When painting portraits of wild flowers it is sometimes not only necessary but also delightful to show them growing in their natural habitats. Woodland floors make particularly interesting subjects to paint with all the dead leaves, Ivy and small plants which are scattered around. Collect leaves in autumn and after painting them store them in a box for future use. Beech, particularly, will curl inwards showing their veins most attractively. Other objects to look for are Beech mast, Acorns, Larch cones, Hazel nuts, conkers, and even small feathers, all of which will form natural 'props' for autumn pictures. Primroses as well as the Oxlips on the opposite page are supreme examples of nature's clean coloured flowers – pure, clear palest yellow, as fresh as their scent and which you can achieve by using a clean brush, fresh water, a scrupulously cleaned dish on which to dilute the paint and taking care not to overdo the shadows. Yellow paints are good and permanent.

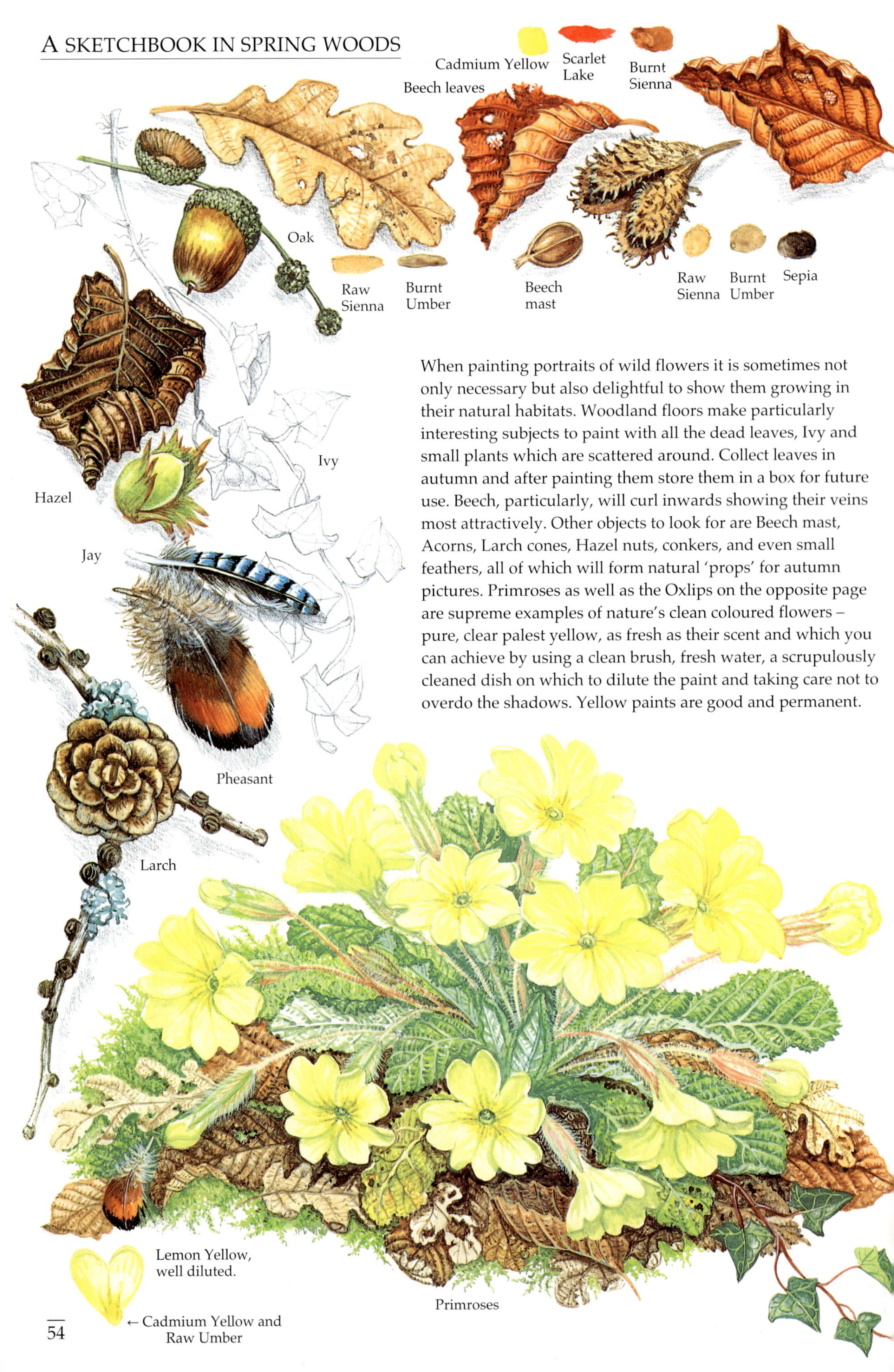

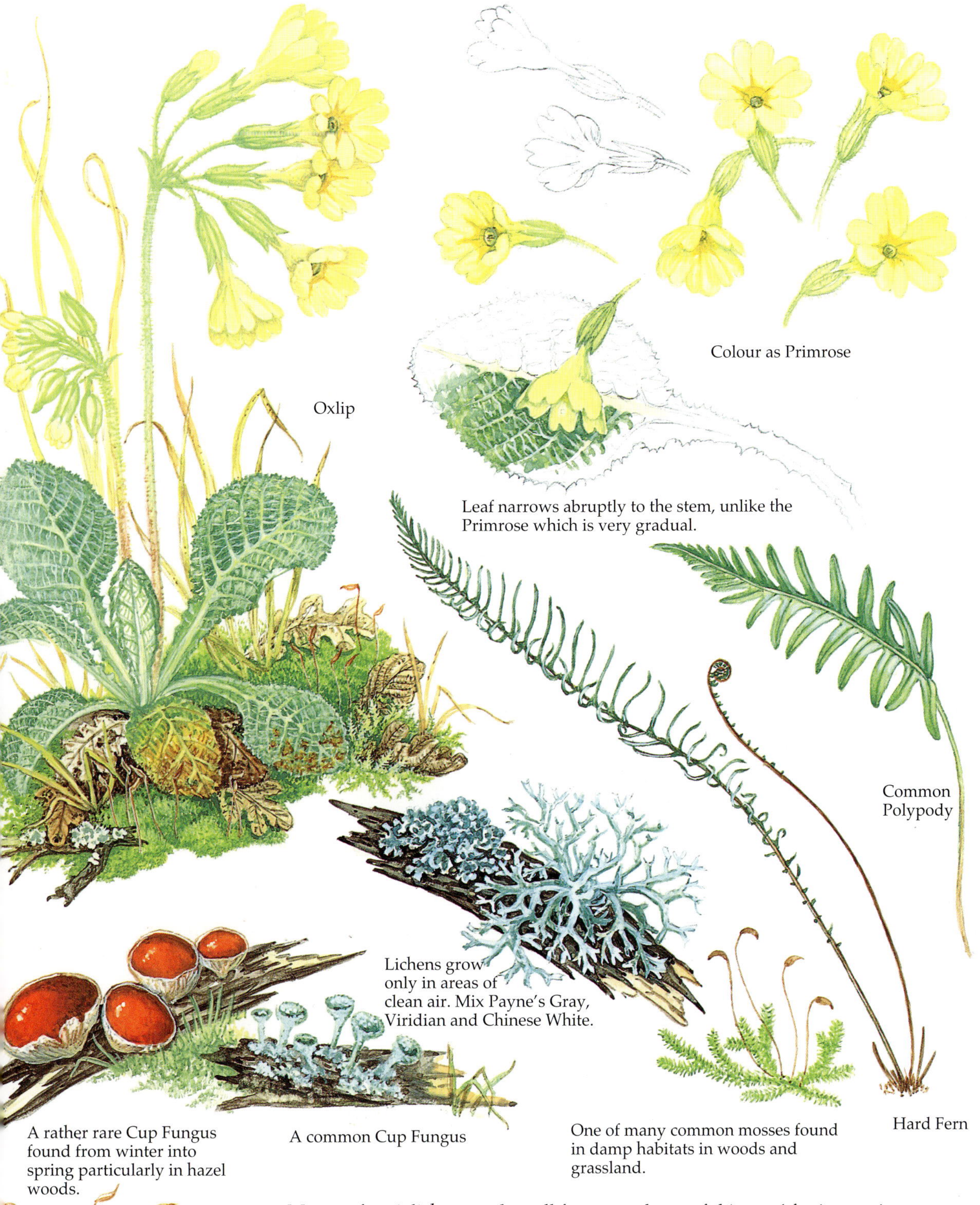

Bright green cushion moss can be found in many woods.

Mosses, fungi, lichens and small ferns are also useful 'props' for interesting foregrounds to a woodland scene. They are also fascinating to paint but do not put too many around any one plant or it will distract attention from the main subject, in this case the rare and delicately coloured Oxlip which grows in damp woods in a few places in S England. It is not difficult to buy a plant, particularly from an Alpine garden nursery, for it grows also in the mountains of Europe. It can be planted in a shady part of the garden and may produce seed but don't put them near Primroses as the resultant plants may well be hybrids called False Oxlip. Fresh pure seed can be bought from many firms.

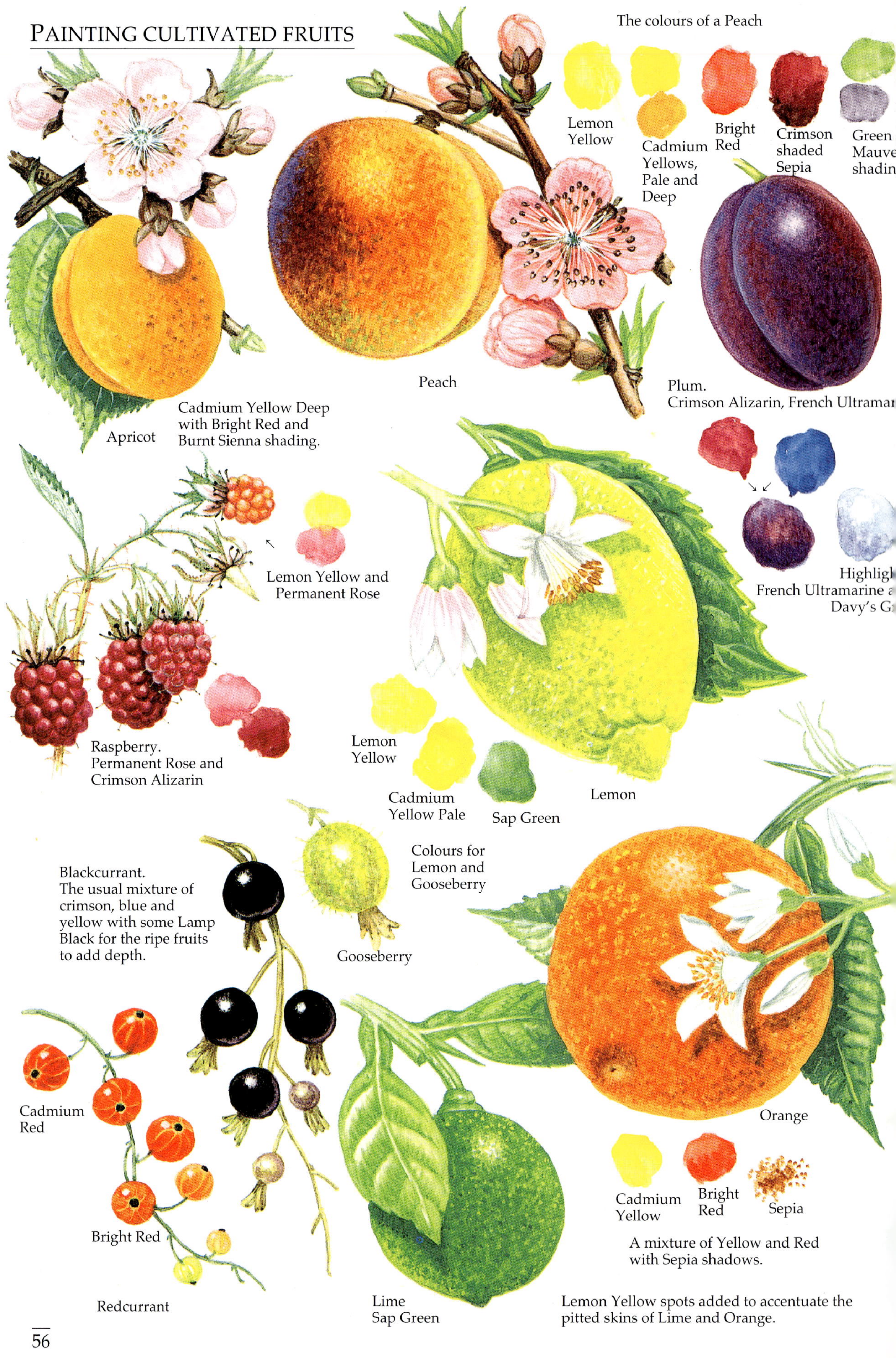
The colours of a Peach
Lemon Yellow
Cadmium Yellows, Pale and Deep
Bright Red
Crimson shaded Sepia
Green Mauve shadin
Apricot
Cadmium Yellow Deep with Bright Red and Burnt Sienna shading.
Peach
Plum.
Crimson Alizarin, French Ultramar
Highligl
French Ultramarine a
Davy's G
Lemon Yellow and Permanent Rose
Raspberry.
Permanent Rose and Crimson Alizarin
Lemon Yellow
Cadmium Yellow Pale
Sap Green
Lemon
Colours for Lemon and Gooseberry
Gooseberry
Blackcurrant.
The usual mixture of crimson, blue and yellow with some Lamp Black for the ripe fruits to add depth.
Cadmium Red
Bright Red
Redcurrant
Orange
Cadmium Yellow
Bright Red
Sepia
A mixture of Yellow and Red with Sepia shadows.
Lime
Sap Green
Lemon Yellow spots added to accentuate the pitted skins of Lime and Orange.

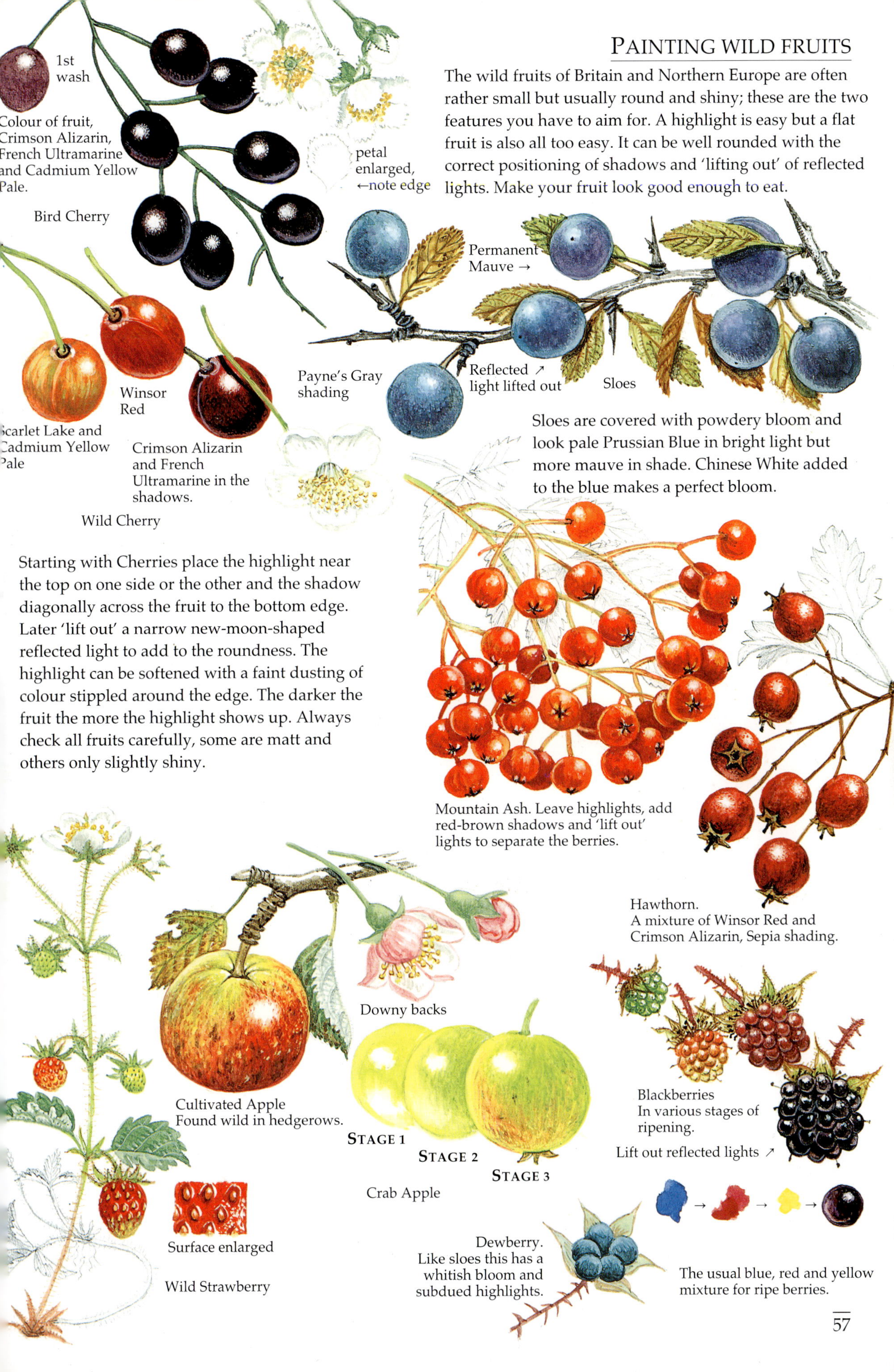

Painting Wild Fruits

The wild fruits of Britain and Northern Europe are often rather small but usually round and shiny; these are the two features you have to aim for. A highlight is easy but a flat fruit is also all too easy. It can be well rounded with the correct positioning of shadows and 'lifting out' of reflected lights. Make your fruit look good enough to eat.

Sloes are covered with powdery bloom and look pale Prussian Blue in bright light but more mauve in shade. Chinese White added to the blue makes a perfect bloom.

Starting with Cherries place the highlight near the top on one side or the other and the shadow diagonally across the fruit to the bottom edge. Later 'lift out' a narrow new-moon-shaped reflected light to add to the roundness. The highlight can be softened with a faint dusting of colour stippled around the edge. The darker the fruit the more the highlight shows up. Always check all fruits carefully, some are matt and others only slightly shiny.

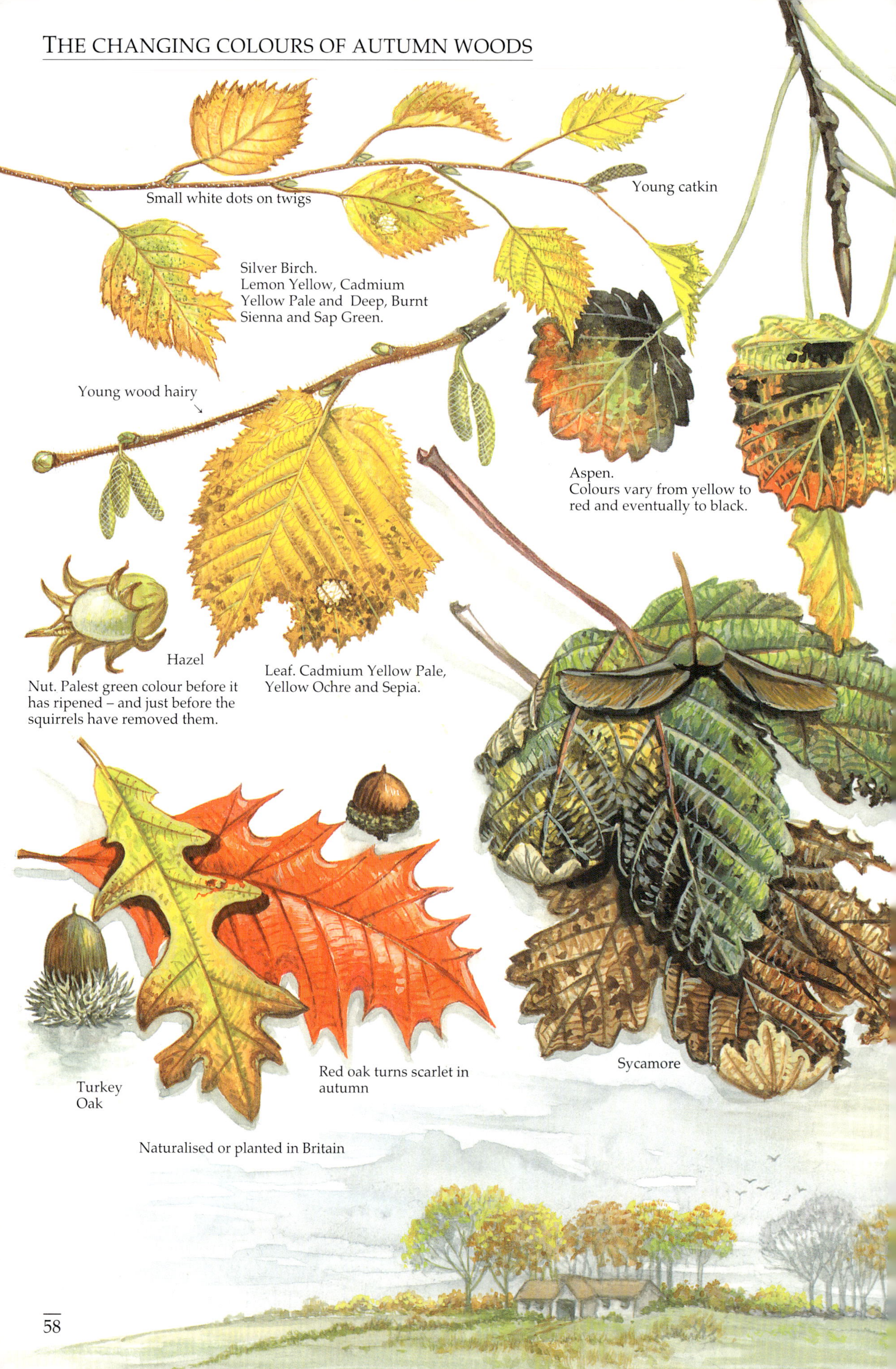
Small white dots on twigs
Young catkin
Silver Birch.
Lemon Yellow, Cadmium Yellow Pale and Deep, Burnt Sienna and Sap Green.
Young wood hairy
Aspen.
Colours vary from yellow to red and eventually to black.
Hazel
Nut. Palest green colour before it has ripened – and just before the squirrels have removed them.
Leaf. Cadmium Yellow Pale, Yellow Ochre and Sepia.
Sycamore
Red oak turns scarlet in autumn
Turkey Oak
Naturalised or planted in Britain

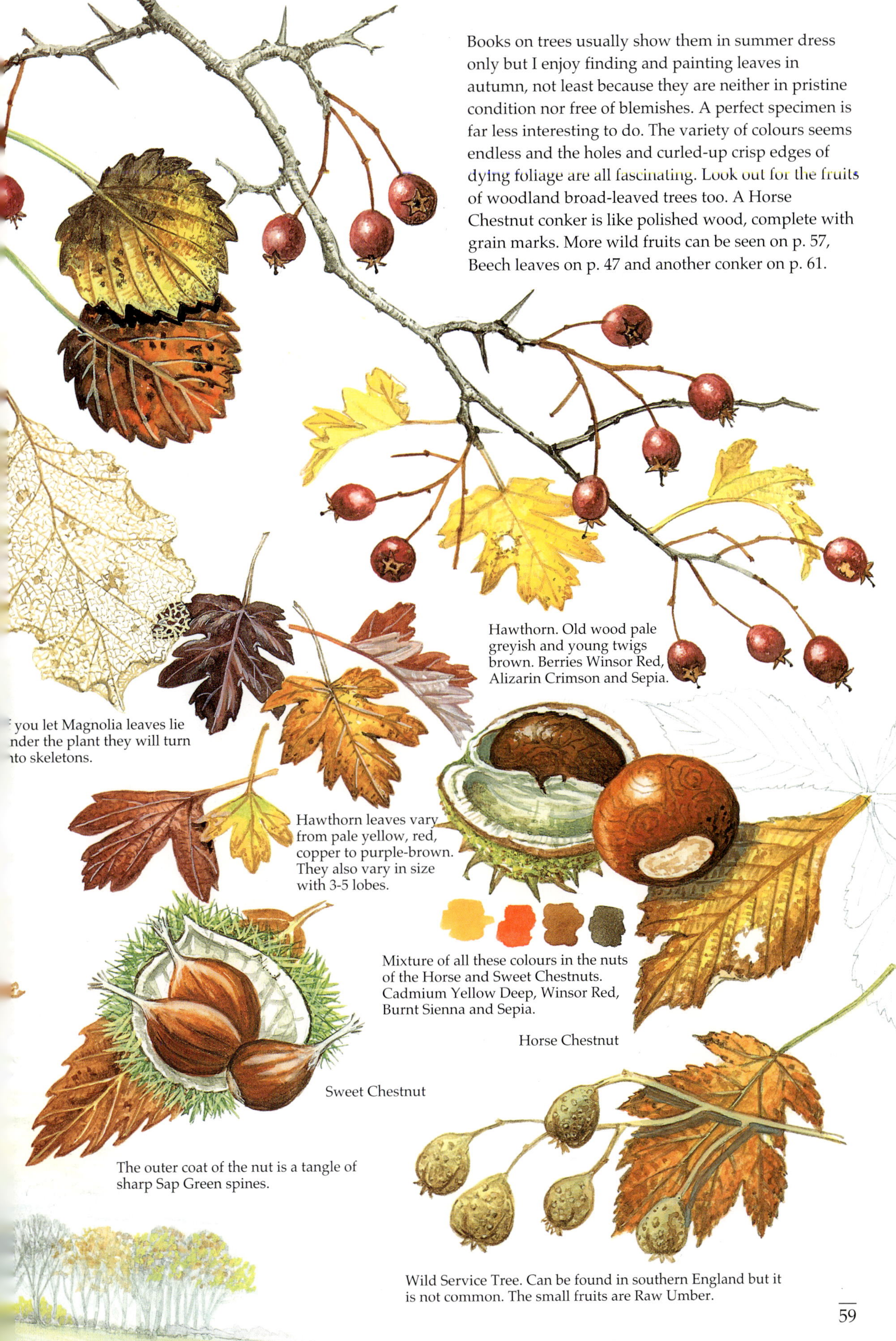

Books on trees usually show them in summer dress only but I enjoy finding and painting leaves in autumn, not least because they are neither in pristine condition nor free of blemishes. A perfect specimen is far less interesting to do. The variety of colours seems endless and the holes and curled-up crisp edges of dying foliage are all fascinating. Look out for the fruits of woodland broad-leaved trees too. A Horse Chestnut conker is like polished wood, complete with grain marks. More wild fruits can be seen on p. 57, Beech leaves on p. 47 and another conker on p. 61.

Hawthorn. Old wood pale greyish and young twigs brown. Berries Winsor Red, Alizarin Crimson and Sepia.

f you let Magnolia leaves lie nder the plant they will turn nto skeletons.

Hawthorn leaves vary from pale yellow, red, copper to purple-brown. They also vary in size with 3-5 lobes.

Mixture of all these colours in the nuts of the Horse and Sweet Chestnuts. Cadmium Yellow Deep, Winsor Red, Burnt Sienna and Sepia.

Horse Chestnut

Sweet Chestnut

The outer coat of the nut is a tangle of sharp Sap Green spines.

Wild Service Tree. Can be found in southern England but it is not common. The small fruits are Raw Umber.

Planning a Picture

'Autumn Harvest'

If you combine the brown beech leaves on p. 47 with some wild fruits on p. 57 you have the basic ingredients for an autumn picture. Then add some extra touches such as a conker, the covering of which I painted in yellow-green with brown-green markings. I then left the woodland floor to reach up to the bushes draped with Old Man's Beard, which are the seeds of Traveller's Joy, the only wild Clematis in Britain. In the hedgerow I found Spindle berries, nature's best and brightest colour clash, also Guelder-rose and Dogwood which provided the right shapes and tones I was was looking for to balance the design.

The fact that the Blackberries I sketched in September on p. 29 have joined forces with the Beech leaves I am now painting on this page in November can be put down to artistic licence, a privilege we cannot enjoy if we hold a camera rather than a paint brush.

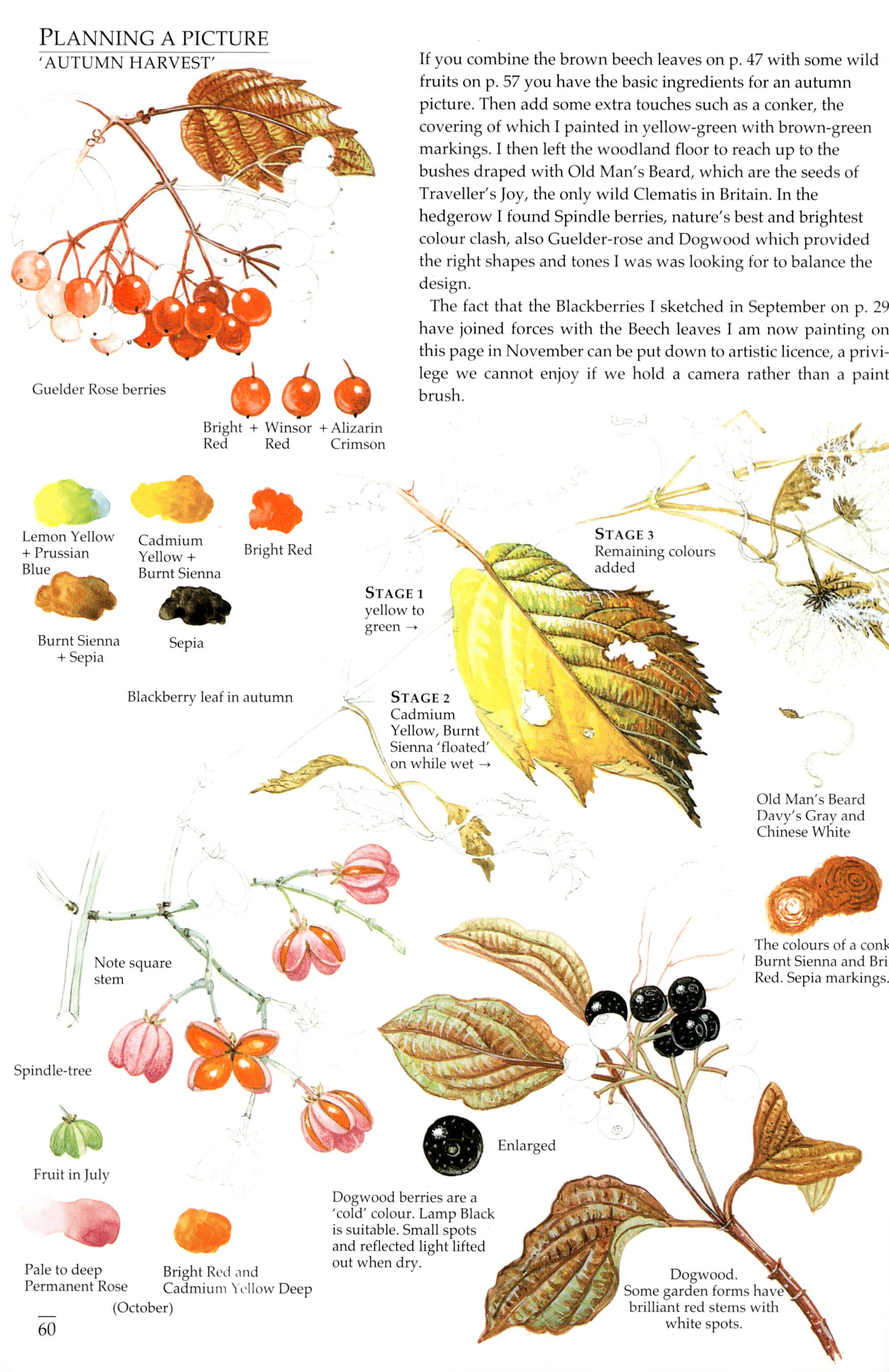

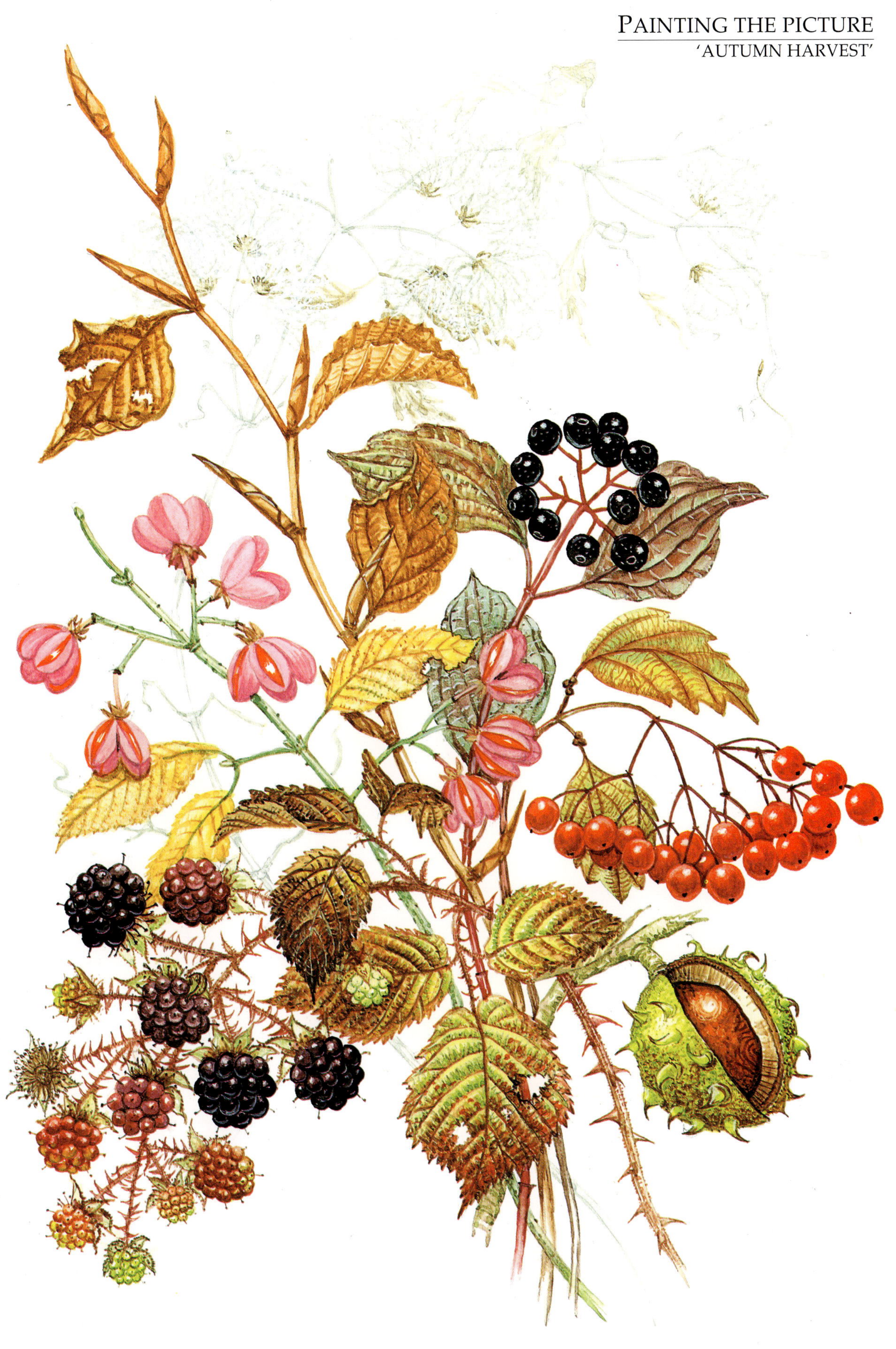

DRIED FLOWERS AND SEEDHEADS
FOR WINTER PICTURES

If you don't dry your own flowers for winter decoration it is now easy to buy them in flower shops and nurseries. Some plants however are simple to grow and almost self-drying such as Achilleas, the straw-like Helichrysums, grasses and seedheads of Opium Poppies and the silvery transparent discs of Honesty.

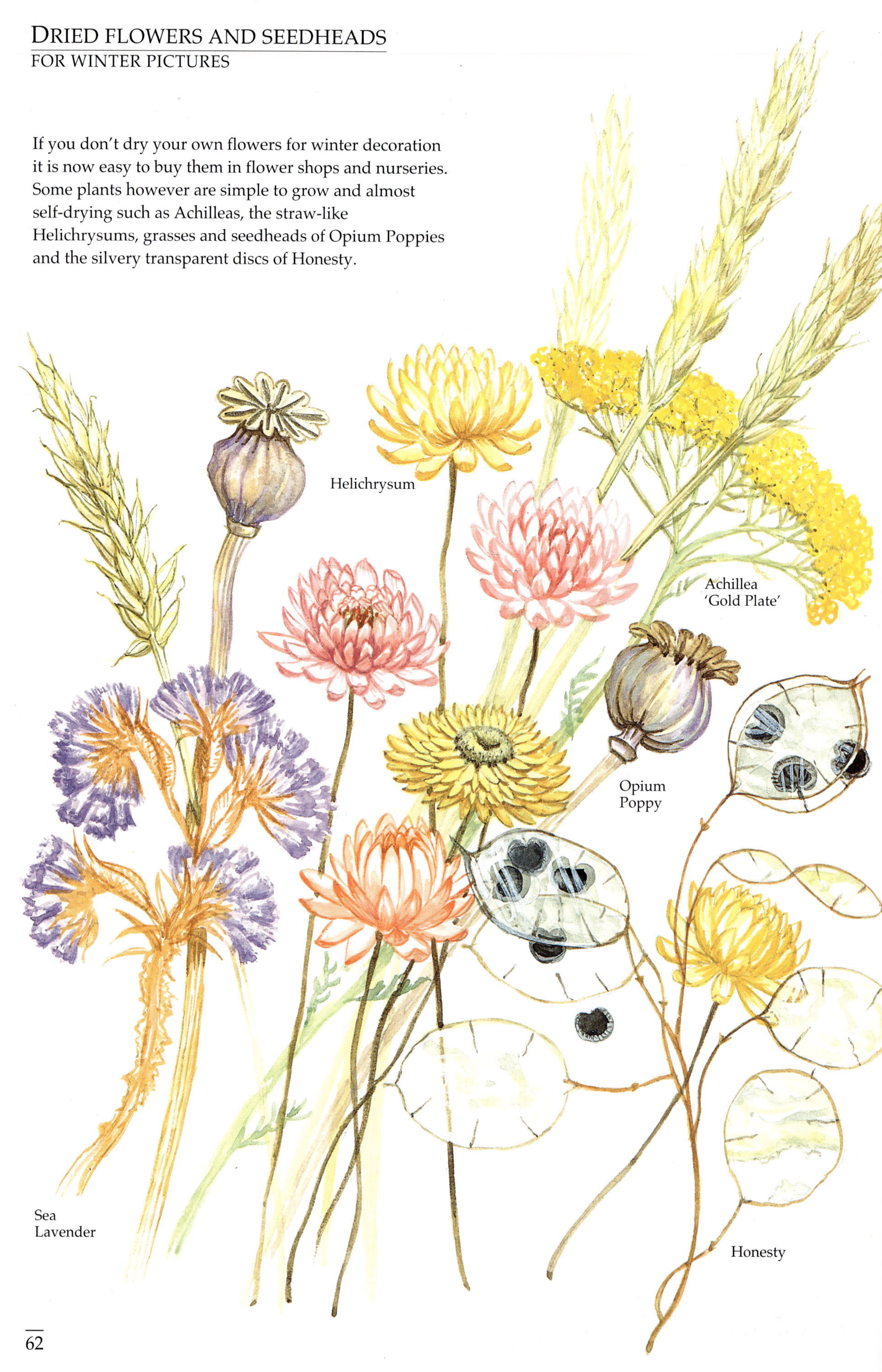

Easily dried grasses which I like to paint when they have really faded, and are soft creamy parchment colours. Some you can grow in the garden include Great Quaking Grass and Hare's-tail. Other grasses grow wild and can be found in the countryside. Paintable seedheads include Love-in-a-mist, Red Campion and some easily found Fir cones. Most of the paints used are the umbers and siennas with Sepia and Naples Yellow.

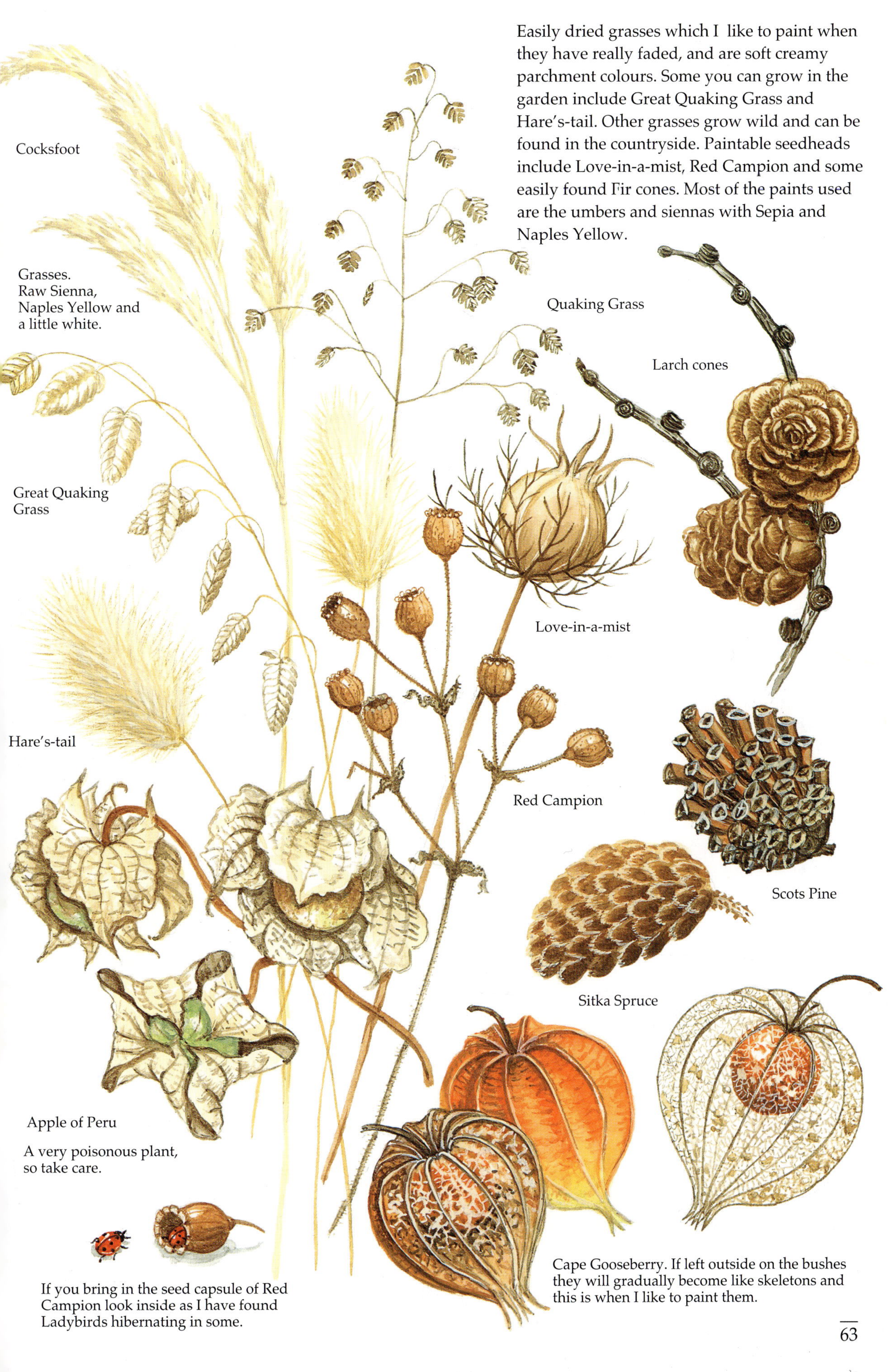

If you bring in the seed capsule of Red Campion look inside as I have found Ladybirds hibernating in some.

Cape Gooseberry. If left outside on the bushes they will gradually become like skeletons and this is when I like to paint them.

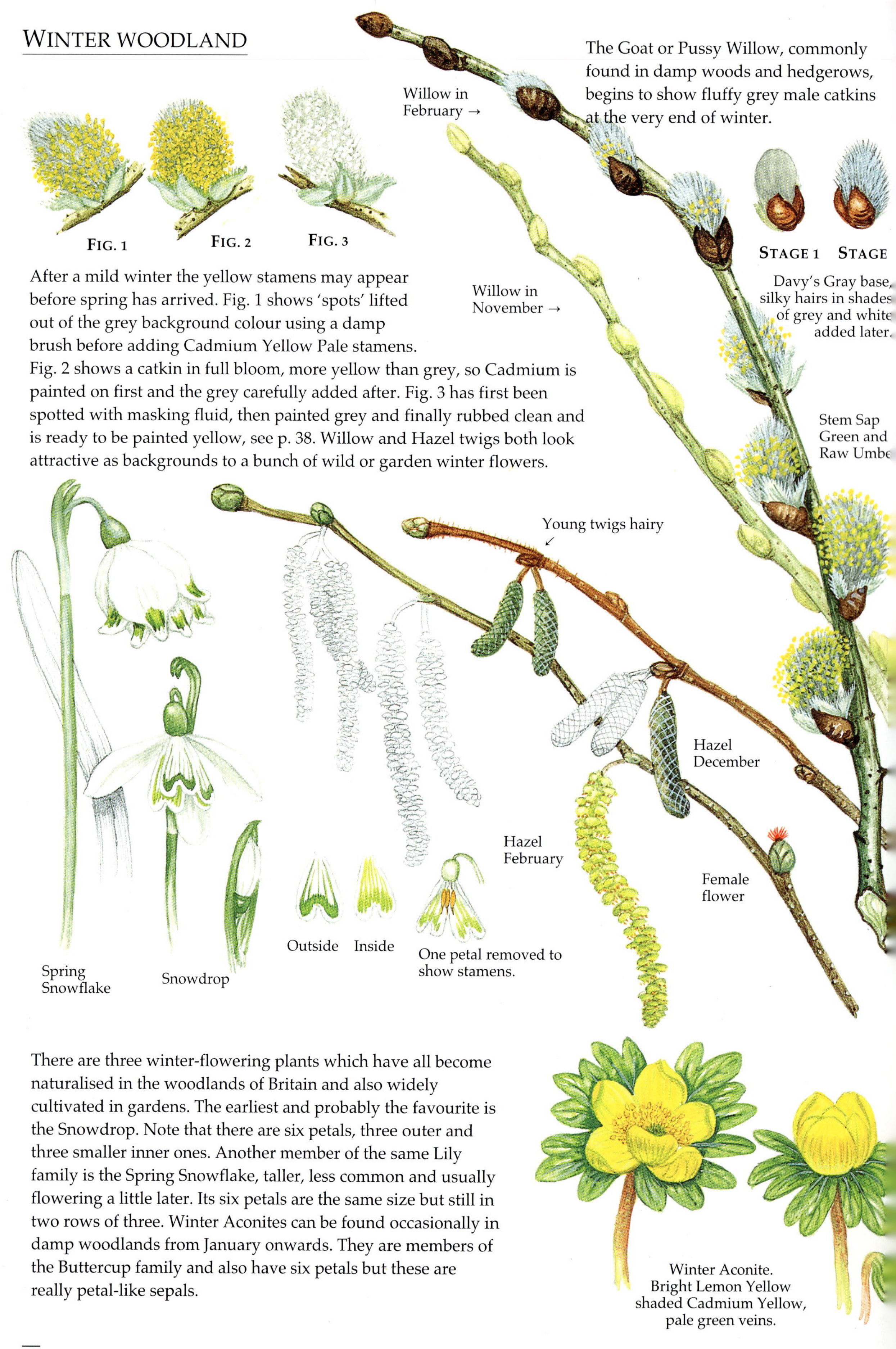

The Goat or Pussy Willow, commonly found in damp woods and hedgerows, begins to show fluffy grey male catkins at the very end of winter.

After a mild winter the yellow stamens may appear before spring has arrived. Fig. 1 shows 'spots' lifted out of the grey background colour using a damp brush before adding Cadmium Yellow Pale stamens. Fig. 2 shows a catkin in full bloom, more yellow than grey, so Cadmium is painted on first and the grey carefully added after. Fig. 3 has first been spotted with masking fluid, then painted grey and finally rubbed clean and is ready to be painted yellow, see p. 38. Willow and Hazel twigs both look attractive as backgrounds to a bunch of wild or garden winter flowers.

There are three winter-flowering plants which have all become naturalised in the woodlands of Britain and also widely cultivated in gardens. The earliest and probably the favourite is the Snowdrop. Note that there are six petals, three outer and three smaller inner ones. Another member of the same Lily family is the Spring Snowflake, taller, less common and usually flowering a little later. Its six petals are the same size but still in two rows of three. Winter Aconites can be found occasionally in damp woodlands from January onwards. They are members of the Buttercup family and also have six petals but these are really petal-like sepals.

Winter Aconite. Bright Lemon Yellow shaded Cadmium Yellow, pale green veins.

Snowdrops in winter with touches of frost on dead leaves but no background as I wanted to convey a pristine cold and uncluttered look to the picture. This is only a small section of a large painting I did, a miniature version of which is sketched below to give an idea of the overall shape of the design. The close-up group of Snowdrops show that they were painted in full detail, but to give an illusion of distance, the flowers in the background were painted in paler shades and with less detail added.

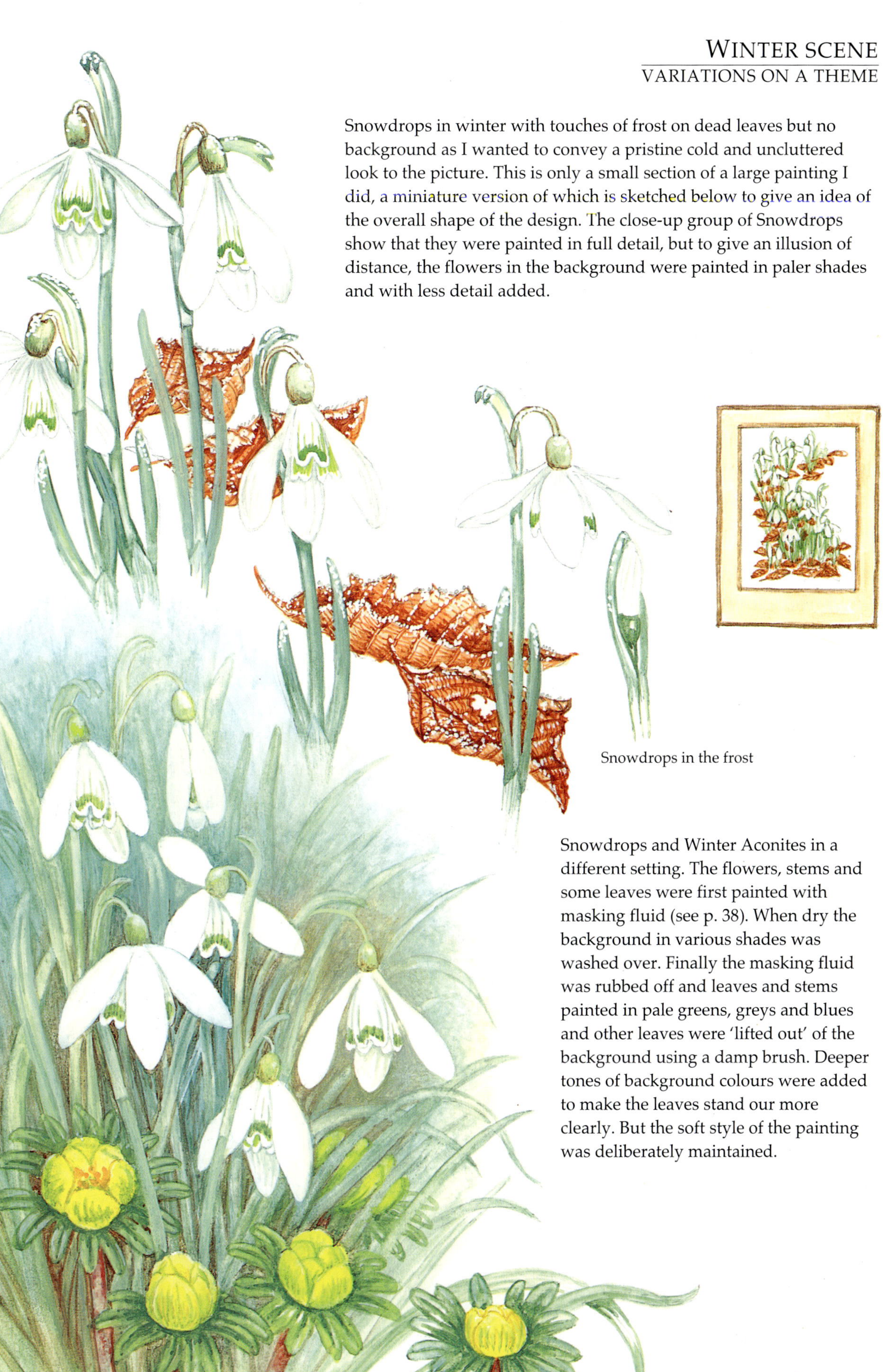

Snowdrops in the frost

Snowdrops and Winter Aconites in a different setting. The flowers, stems and some leaves were first painted with masking fluid (see p. 38). When dry the background in various shades was washed over. Finally the masking fluid was rubbed off and leaves and stems painted in pale greens, greys and blues and other leaves were 'lifted out' of the background using a damp brush. Deeper tones of background colours were added to make the leaves stand our more clearly. But the soft style of the painting was deliberately maintained.

TREES IN THE BACKGROUND

Trees can be most useful as backgrounds to flower scenes, varying from Bluebells in a wood, herbaceous borders backed by hedges or Scots Pines in a heather moorland setting. Silver Birches and Willows are particularly attractive to draw or paint and are not overpowering.

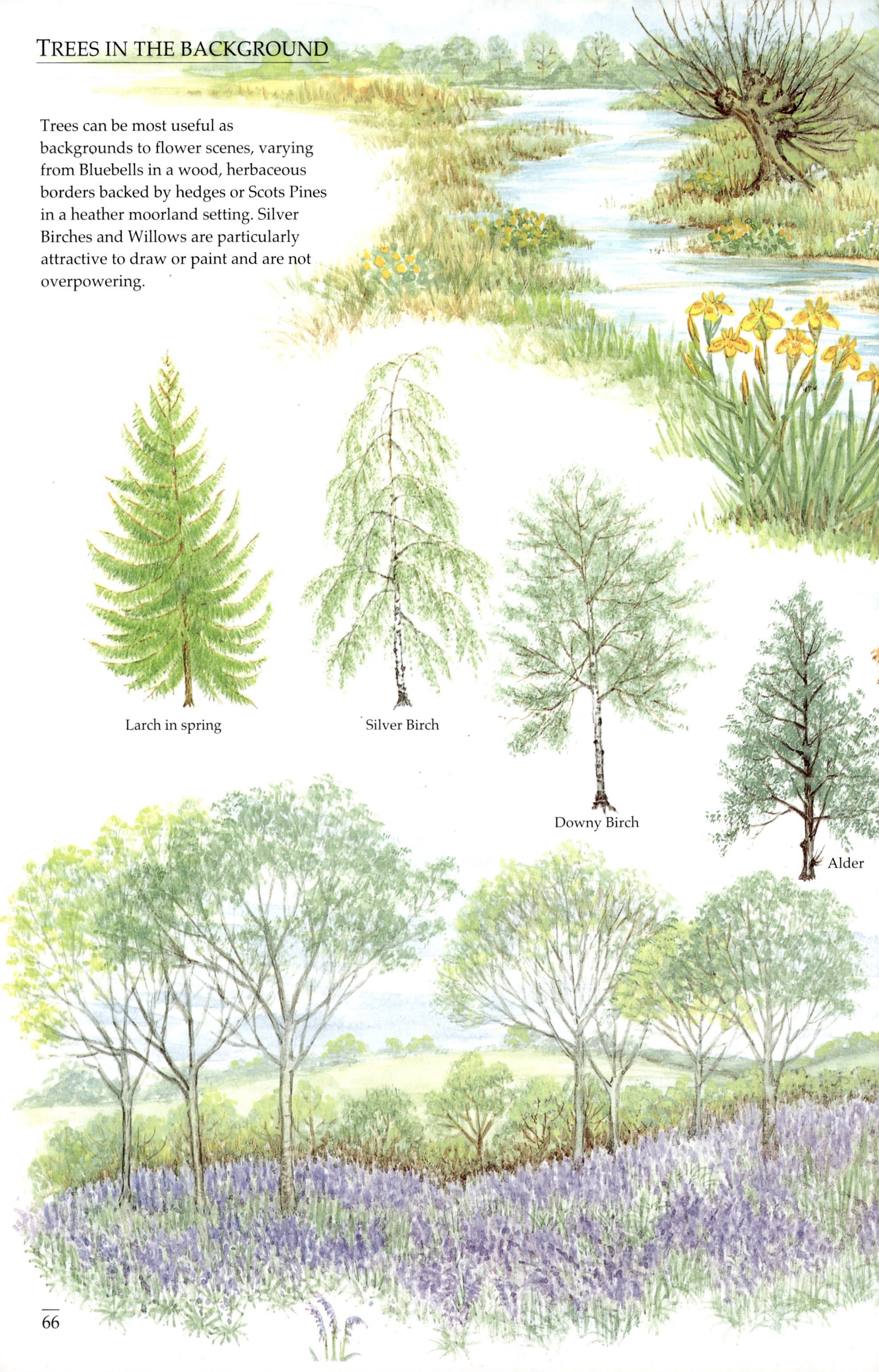

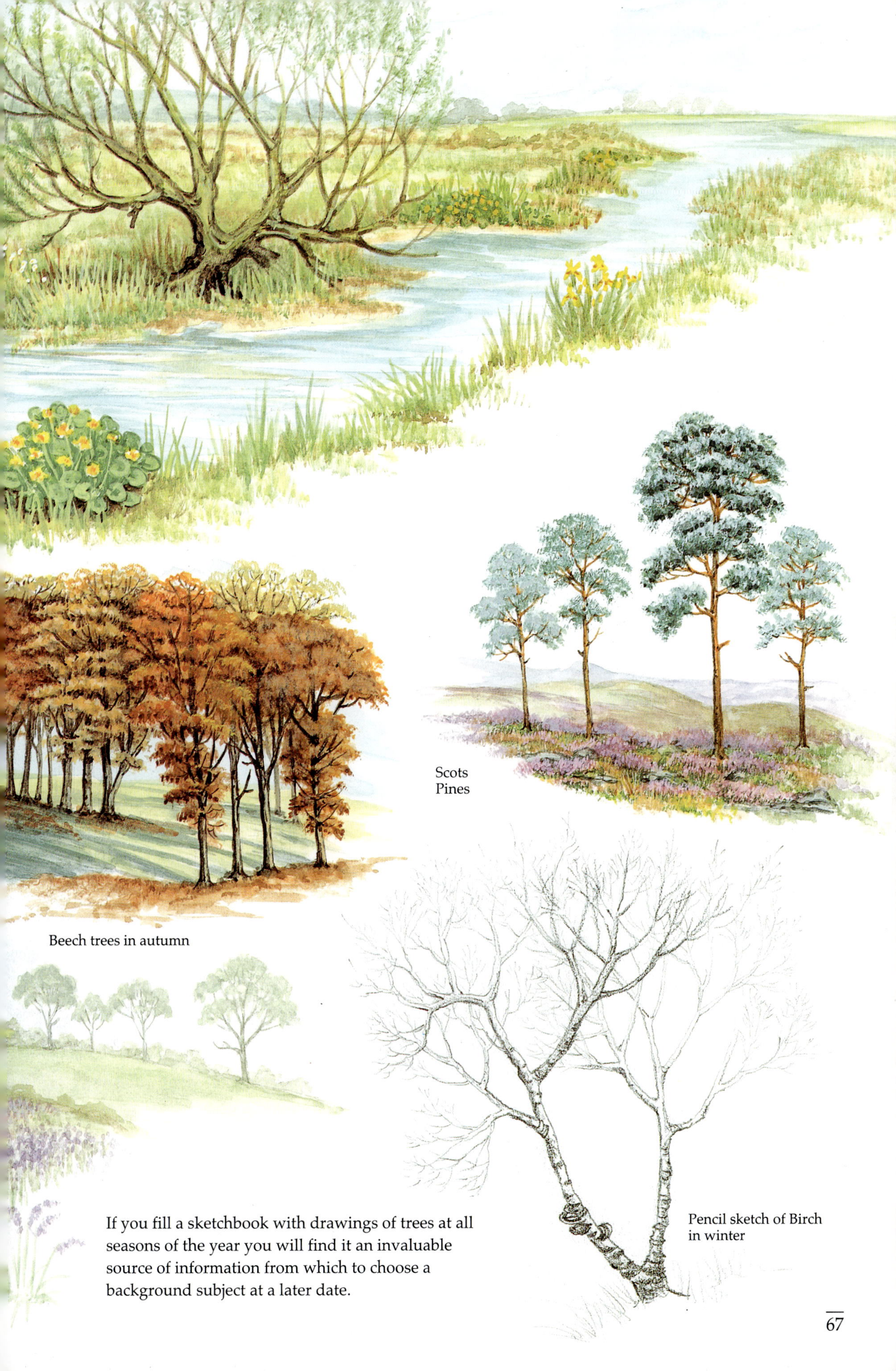

Scots Pines

Beech trees in autumn

Pencil sketch of Birch in winter

If you fill a sketchbook with drawings of trees at all seasons of the year you will find it an invaluable source of information from which to choose a background subject at a later date.

WILD FLOWERS IN THEIR HABITATS

CHALK GRASSLAND

Flowers that grow on chalk or limestone grassland are very distinctive. Many are rare and protected plants. The two Bellflowers can be bought for the garden and painted at leisure but the orchids – only two of many species on chalk downland – have to be painted where they grow.

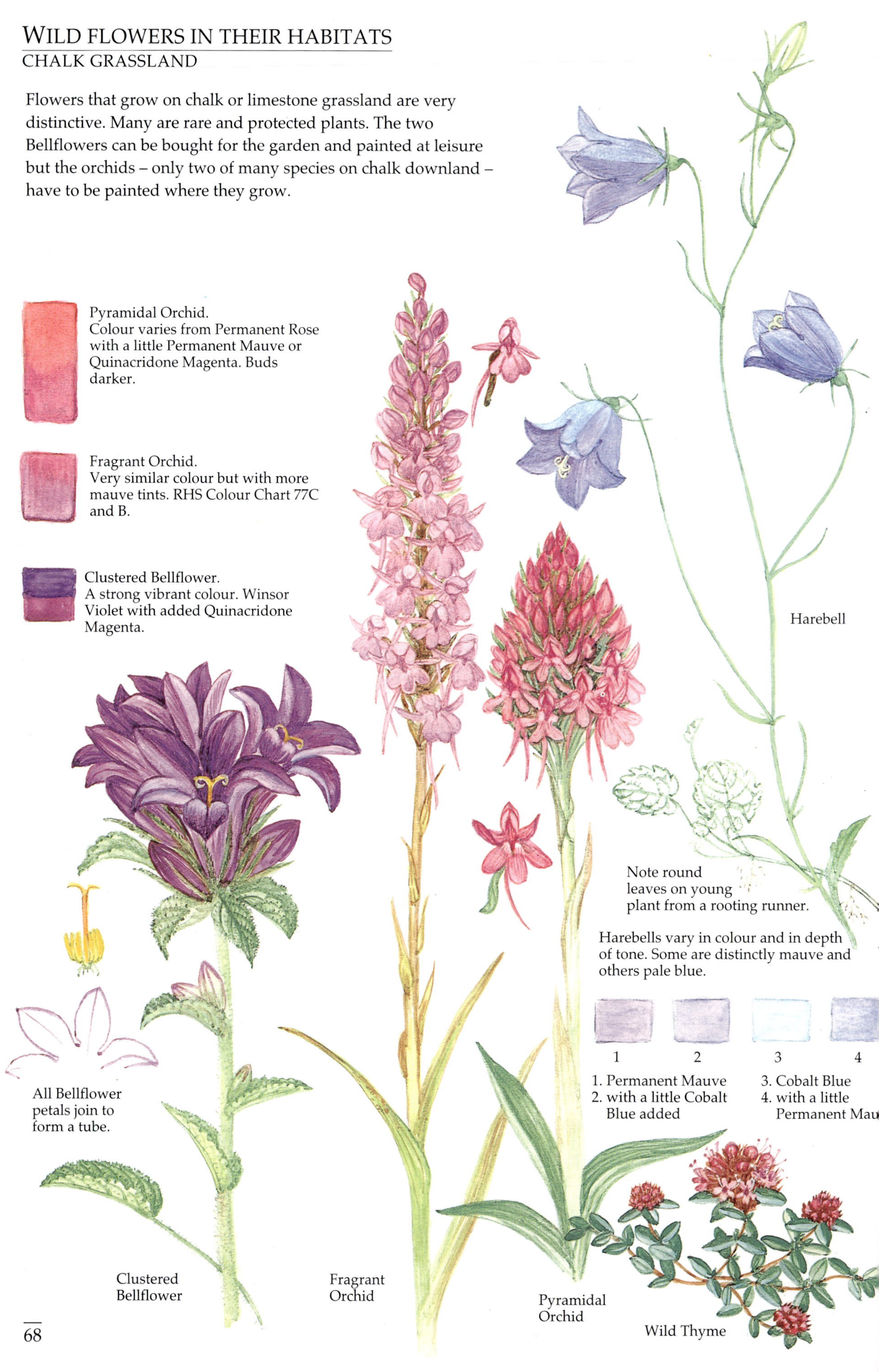

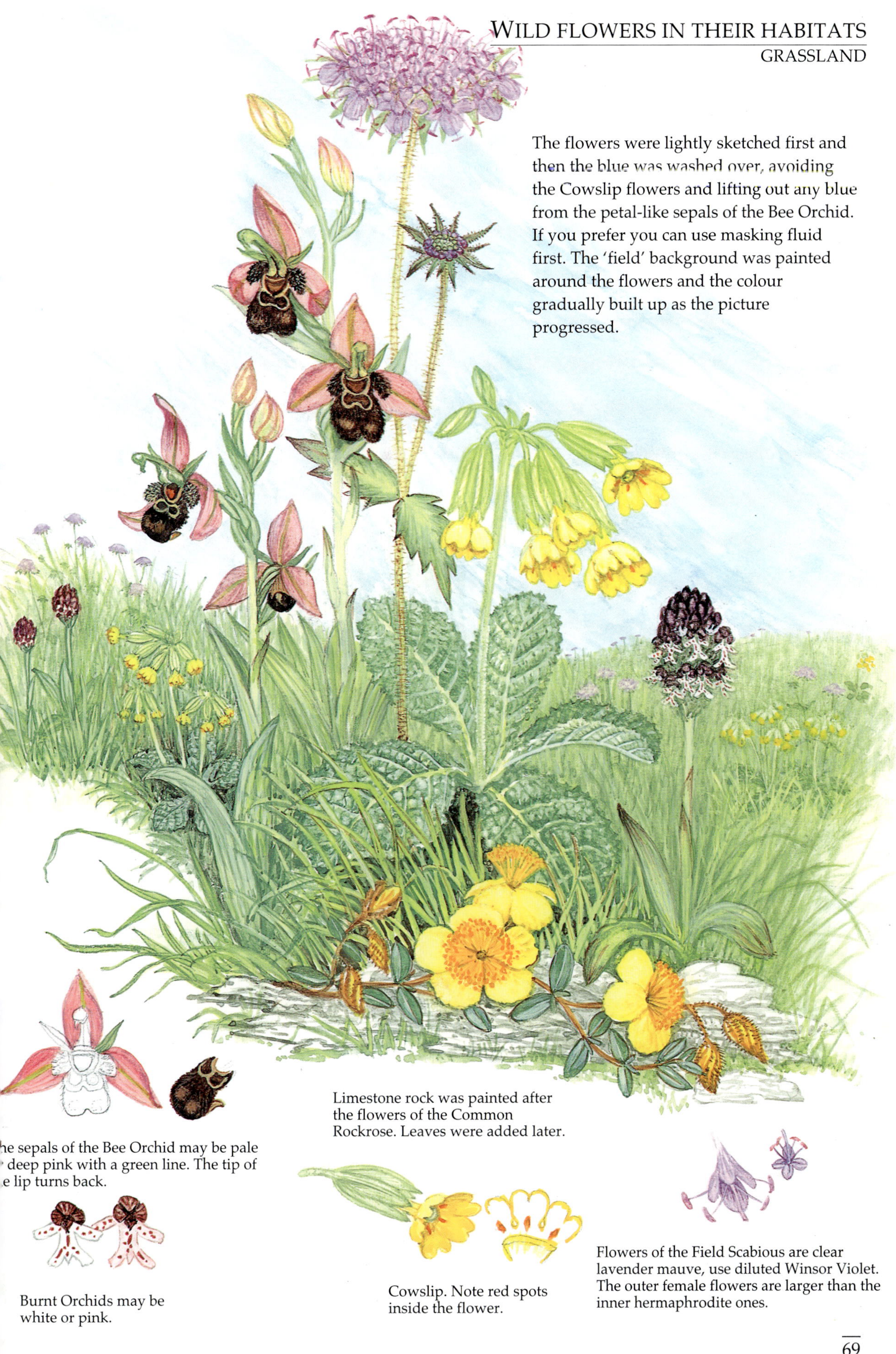

The flowers were lightly sketched first and then the blue was washed over, avoiding the Cowslip flowers and lifting out any blue from the petal-like sepals of the Bee Orchid. If you prefer you can use masking fluid first. The 'field' background was painted around the flowers and the colour gradually built up as the picture progressed.

Limestone rock was painted after the flowers of the Common Rockrose. Leaves were added later.

he sepals of the Bee Orchid may be pale deep pink with a green line. The tip of e lip turns back.

Burnt Orchids may be white or pink.

Cowslip. Note red spots inside the flower.

Flowers of the Field Scabious are clear lavender mauve, use diluted Winsor Violet. The outer female flowers are larger than the inner hermaphrodite ones.

Meadowland is really another name for a farm field which is sown with grass for cattle fodder. Such fields are therefore 'man-made' and sadly bare of 'weeds' in other words our native flora! Around the margins you may find a few attractive ones. I did the painting below in the same labour-intensive style I used on the previous page. First the pencil sketch then the sky avoiding the white Bladder Campion flowers on the left. Background next, field by field and finally the frieze of flowers. I broke the purist rule and mixed some Zinc White gouache with the greens for the heads of the grasses. The two remaining flowers are the Common Poppy and the blue Meadow Crane's-bill.

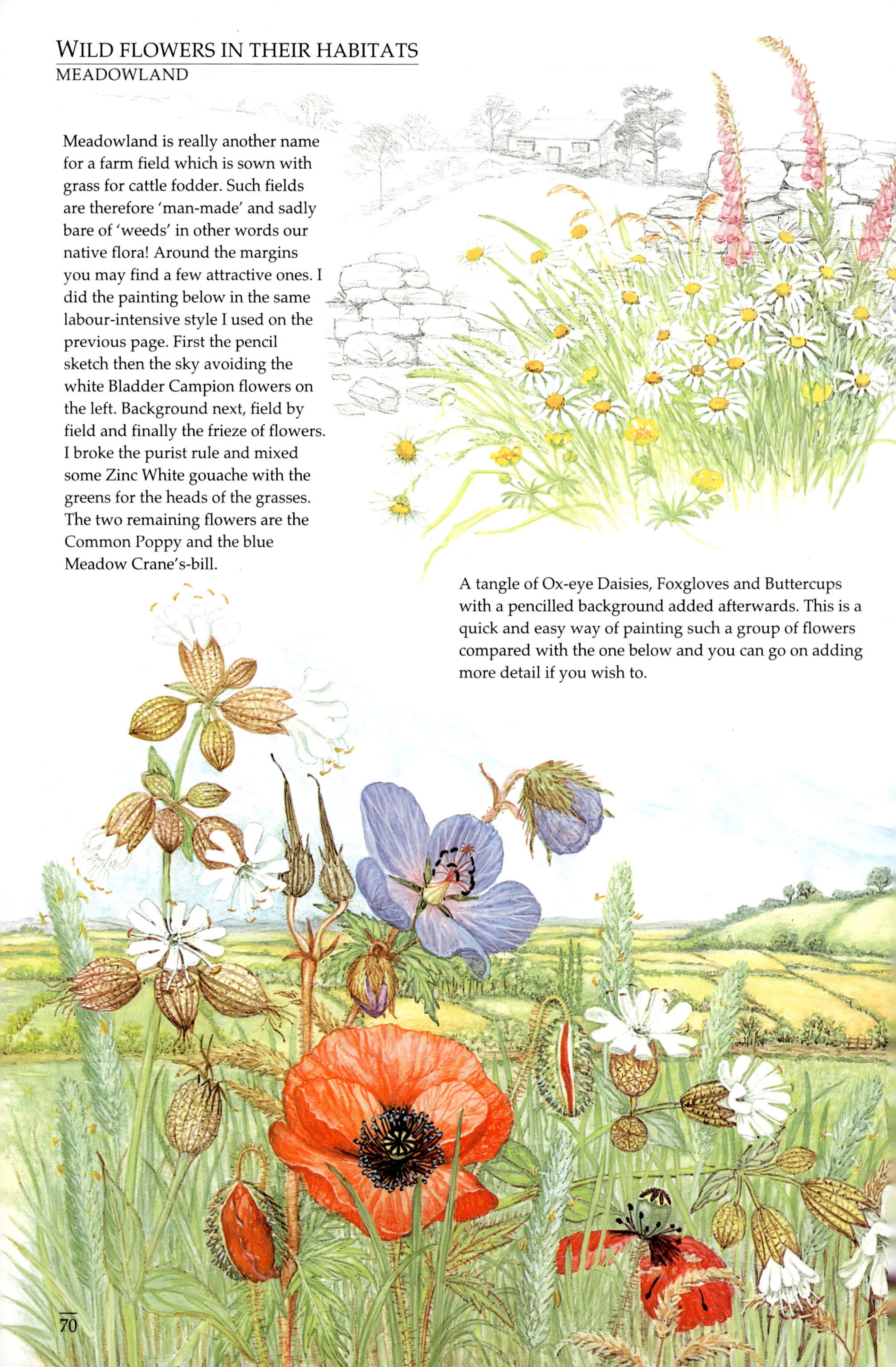

A tangle of Ox-eye Daisies, Foxgloves and Buttercups with a pencilled background added afterwards. This is a quick and easy way of painting such a group of flowers compared with the one below and you can go on adding more detail if you wish to.

Wetlands are becoming increasingly rare and beautiful plants can be found there. The tall Yellow Iris is very noticeable in marshes with its bright flowers but many other species found growing actually in water are white or very pale pink and often three-petalled such as Arrowheads, Water Plantains and Frogbits or the multi-petalled Water Lilies which everyone knows. If you are looking for really colourful flowers to paint then the well stocked garden pool is probably the best place to visit (p. 93). There are several species of Water Crowfoot, some growing in muddy ditches and others surviving in fast flowing rivers with long strong stems anchored to the bottom. Some have aerial leaves and quite different feathery submerged ones.

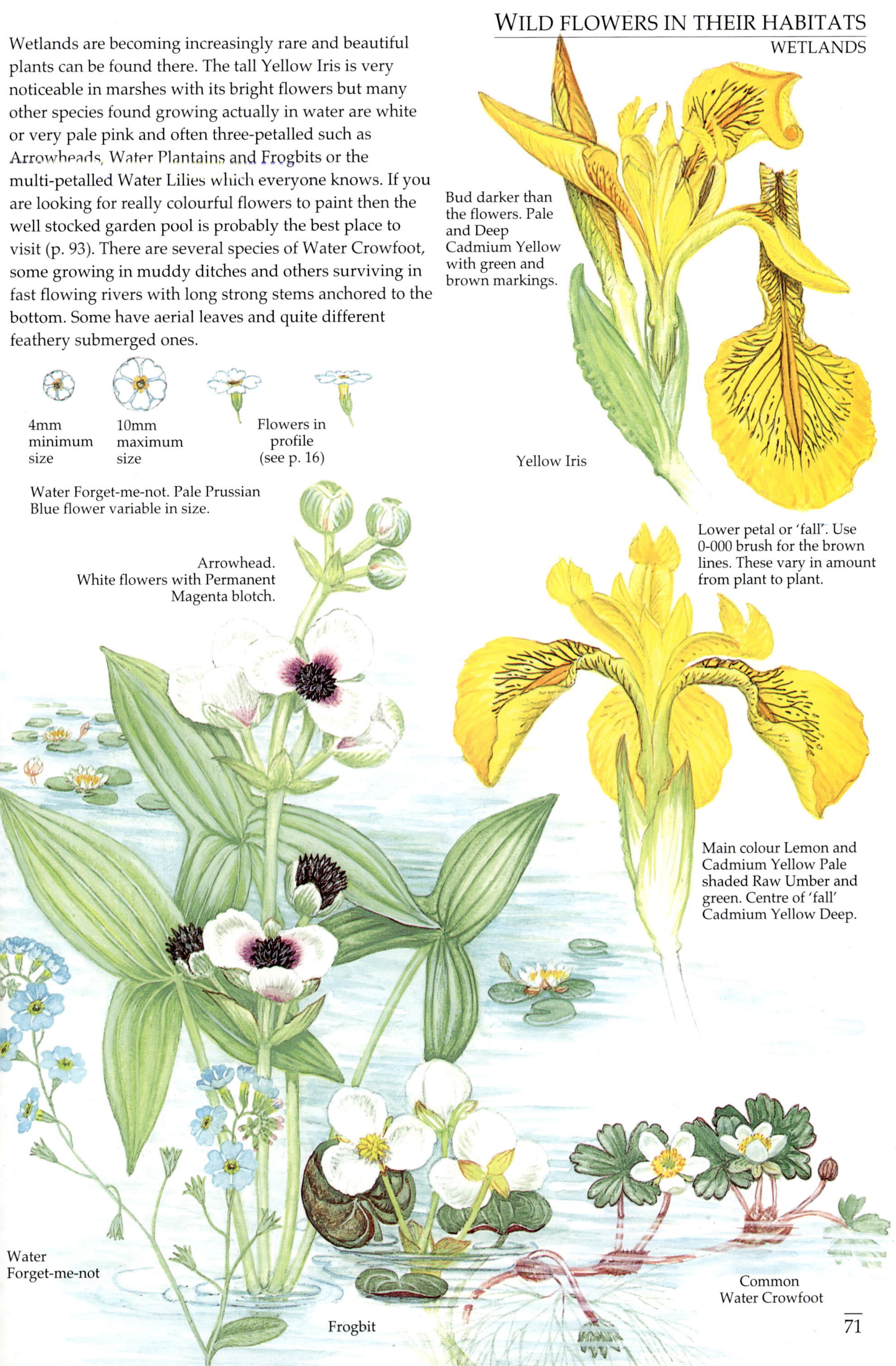

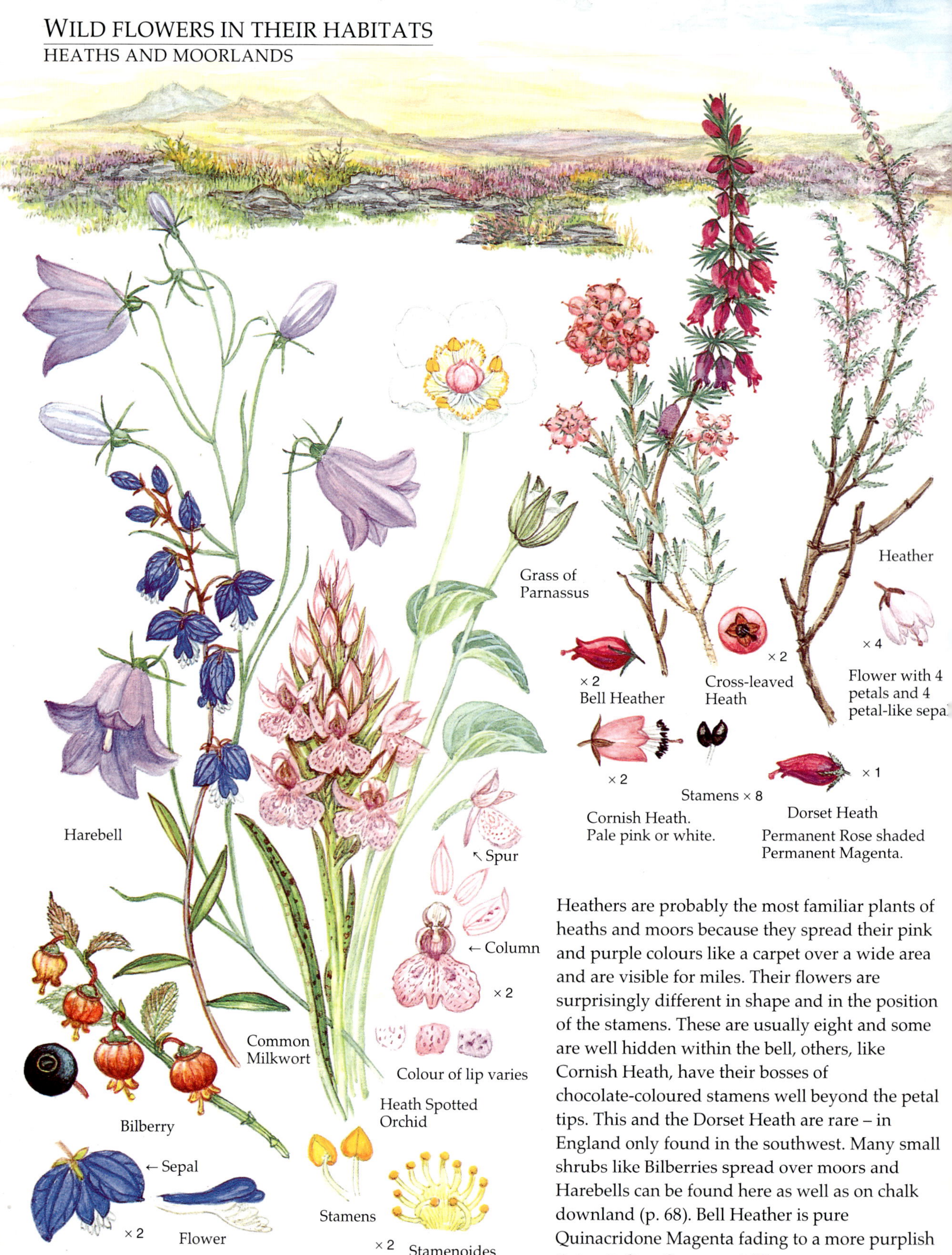

Heathers are probably the most familiar plants of heaths and moors because they spread their pink and purple colours like a carpet over a wide area and are visible for miles. Their flowers are surprisingly different in shape and in the position of the stamens. These are usually eight and some are well hidden within the bell, others, like Cornish Heath, have their bosses of chocolate-coloured stamens well beyond the petal tips. This and the Dorset Heath are rare – in England only found in the southwest. Many small shrubs like Bilberries spread over moors and Harebells can be found here as well as on chalk downland (p. 68). Bell Heather is pure Quinacridone Magenta fading to a more purplish tint as it dies. Common Milkworts are more variable and can be white, magenta or bright blue.

Other plants found in these habitats include Heath Spotted Orchids and in damp areas Grass of Parnassus.

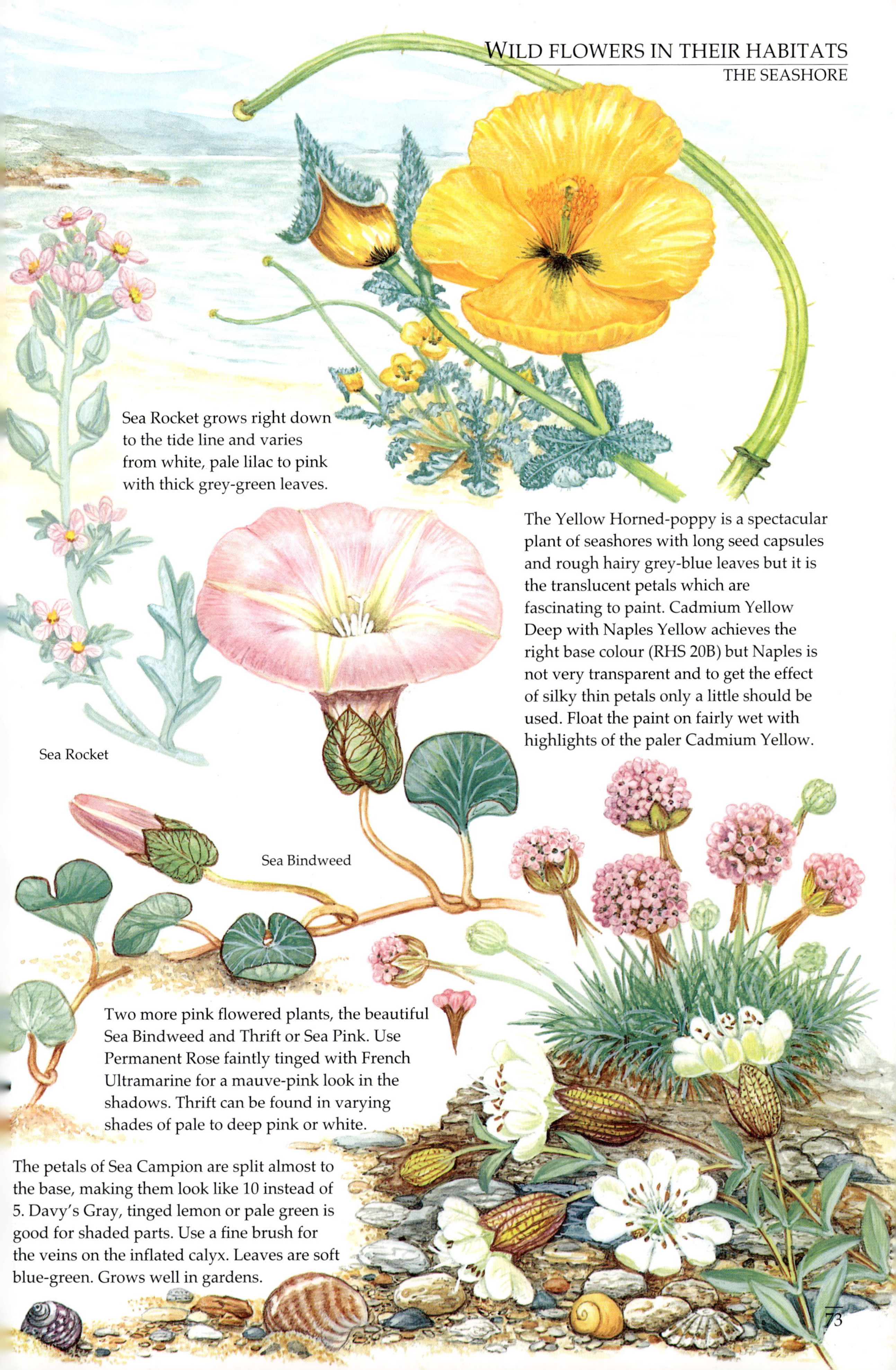

Sea Rocket grows right down to the tide line and varies from white, pale lilac to pink with thick grey-green leaves.

The Yellow Horned-poppy is a spectacular plant of seashores with long seed capsules and rough hairy grey-blue leaves but it is the translucent petals which are fascinating to paint. Cadmium Yellow Deep with Naples Yellow achieves the right base colour (RHS 20B) but Naples is not very transparent and to get the effect of silky thin petals only a little should be used. Float the paint on fairly wet with highlights of the paler Cadmium Yellow.

Two more pink flowered plants, the beautiful Sea Bindweed and Thrift or Sea Pink. Use Permanent Rose faintly tinged with French Ultramarine for a mauve-pink look in the shadows. Thrift can be found in varying shades of pale to deep pink or white.

The petals of Sea Campion are split almost to the base, making them look like 10 instead of 5. Davy's Gray, tinged lemon or pale green is good for shaded parts. Use a fine brush for the veins on the inflated calyx. Leaves are soft blue-green. Grows well in gardens.

Garden Flowers in Spring

Bulbs are the most popular group of plants for this time of the year in the garden. A small area of grass, or a sloping bank, can be transformed if small-flowered bulbs are planted in a scattered natural way and allowed to spread, providing many beautiful subjects to paint.

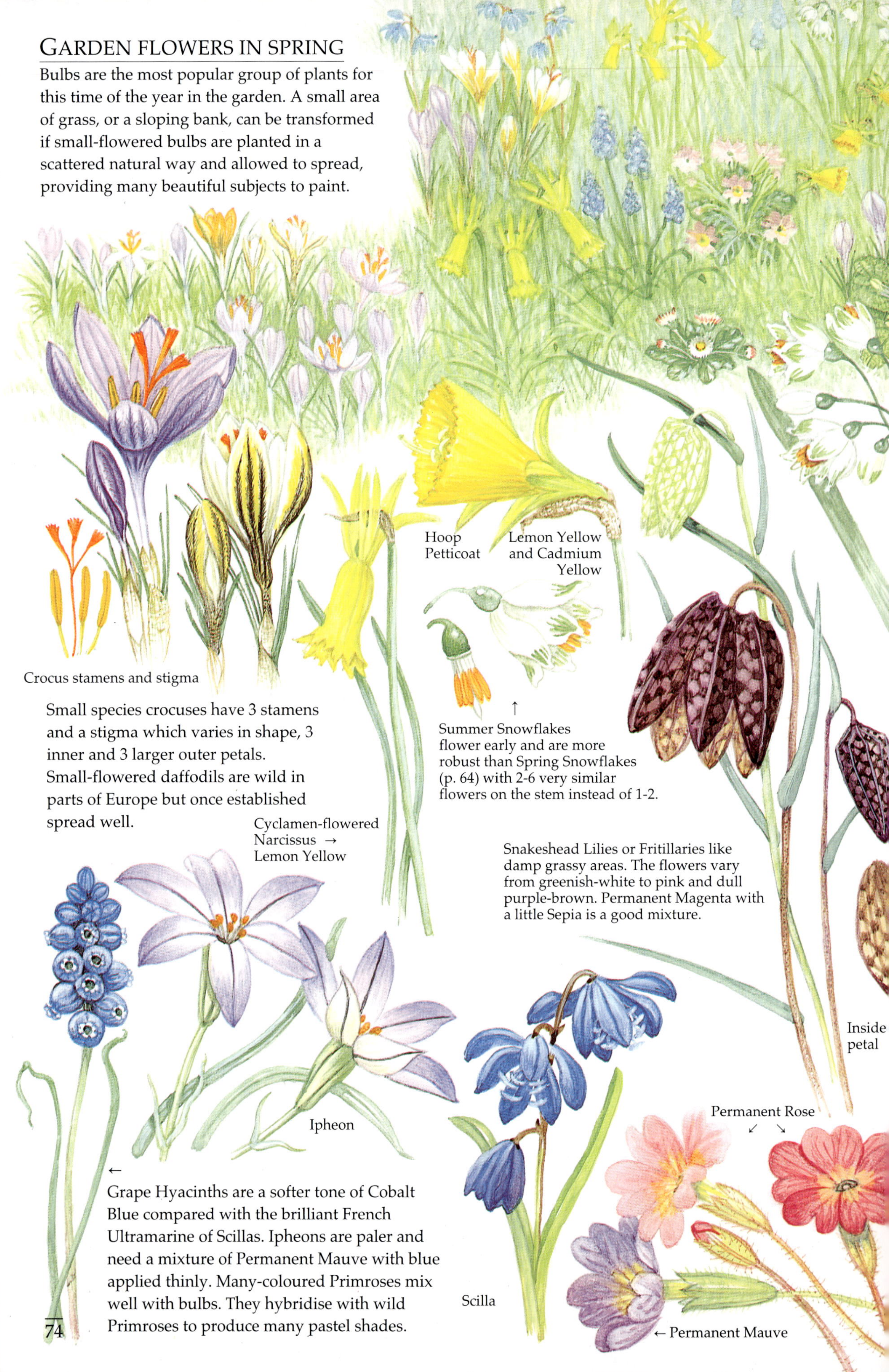

Small species crocuses have 3 stamens and a stigma which varies in shape, 3 inner and 3 larger outer petals. Small-flowered daffodils are wild in parts of Europe but once established spread well.

Grape Hyacinths are a softer tone of Cobalt Blue compared with the brilliant French Ultramarine of Scillas. Ipheons are paler and need a mixture of Permanent Mauve with blue applied thinly. Many-coloured Primroses mix well with bulbs. They hybridise with wild Primroses to produce many pastel shades.

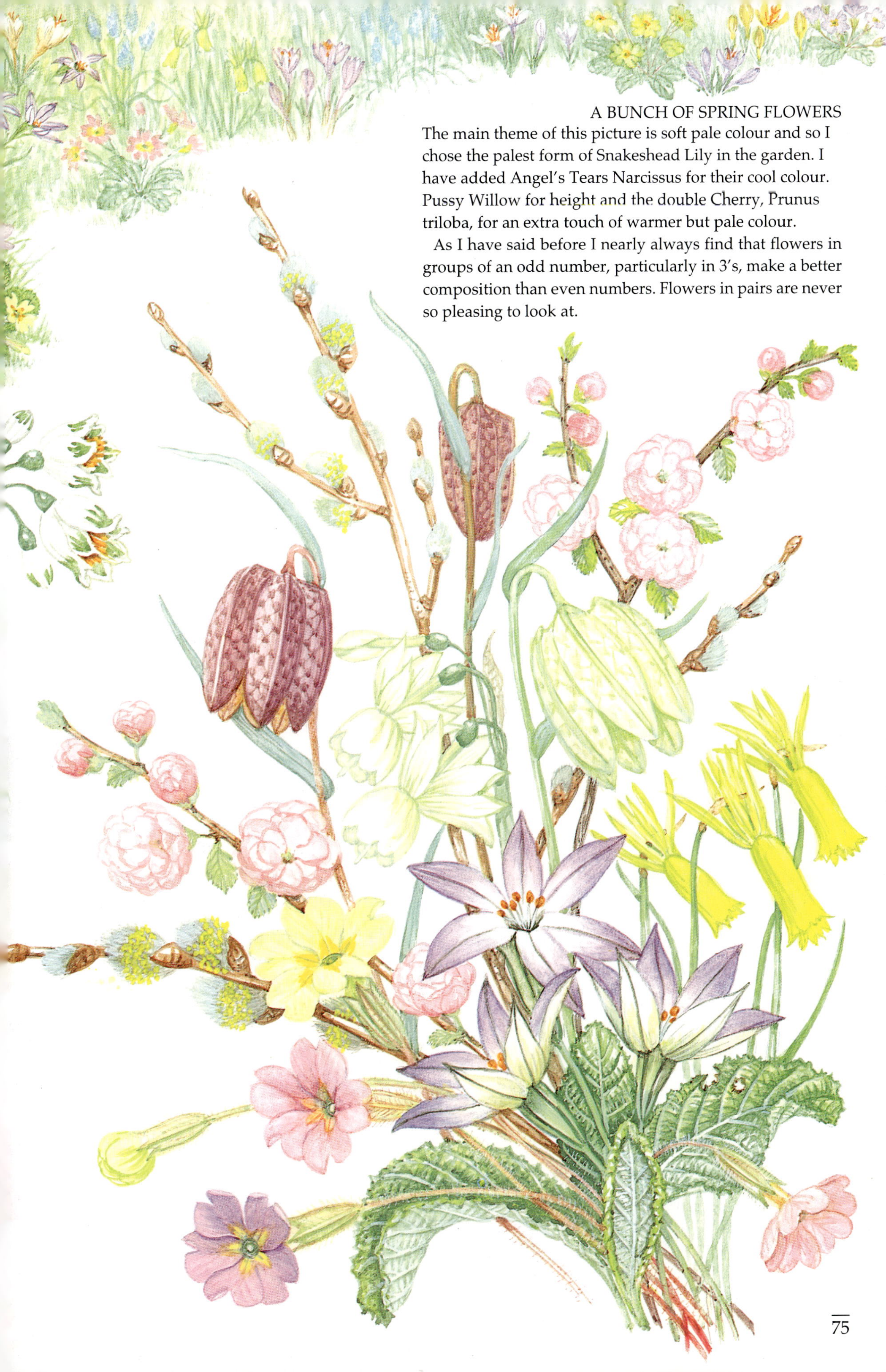

A BUNCH OF SPRING FLOWERS

The main theme of this picture is soft pale colour and so I chose the palest form of Snakeshead Lily in the garden. I have added Angel's Tears Narcissus for their cool colour. Pussy Willow for height and the double Cherry, Prunus triloba, for an extra touch of warmer but pale colour.

As I have said before I nearly always find that flowers in groups of an odd number, particularly in 3's, make a better composition than even numbers. Flowers in pairs are never so pleasing to look at.

Magnolia soulangiana is a popular garden plant but if you do not like the magenta colour on the back of the petals try the soft colours of *Magnolia veitchii* or any of the white ones. Their petals, known as tepals, are thick and opaque and feel like fine smooth suede.

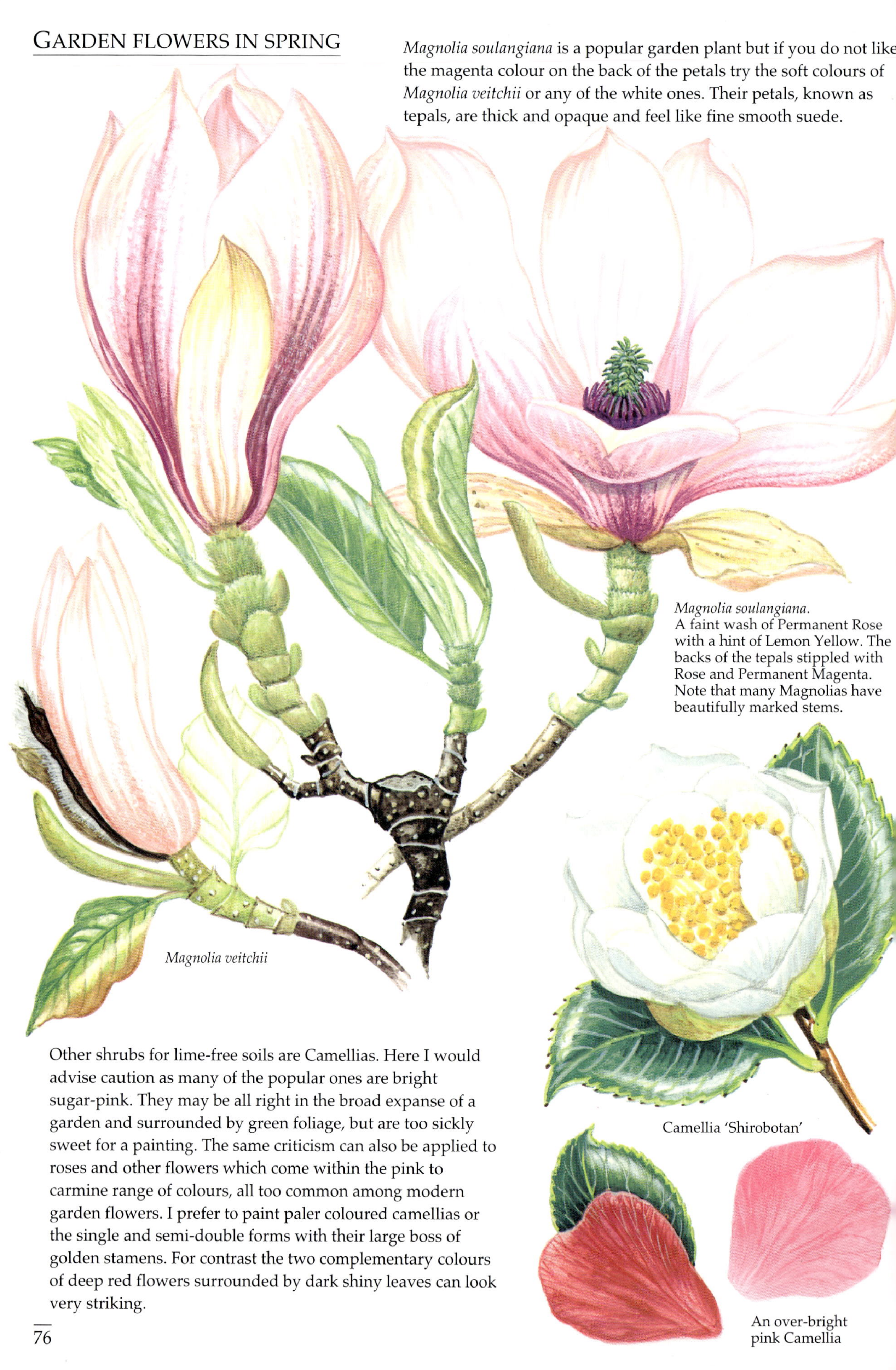

Magnolia soulangiana.
A faint wash of Permanent Rose with a hint of Lemon Yellow. The backs of the tepals stippled with Rose and Permanent Magenta. Note that many Magnolias have beautifully marked stems.

Magnolia veitchii

Camellia 'Shirobotan'

An over-bright pink Camellia

Other shrubs for lime-free soils are Camellias. Here I would advise caution as many of the popular ones are bright sugar-pink. They may be all right in the broad expanse of a garden and surrounded by green foliage, but are too sickly sweet for a painting. The same criticism can also be applied to roses and other flowers which come within the pink to carmine range of colours, all too common among modern garden flowers. I prefer to paint paler coloured camellias or the single and semi-double forms with their large boss of golden stamens. For contrast the two complementary colours of deep red flowers surrounded by dark shiny leaves can look very striking.

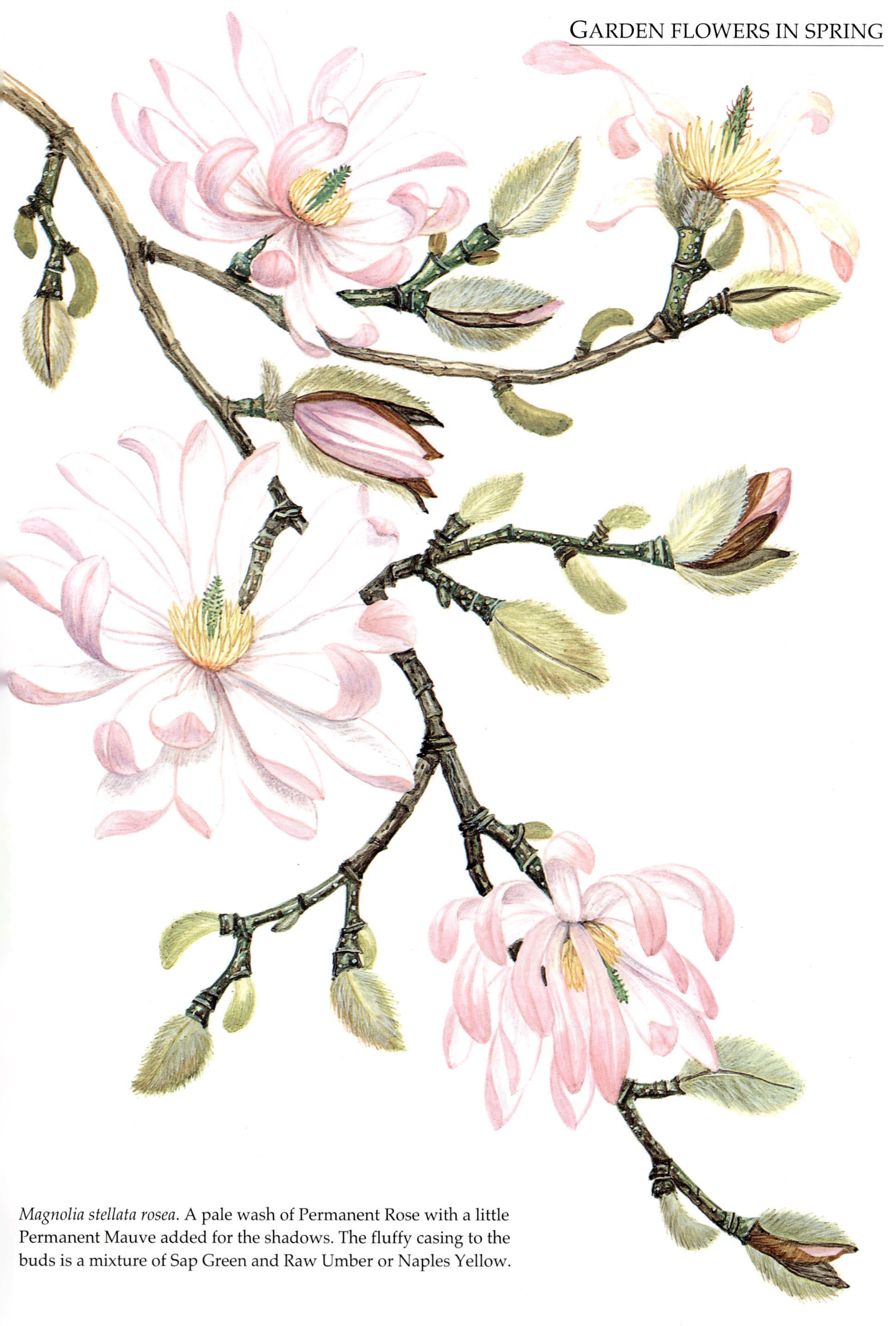

Magnolia stellata rosea. A pale wash of Permanent Rose with a little Permanent Mauve added for the shadows. The fluffy casing to the buds is a mixture of Sap Green and Raw Umber or Naples Yellow.

TULIPS AND LILIES-OF-THE-VALLEY

There are many different Tulips which flower throughout spring into early summer. They are rather too formal for the wild garden but Lily-of-the-Valley can be grown – and will spread – in any shady part of the garden.

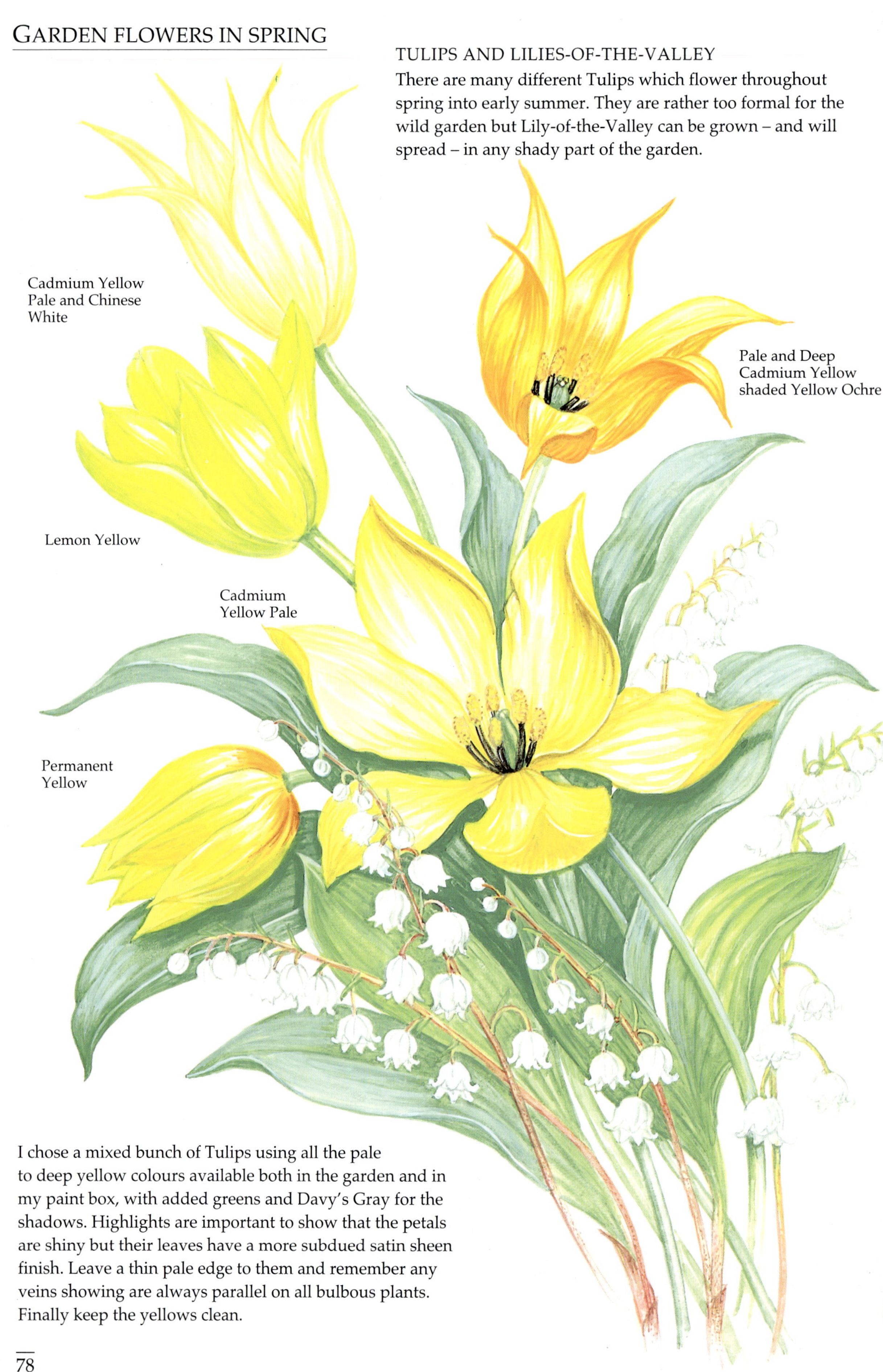

I chose a mixed bunch of Tulips using all the pale to deep yellow colours available both in the garden and in my paint box, with added greens and Davy's Gray for the shadows. Highlights are important to show that the petals are shiny but their leaves have a more subdued satin sheen finish. Leave a thin pale edge to them and remember any veins showing are always parallel on all bulbous plants. Finally keep the yellows clean.

The Almond, *Prunus dulcis*, is widely grown in this country for its early spring flowers and not for its nuts which are very bitter. Ornamental garden cherries too are grown purely for their wonderful display of flowers. All are attractive subjects for the painter though I find some of the pink ones over bright and prefer to paint the paler pink and white forms.

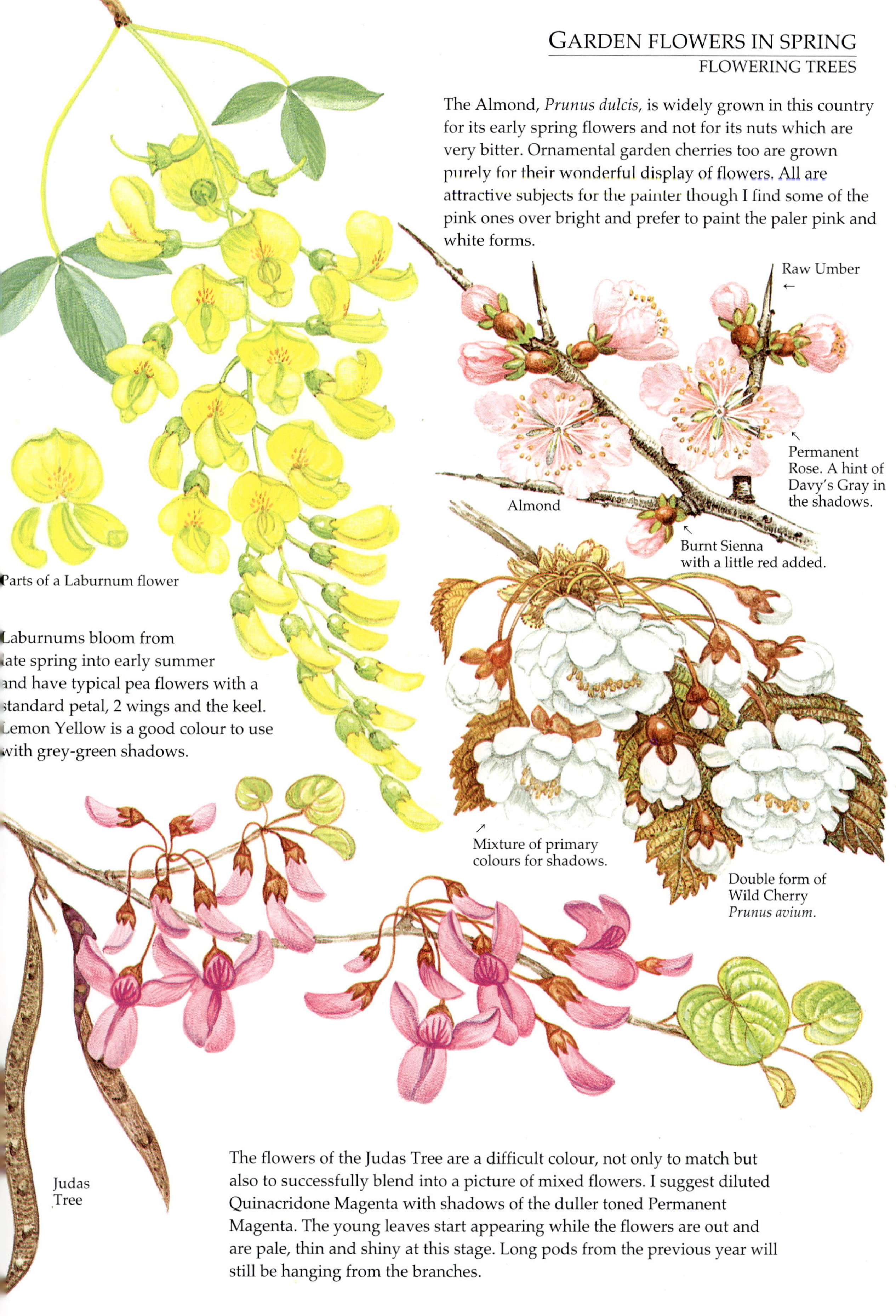

Laburnums bloom from late spring into early summer and have typical pea flowers with a standard petal, 2 wings and the keel. Lemon Yellow is a good colour to use with grey-green shadows.

The flowers of the Judas Tree are a difficult colour, not only to match but also to successfully blend into a picture of mixed flowers. I suggest diluted Quinacridone Magenta with shadows of the duller toned Permanent Magenta. The young leaves start appearing while the flowers are out and are pale, thin and shiny at this stage. Long pods from the previous year will still be hanging from the branches.

GARDEN FLOWERS IN SUMMER

I like to choose old Shrub Roses for my pictures because I prefer their often untidy blooms and soft tones to the even perfection of modern roses. A warm colour is the main theme of this picture and I have used Permanent Rose for all the pink flowers to demonstrate how much one can vary the shade by using thin washes or concentrated dryer applications as shown on the petals of *Rosa mundi*, some French Ultramarine is added for the shadows.

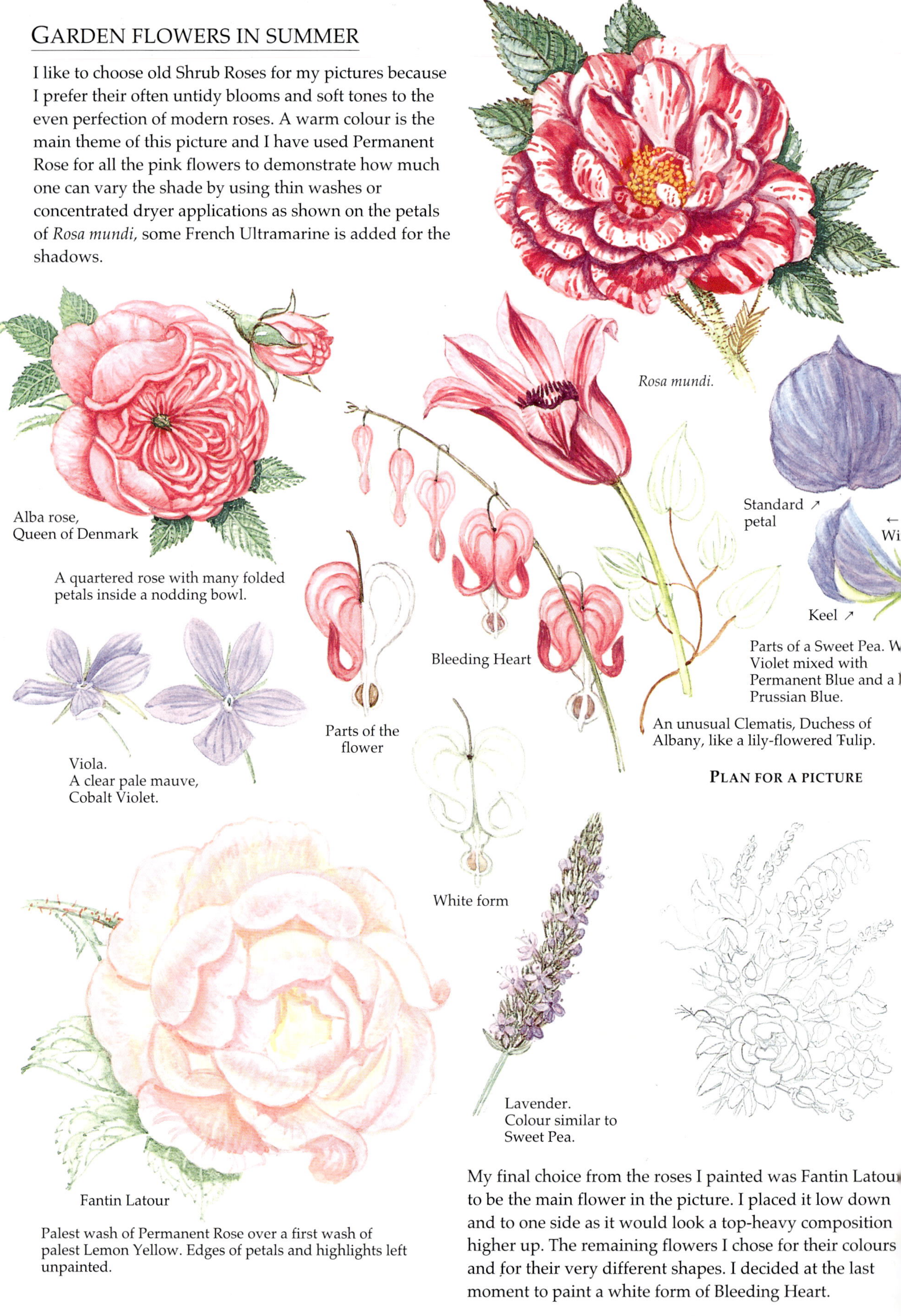

Rosa mundi.

Alba rose,
Queen of Denmark

A quartered rose with many folded petals inside a nodding bowl.

Viola.
A clear pale mauve, Cobalt Violet.

Parts of the flower

Bleeding Heart

White form

Parts of a Sweet Pea. W Violet mixed with Permanent Blue and a Prussian Blue.

An unusual Clematis, Duchess of Albany, like a lily-flowered Tulip.

PLAN FOR A PICTURE

Fantin Latour

Palest wash of Permanent Rose over a first wash of palest Lemon Yellow. Edges of petals and highlights left unpainted.

Lavender.
Colour similar to Sweet Pea.

My final choice from the roses I painted was Fantin Latour to be the main flower in the picture. I placed it low down and to one side as it would look a top-heavy composition higher up. The remaining flowers I chose for their colours and for their very different shapes. I decided at the last moment to paint a white form of Bleeding Heart.

A BUNCH OF SUMMER FLOWERS

The size of this page and the lack of a mount which always gives a feeling of space restricts the effect of such a painting. When planning a similar one which is to be mounted and framed always allow several centimetres of paper beyond the painting which can be trimmed back a little if necessary – but be generous. A soft grey-green mount surrounding it, at least 5cm wide, and finally a light-coloured frame completes the effect.

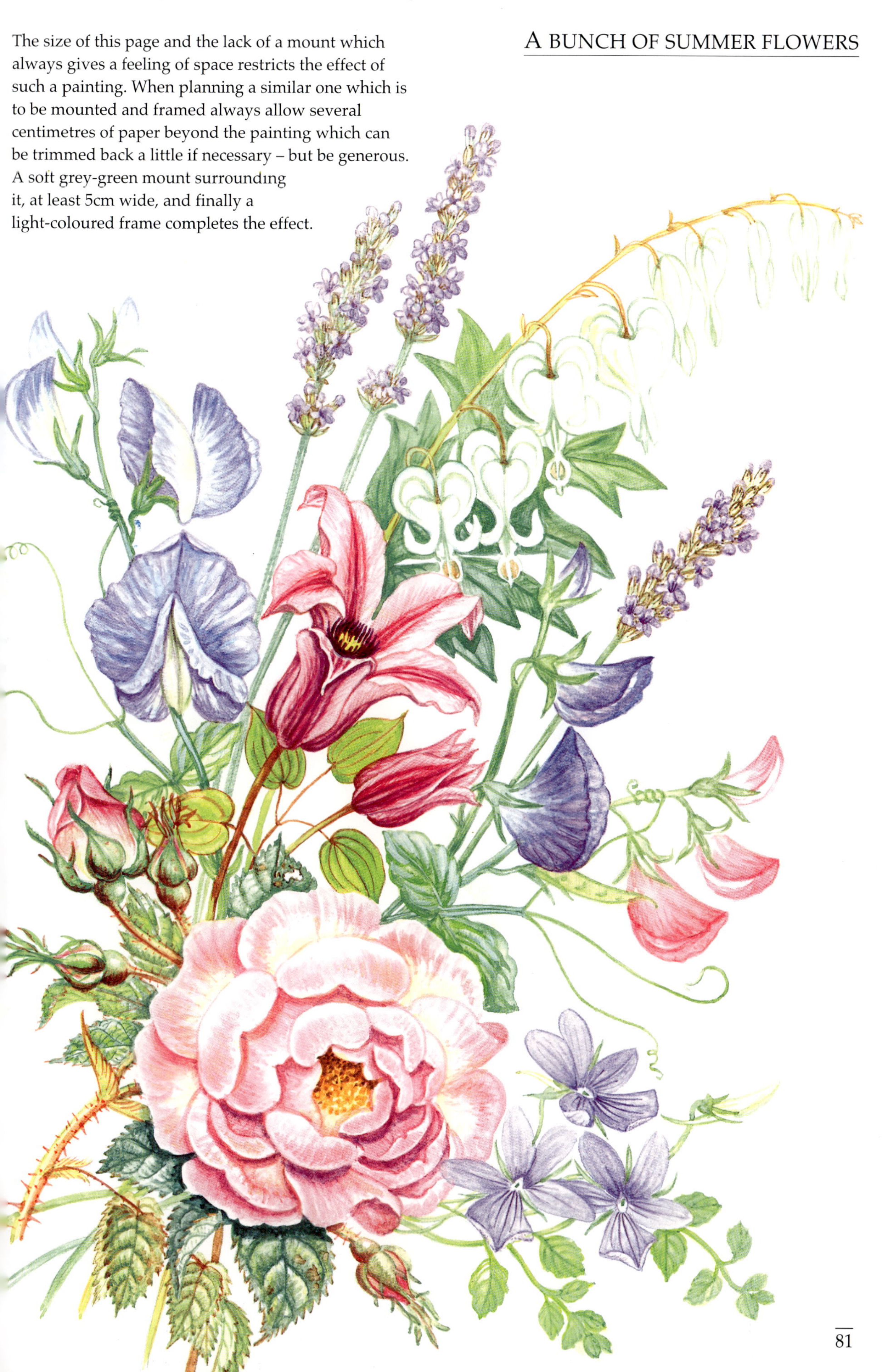

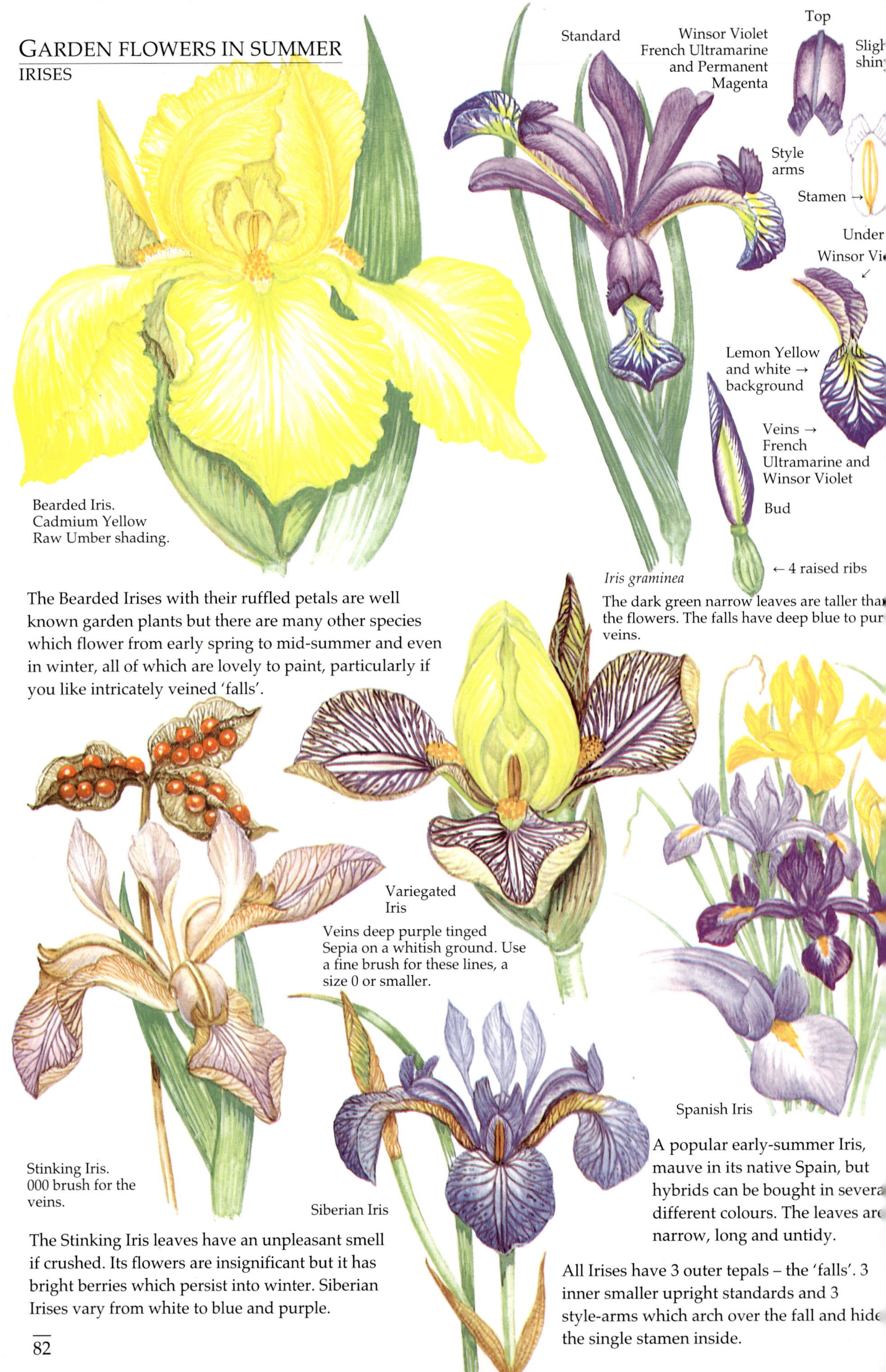

Bearded Iris. Cadmium Yellow Raw Umber shading.

Iris graminea

The dark green narrow leaves are taller tha the flowers. The falls have deep blue to pur veins.

The Bearded Irises with their ruffled petals are well known garden plants but there are many other species which flower from early spring to mid-summer and even in winter, all of which are lovely to paint, particularly if you like intricately veined 'falls'.

Variegated Iris

Veins deep purple tinged Sepia on a whitish ground. Use a fine brush for these lines, a size 0 or smaller.

Spanish Iris

A popular early-summer Iris, mauve in its native Spain, but hybrids can be bought in severa different colours. The leaves are narrow, long and untidy.

Stinking Iris. 000 brush for the veins.

Siberian Iris

The Stinking Iris leaves have an unpleasant smell if crushed. Its flowers are insignificant but it has bright berries which persist into winter. Siberian Irises vary from white to blue and purple.

All Irises have 3 outer tepals – the 'falls'. 3 inner smaller upright standards and 3 style-arms which arch over the fall and hide the single stamen inside.

A clear mauve-blue Bearded Iris with yellow beard. I used Cobalt Blue tinged with well diluted Winsor Violet in the shadows. The buds are much darker and shiny.

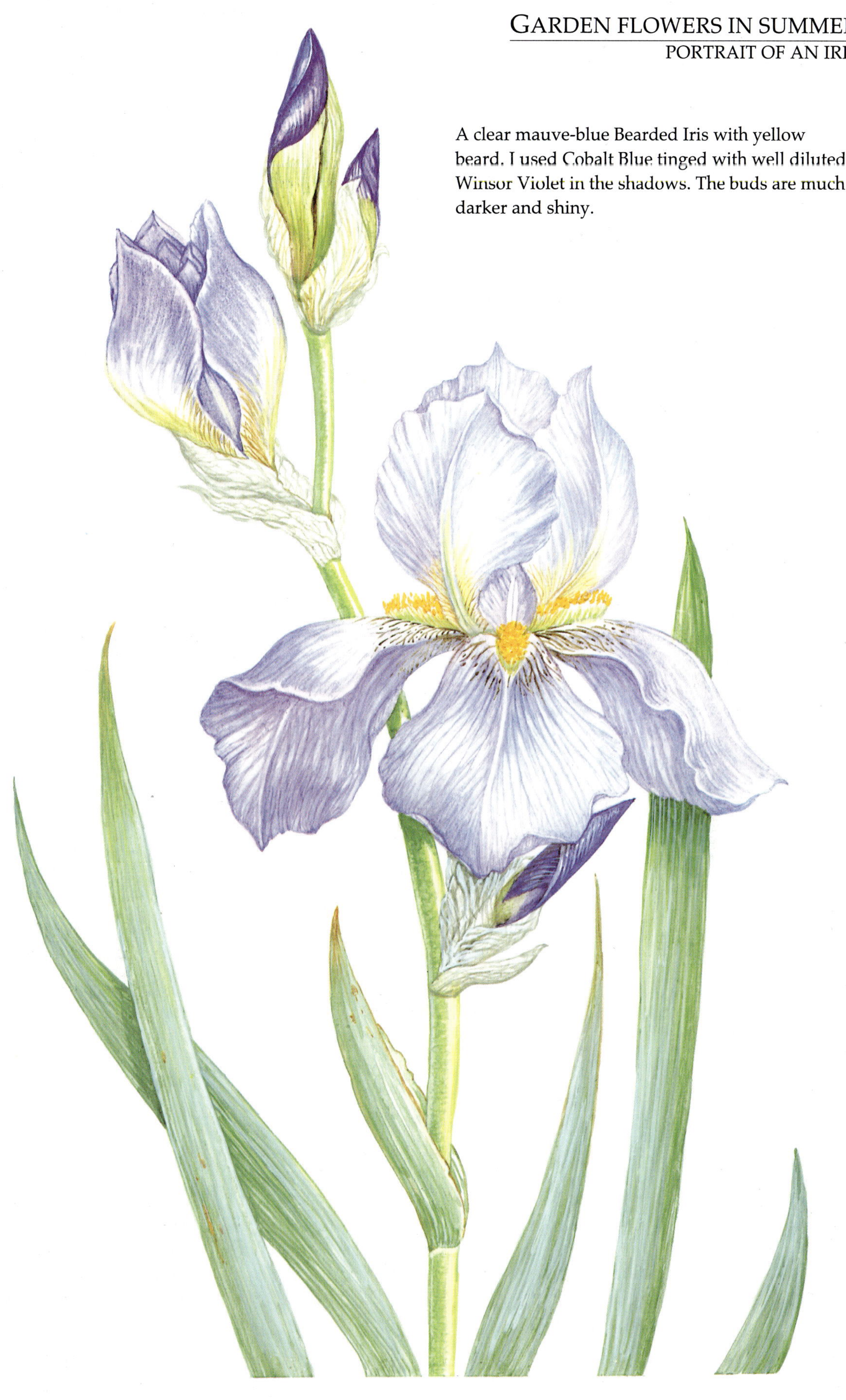

LILIES

Lilies are superbly shaped. From the curve of each petal (or more accurately tepal) to the spreading stamens they are a marvel of design. As with all bulbous plants they have six petals, six stamens and one long three-lobed stigma. To correctly reproduce such perfection of shape requires practice and my suggestion on p. 19 regarding leaves of 'glass' applies here for the backward curve of each petal has to be smooth and continuous with no breaks in the line.

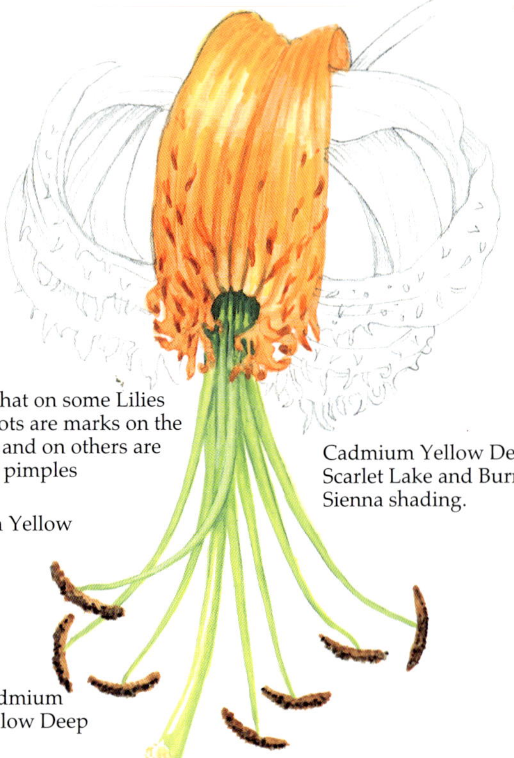

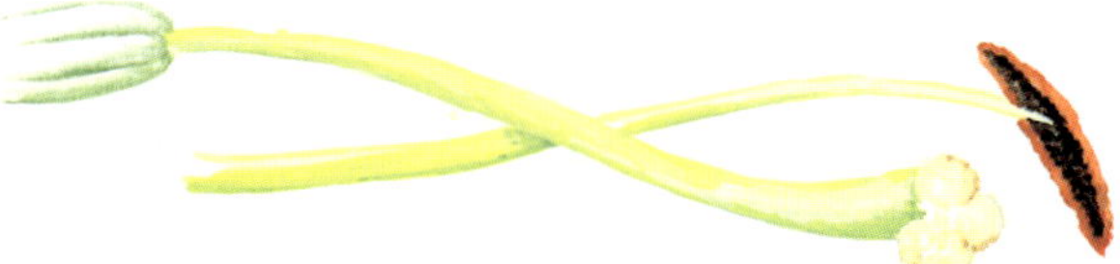

Note that on some Lilies the spots are marks on the petals and on others are raised pimples

Cadmium Yellow Dee Scarlet Lake and Burn Sienna shading.

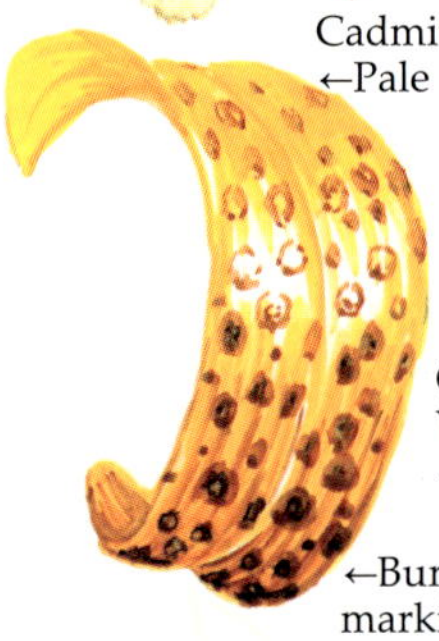

Cadmium Yellow ←Pale

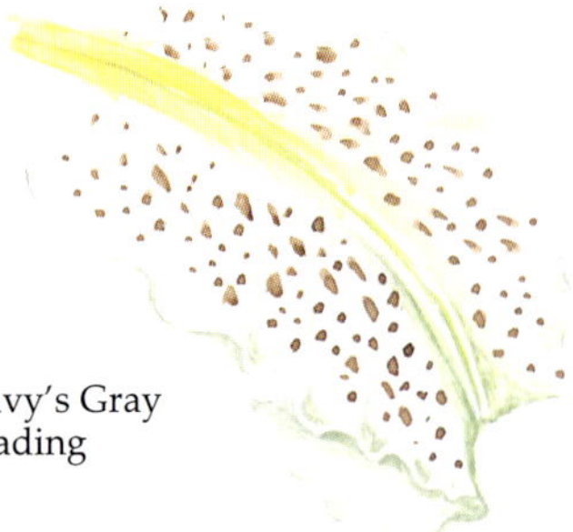

Davy's Gray shading

Cadmium Yellow Deep ←

←Burnt Sienna and Sepia markings

A warning. Avoid touching the stamens, as dropped pollen on clothing, hands or, worse still, your sheet of paper, stains badly and is difficult to remove. It is best to snip off the pollen-bearing tips before handling the flowers but sketch them first for adding later.

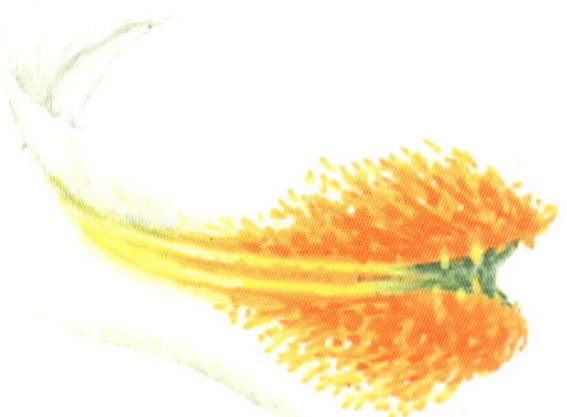

'Bright Star' white with Cadmium Yellow Deep mixed with Bright Red

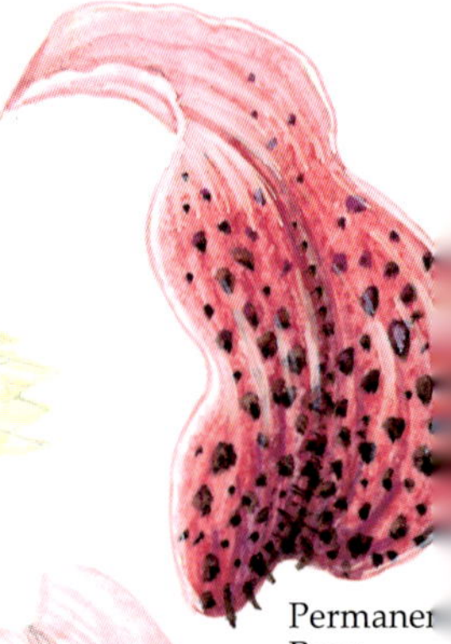

Permaner Rose

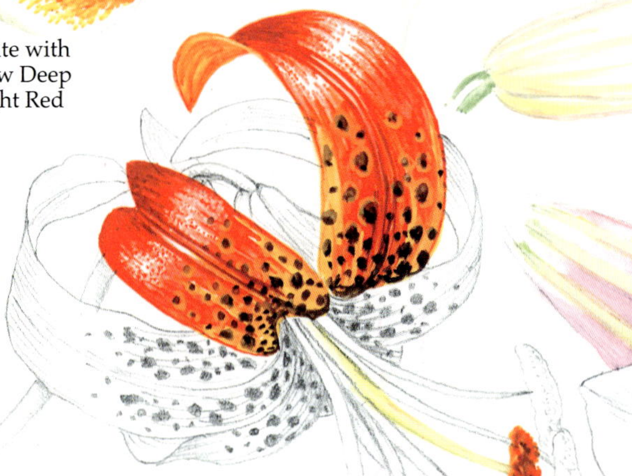

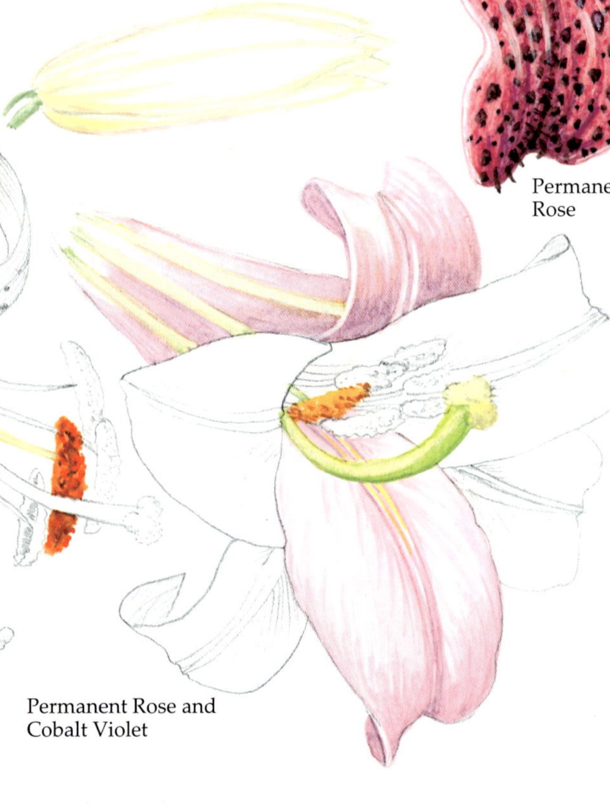

Many lilies have shiny petals, especially noticeable in the darker coloured ones. Here I first left the highlights unpainted and later softened them by stippling over with a very fine brush. Basic colours, Cadmium Yellow Deep overpainted with red such as Bright Red, and Sepia for the spots.

Permanent Rose and Cobalt Violet

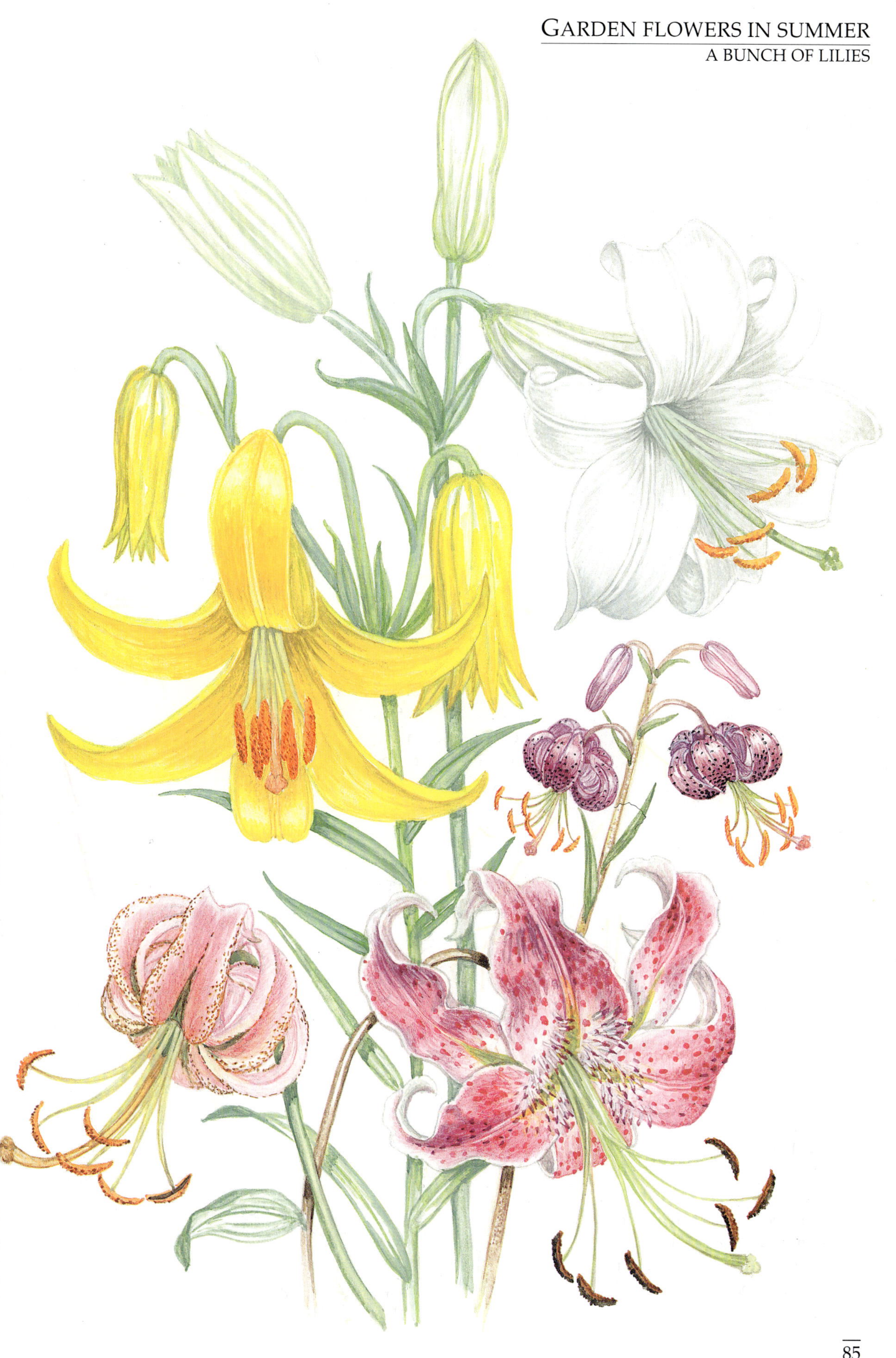

Garden Flowers in Autumn

Dahlias and Chrysanthemums may be the most popular garden flowers of late summer and autumn but there are many others from which to choose that are perhaps less well known and more attractive to paint, such as *Clematis tangutica* with strong Lemon Yellow flowers and silky seed heads which shine in the sun. Mix the same yellow with a little Sap Green and Raw Umber for these and leave some highlights unpainted. *Clematis rehderiana* is paler than a primrose and looks delicate but will soon cover a small tree if allowed a free hand

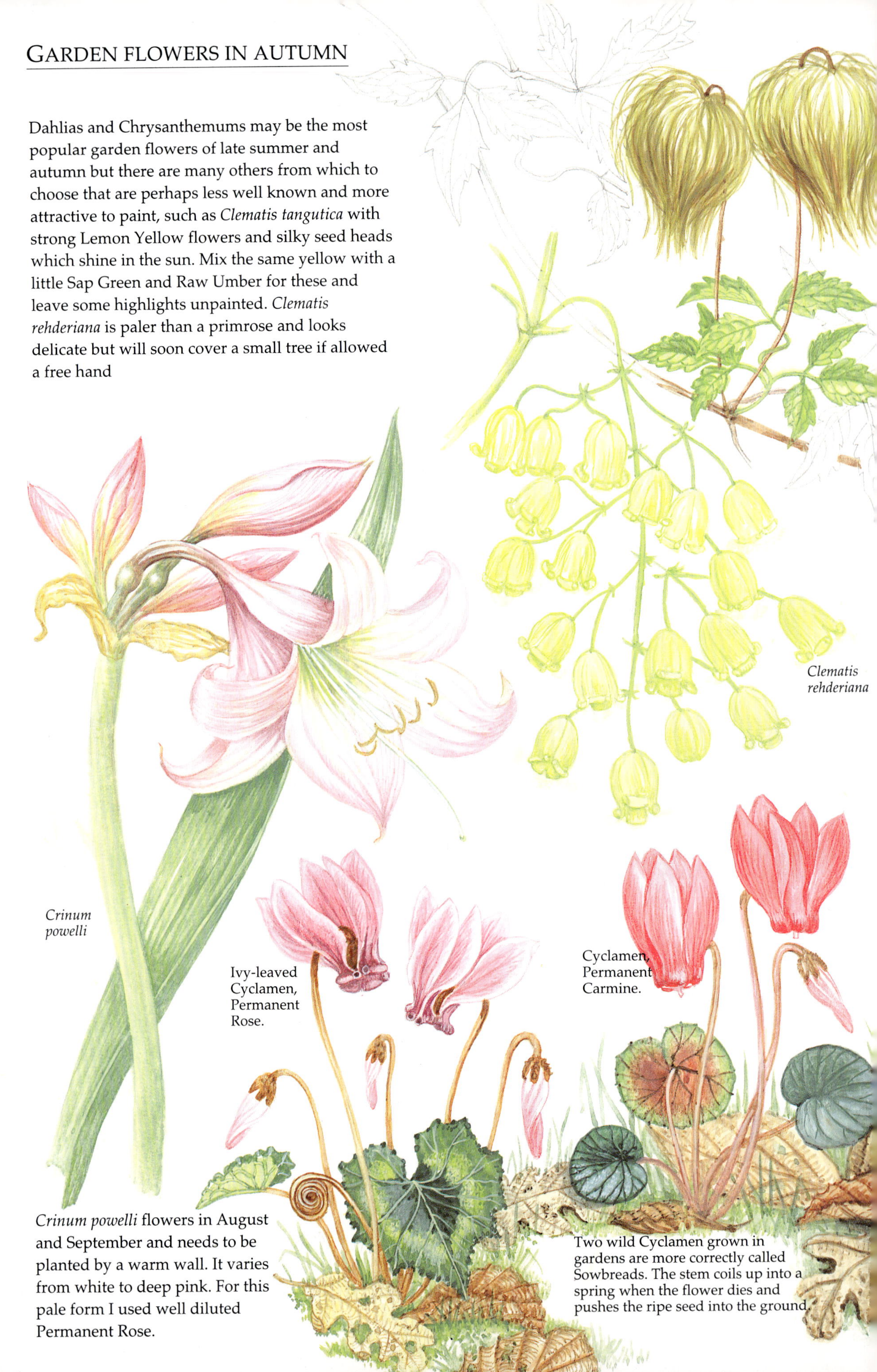

Clematis rehderiana

Crinum powelli

Ivy-leaved Cyclamen, Permanent Rose.

Cyclamen, Permanent Carmine.

Crinum powelli flowers in August and September and needs to be planted by a warm wall. It varies from white to deep pink. For this pale form I used well diluted Permanent Rose.

Two wild Cyclamen grown in gardens are more correctly called Sowbreads. The stem coils up into a spring when the flower dies and pushes the ripe seed into the ground.

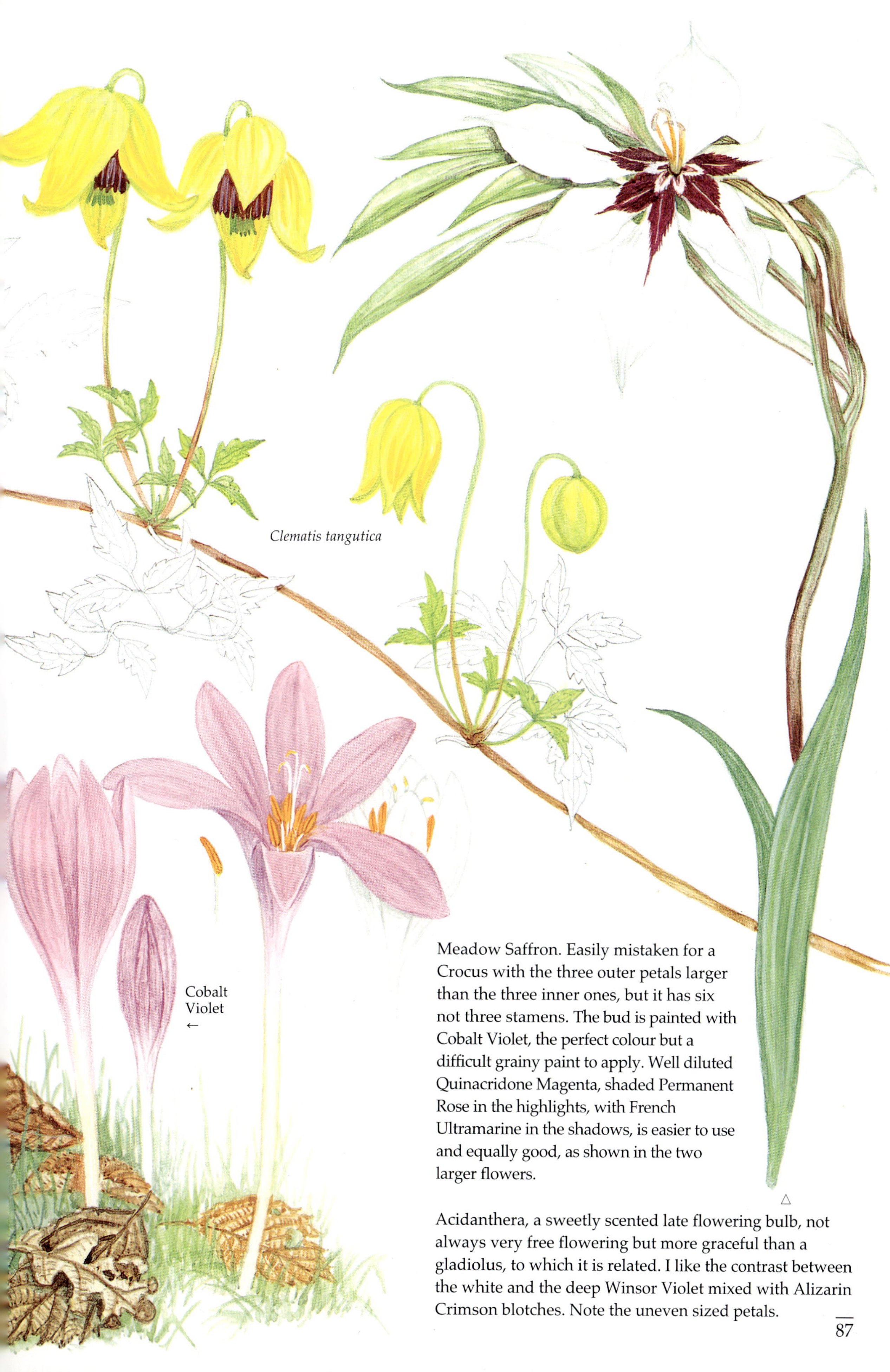

Meadow Saffron. Easily mistaken for a Crocus with the three outer petals larger than the three inner ones, but it has six not three stamens. The bud is painted with Cobalt Violet, the perfect colour but a difficult grainy paint to apply. Well diluted Quinacridone Magenta, shaded Permanent Rose in the highlights, with French Ultramarine in the shadows, is easier to use and equally good, as shown in the two larger flowers.

△

Acidanthera, a sweetly scented late flowering bulb, not always very free flowering but more graceful than a gladiolus, to which it is related. I like the contrast between the white and the deep Winsor Violet mixed with Alizarin Crimson blotches. Note the uneven sized petals.

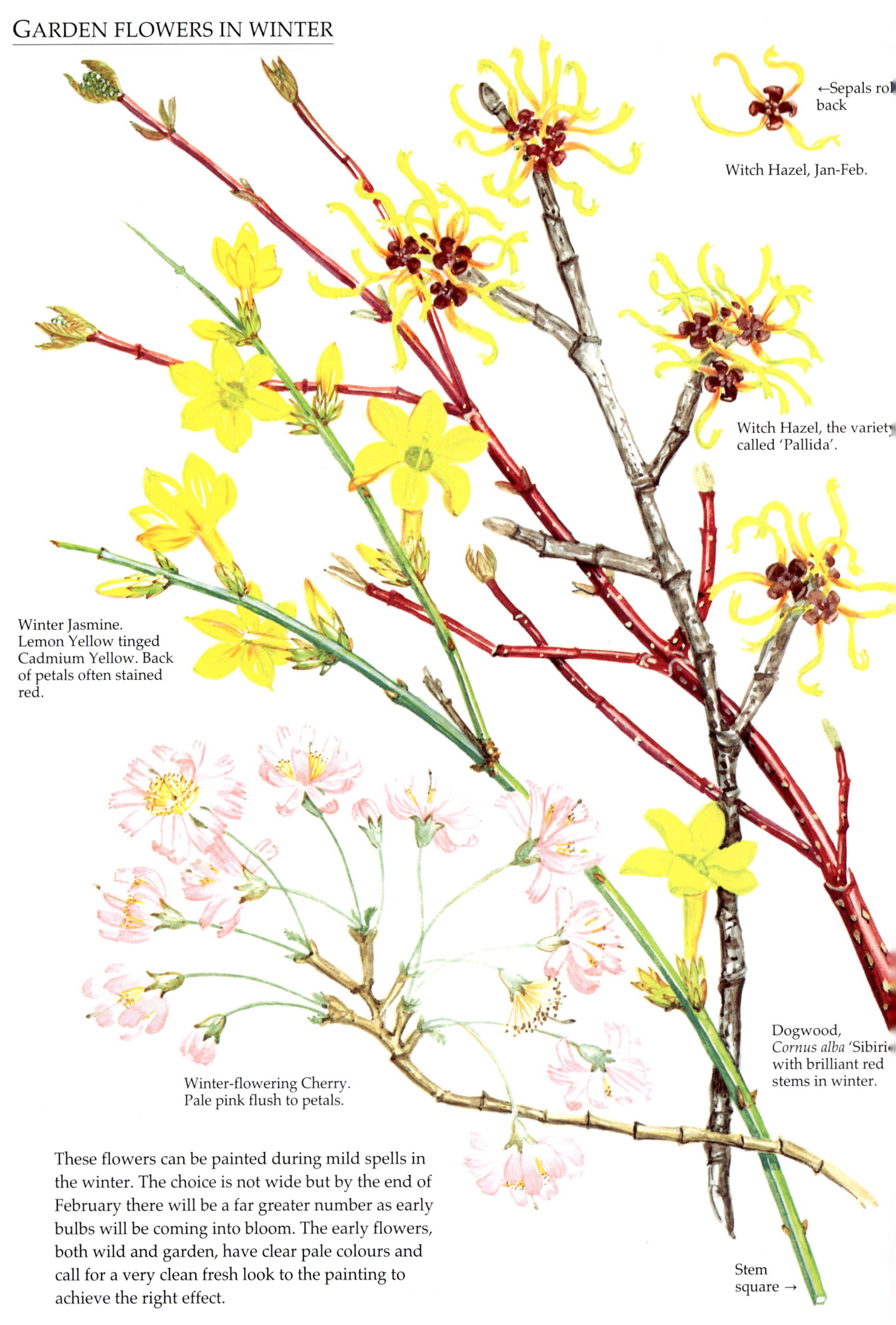

Witch Hazel, Jan-Feb.

Witch Hazel, the variety called 'Pallida'.

Winter Jasmine. Lemon Yellow tinged Cadmium Yellow. Back of petals often stained red.

Dogwood, *Cornus alba* 'Sibiri with brilliant red stems in winter.

Winter-flowering Cherry. Pale pink flush to petals.

These flowers can be painted during mild spells in the winter. The choice is not wide but by the end of February there will be a far greater number as early bulbs will be coming into bloom. The early flowers, both wild and garden, have clear pale colours and call for a very clean fresh look to the painting to achieve the right effect.

Of all the garden flowers available, flowering bulbs can probably provide the painter with enough desirable subjects to last throughout many months. As well as Wild Snowdrops there are various larger-flowered forms and many small crocuses with attractive feathery markings on the back of the petals. They bloom at varying times through the winter months and into early Spring.

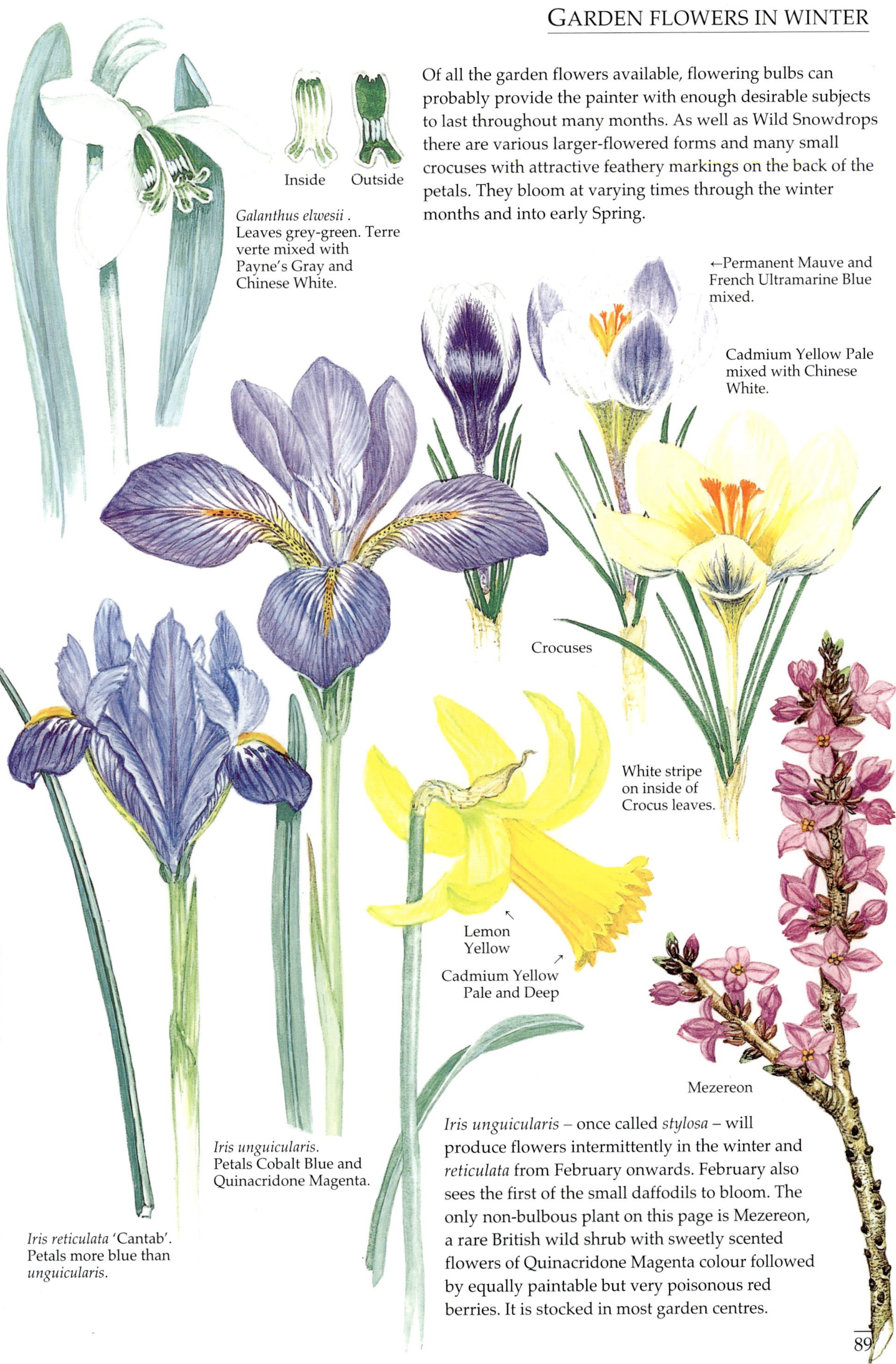

Galanthus elwesii. Leaves grey-green. Terre verte mixed with Payne's Gray and Chinese White.

Crocuses

Mezereon

Iris unguicularis. Petals Cobalt Blue and Quinacridone Magenta.

Iris reticulata 'Cantab'. Petals more blue than *unguicularis*.

Iris unguicularis – once called *stylosa* – will produce flowers intermittently in the winter and *reticulata* from February onwards. February also sees the first of the small daffodils to bloom. The only non-bulbous plant on this page is Mezereon, a rare British wild shrub with sweetly scented flowers of Quinacridone Magenta colour followed by equally paintable but very poisonous red berries. It is stocked in most garden centres.

BEDS AND BORDERS

Garden scenes like these can be painted to any size you like, even when reduced to a tiny miniature they can look attractive. In order to achieve a feeling of distance the background is painted slightly 'out of focus' and in varying shades of greens to avoid monotony. Full details and brighter colours are reserved for the foreground.

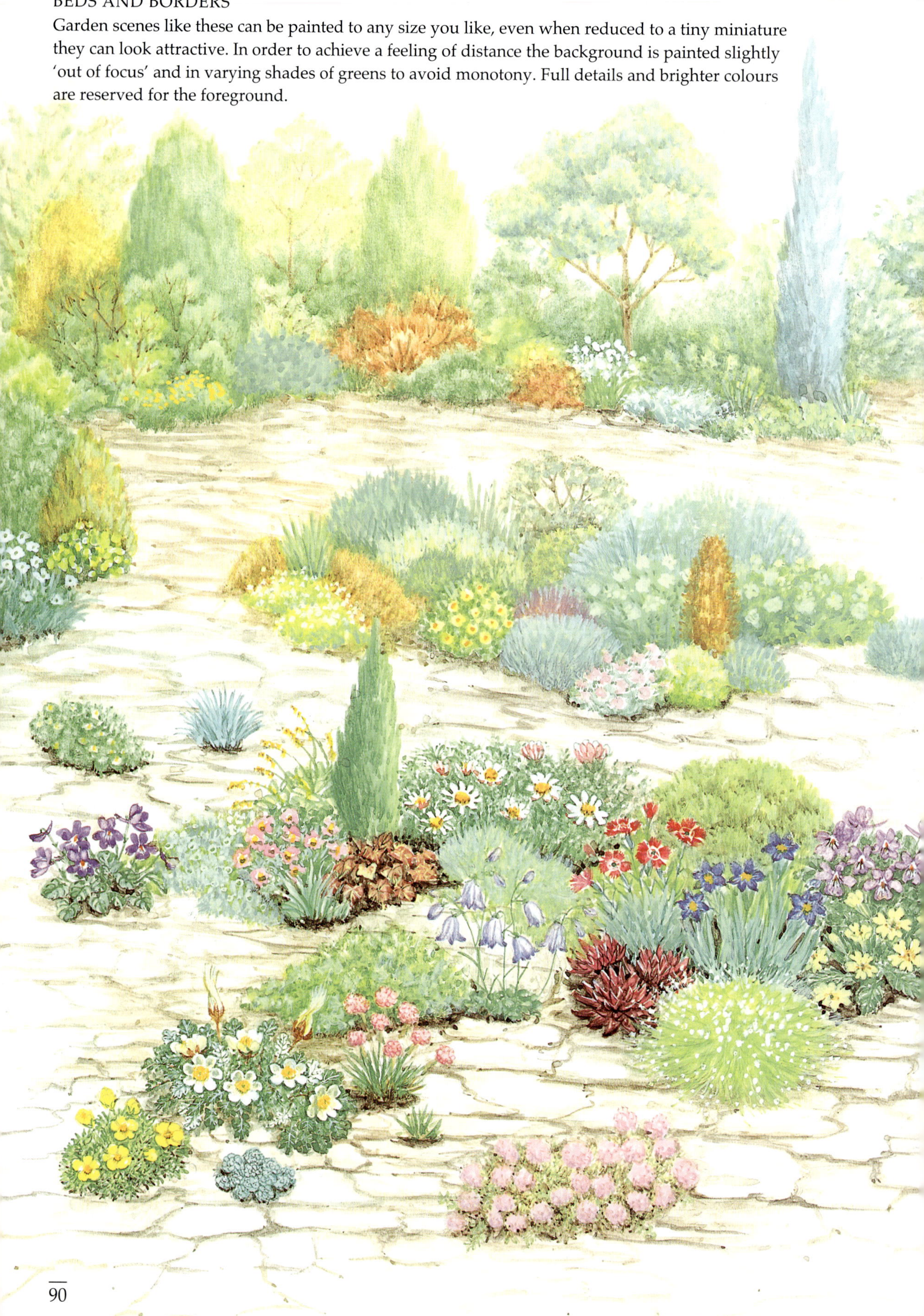

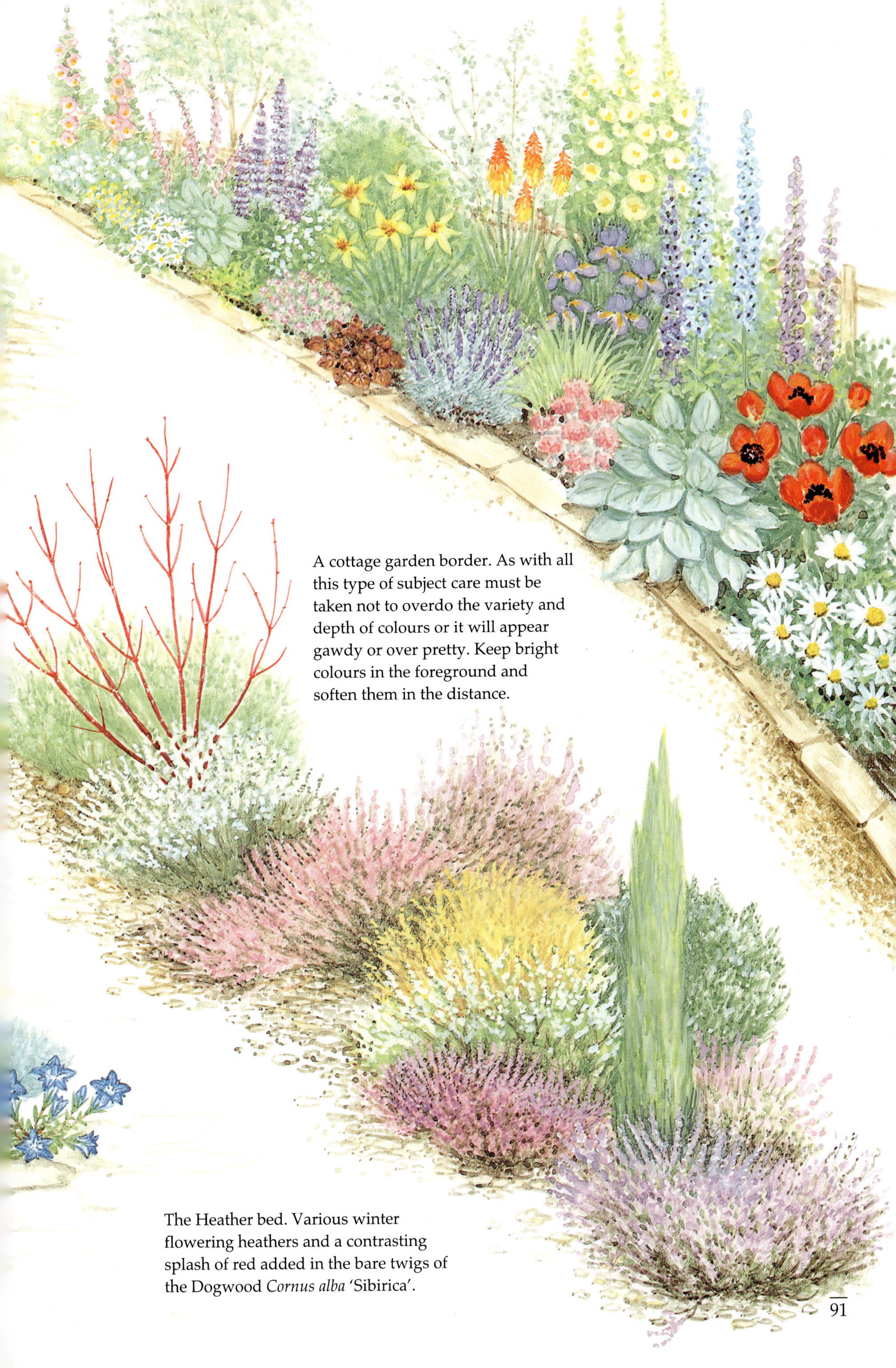

A cottage garden border. As with all this type of subject care must be taken not to overdo the variety and depth of colours or it will appear gawdy or over pretty. Keep bright colours in the foreground and soften them in the distance.

The Heather bed. Various winter flowering heathers and a contrasting splash of red added in the bare twigs of the Dogwood *Cornus alba* 'Sibirica'.

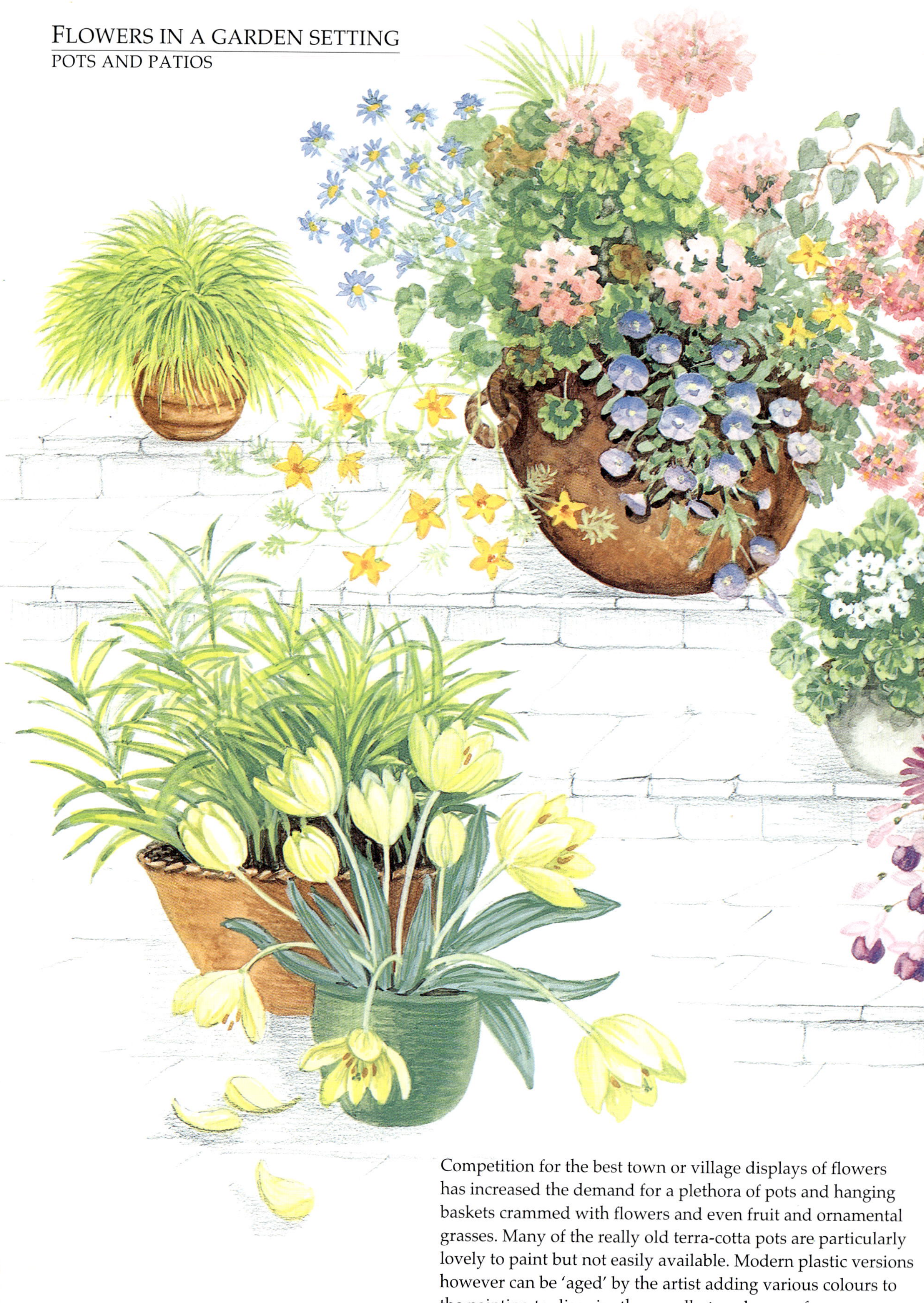

Competition for the best town or village displays of flowers has increased the demand for a plethora of pots and hanging baskets crammed with flowers and even fruit and ornamental grasses. Many of the really old terra-cotta pots are particularly lovely to paint but not easily available. Modern plastic versions however can be 'aged' by the artist adding various colours to the painting to disguise the usually too clean surface.

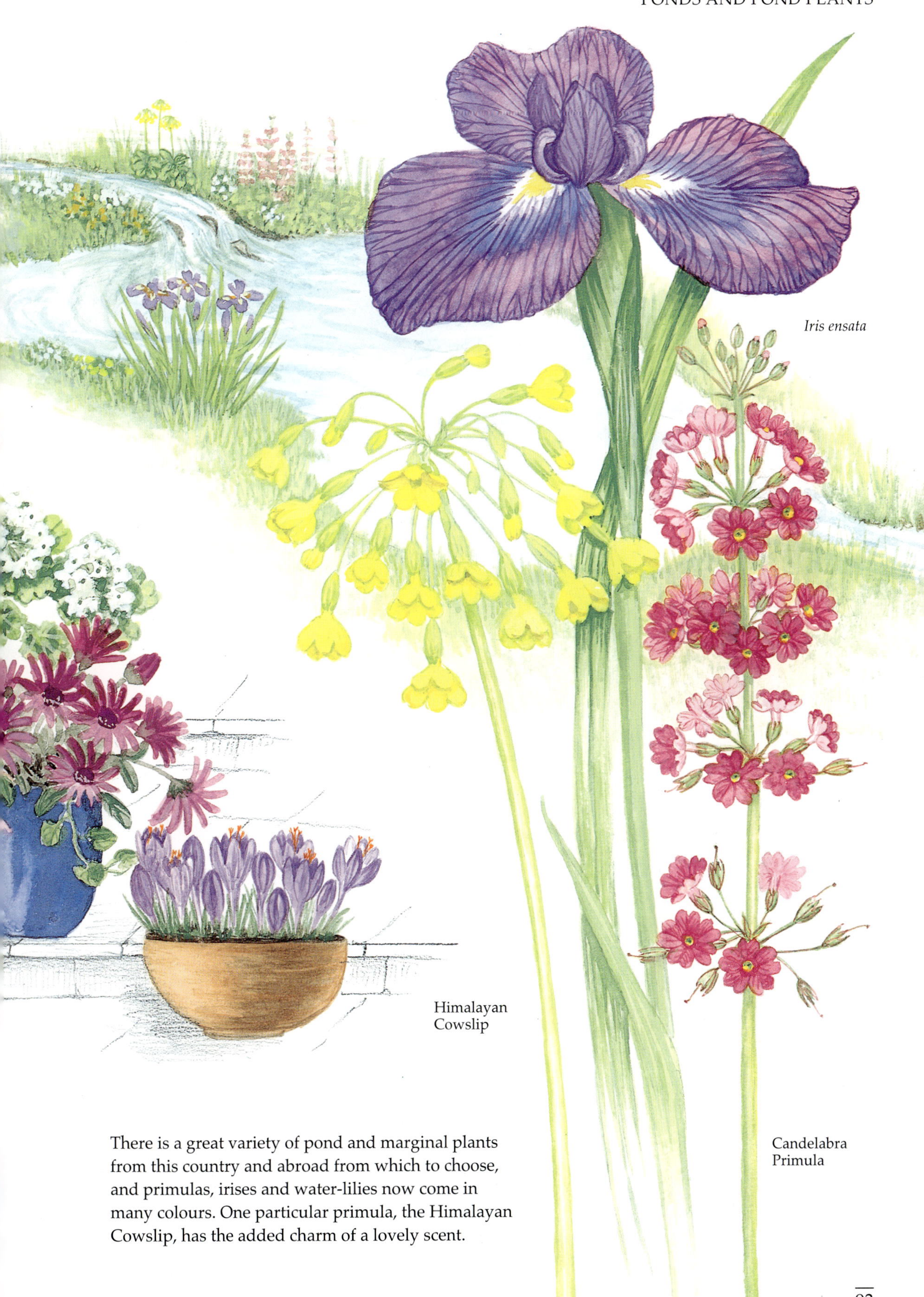

Iris ensata

Himalayan Cowslip

Candelabra Primula

There is a great variety of pond and marginal plants from this country and abroad from which to choose, and primulas, irises and water-lilies now come in many colours. One particular primula, the Himalayan Cowslip, has the added charm of a lovely scent.

CLIMBING PLANTS

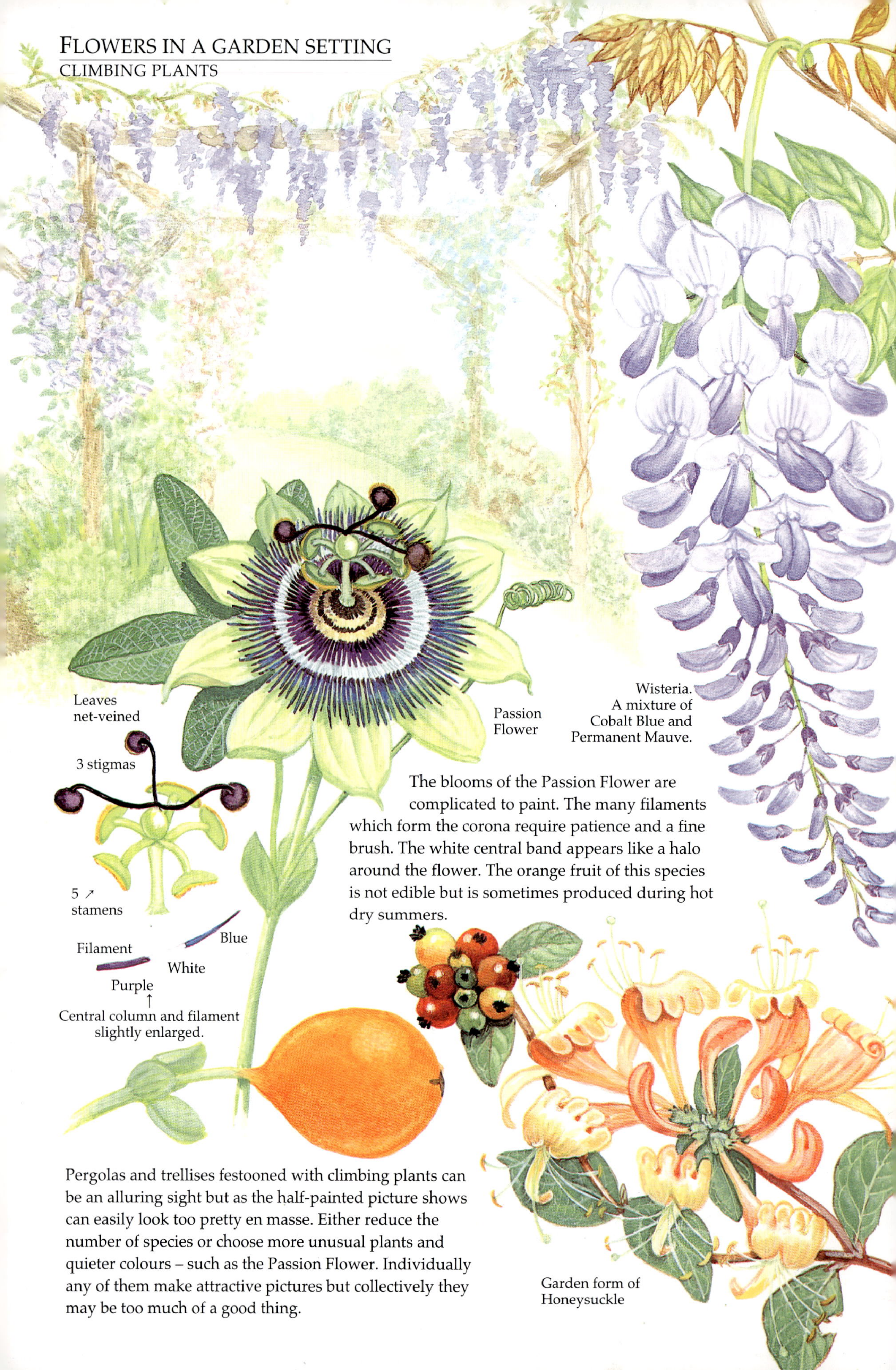

Central column and filament slightly enlarged.

Passion Flower

Wisteria. A mixture of Cobalt Blue and Permanent Mauve.

The blooms of the Passion Flower are complicated to paint. The many filaments which form the corona require patience and a fine brush. The white central band appears like a halo around the flower. The orange fruit of this species is not edible but is sometimes produced during hot dry summers.

Pergolas and trellises festooned with climbing plants can be an alluring sight but as the half-painted picture shows can easily look too pretty en masse. Either reduce the number of species or choose more unusual plants and quieter colours – such as the Passion Flower. Individually any of them make attractive pictures but collectively they may be too much of a good thing.

Garden form of Honeysuckle

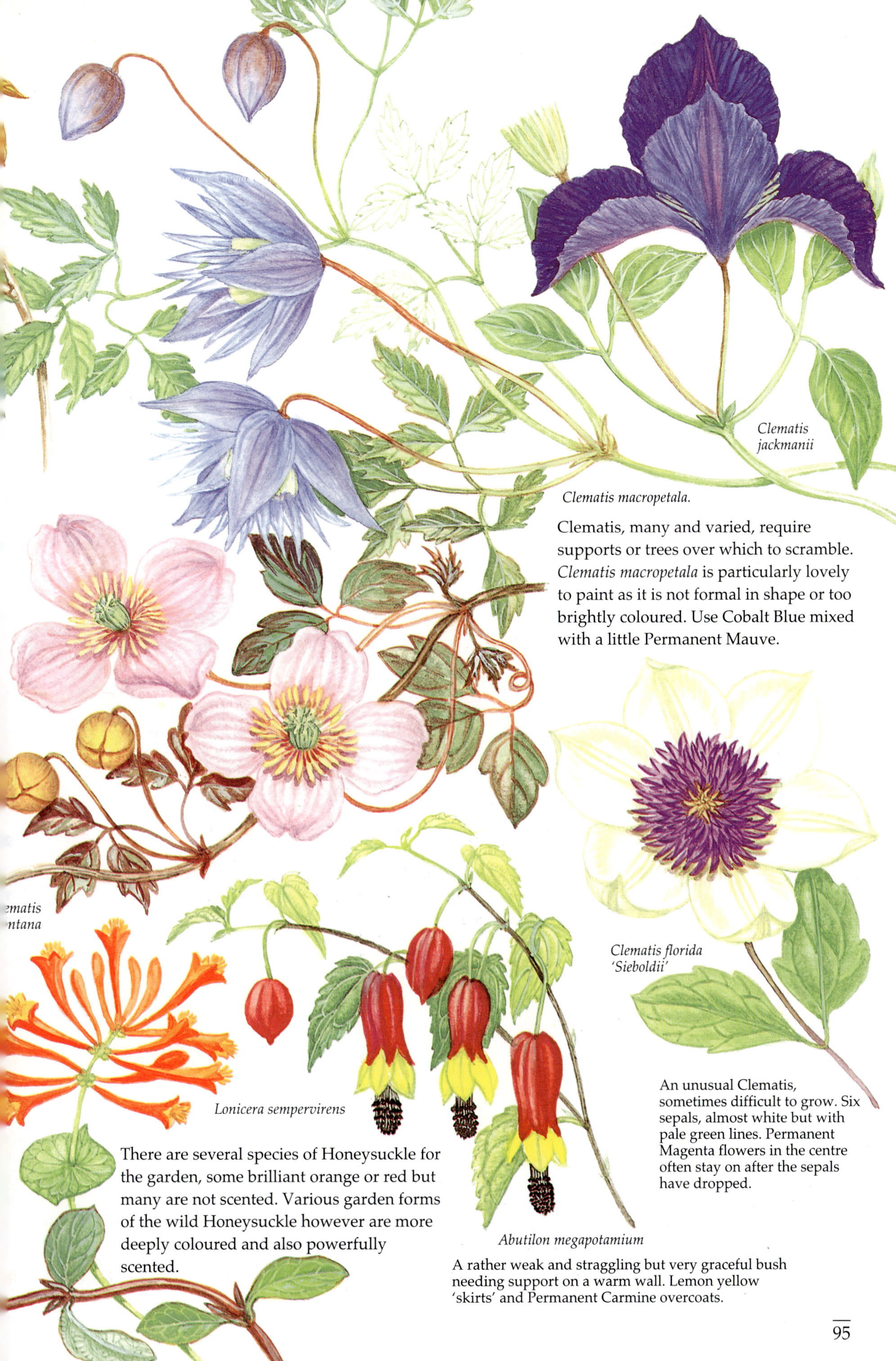

Clematis jackmanii

Clematis macropetala.

Clematis, many and varied, require supports or trees over which to scramble. *Clematis macropetala* is particularly lovely to paint as it is not formal in shape or too brightly coloured. Use Cobalt Blue mixed with a little Permanent Mauve.

Clematis florida 'Sieboldii'

An unusual Clematis, sometimes difficult to grow. Six sepals, almost white but with pale green lines. Permanent Magenta flowers in the centre often stay on after the sepals have dropped.

Lonicera sempervirens

There are several species of Honeysuckle for the garden, some brilliant orange or red but many are not scented. Various garden forms of the wild Honeysuckle however are more deeply coloured and also powerfully scented.

Abutilon megapotamium

A rather weak and straggling but very graceful bush needing support on a warm wall. Lemon yellow 'skirts' and Permanent Carmine overcoats.

WHITE ON WHITE

THE ALL-IMPORTANT SHADOWS

The primary colour mix used here is shown on p. 47 but you can use manufactured colours instead.

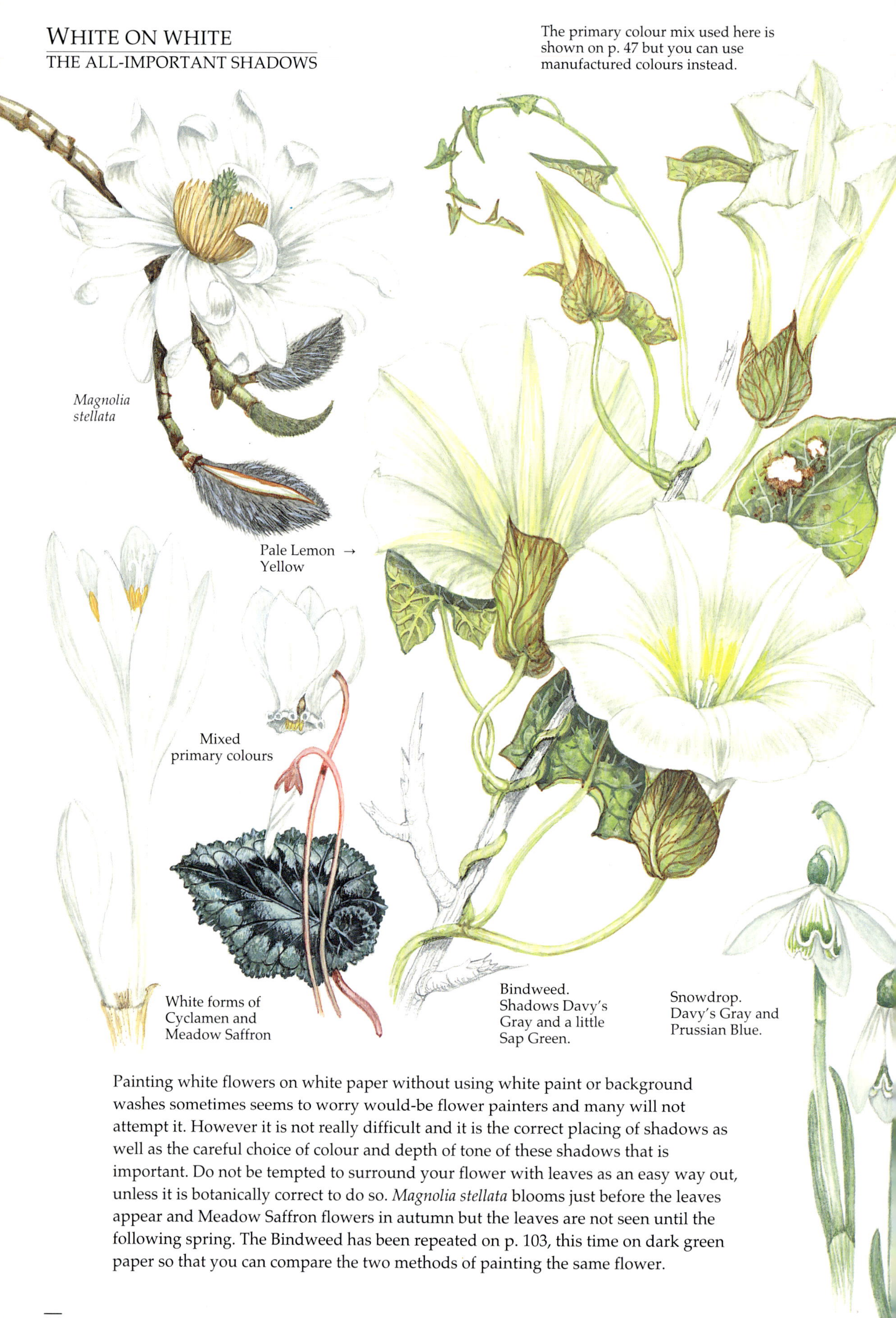

White forms of Cyclamen and Meadow Saffron

Bindweed. Shadows Davy's Gray and a little Sap Green.

Snowdrop. Davy's Gray and Prussian Blue.

Painting white flowers on white paper without using white paint or background washes sometimes seems to worry would-be flower painters and many will not attempt it. However it is not really difficult and it is the correct placing of shadows as well as the careful choice of colour and depth of tone of these shadows that is important. Do not be tempted to surround your flower with leaves as an easy way out, unless it is botanically correct to do so. *Magnolia stellata* blooms just before the leaves appear and Meadow Saffron flowers in autumn but the leaves are not seen until the following spring. The Bindweed has been repeated on p. 103, this time on dark green paper so that you can compare the two methods of painting the same flower.

Working drawings of Magnolias for a book. For the shading use Davy's Gray with varying amounts of Lemon Yellow and Prussian Blue if you find it easier than mixing your own.

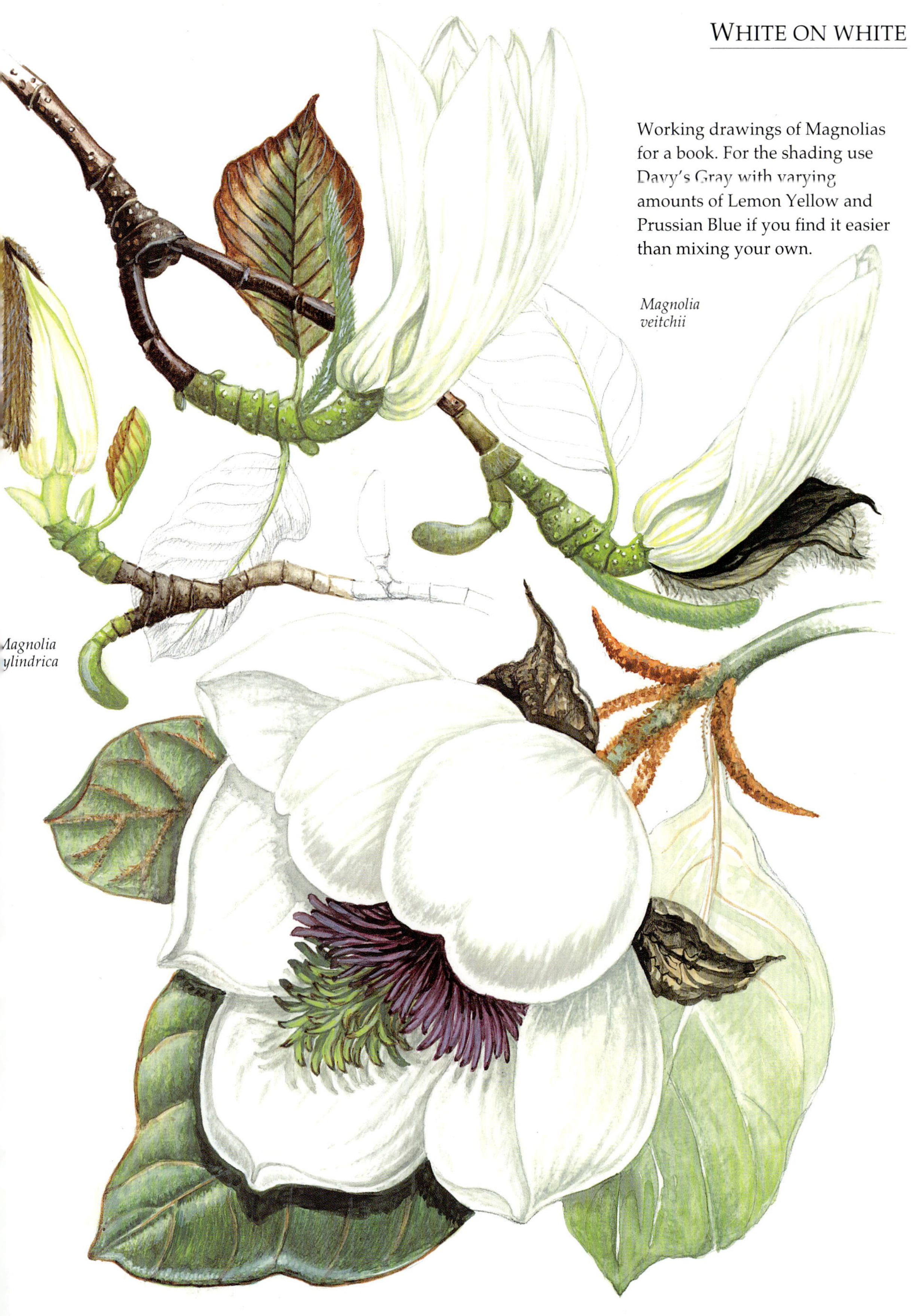

Magnolia veitchii

Magnolia cylindrica

Magnolia globosa

More White Flowers

Planning a Picture

White flowers picked at random from the garden and greenhouse. From my file cards I chose St Bernard's Lily because it is one of the purest white flowers I have seen. It seemed to glow with light when I found a group in a woodland clearing in France.

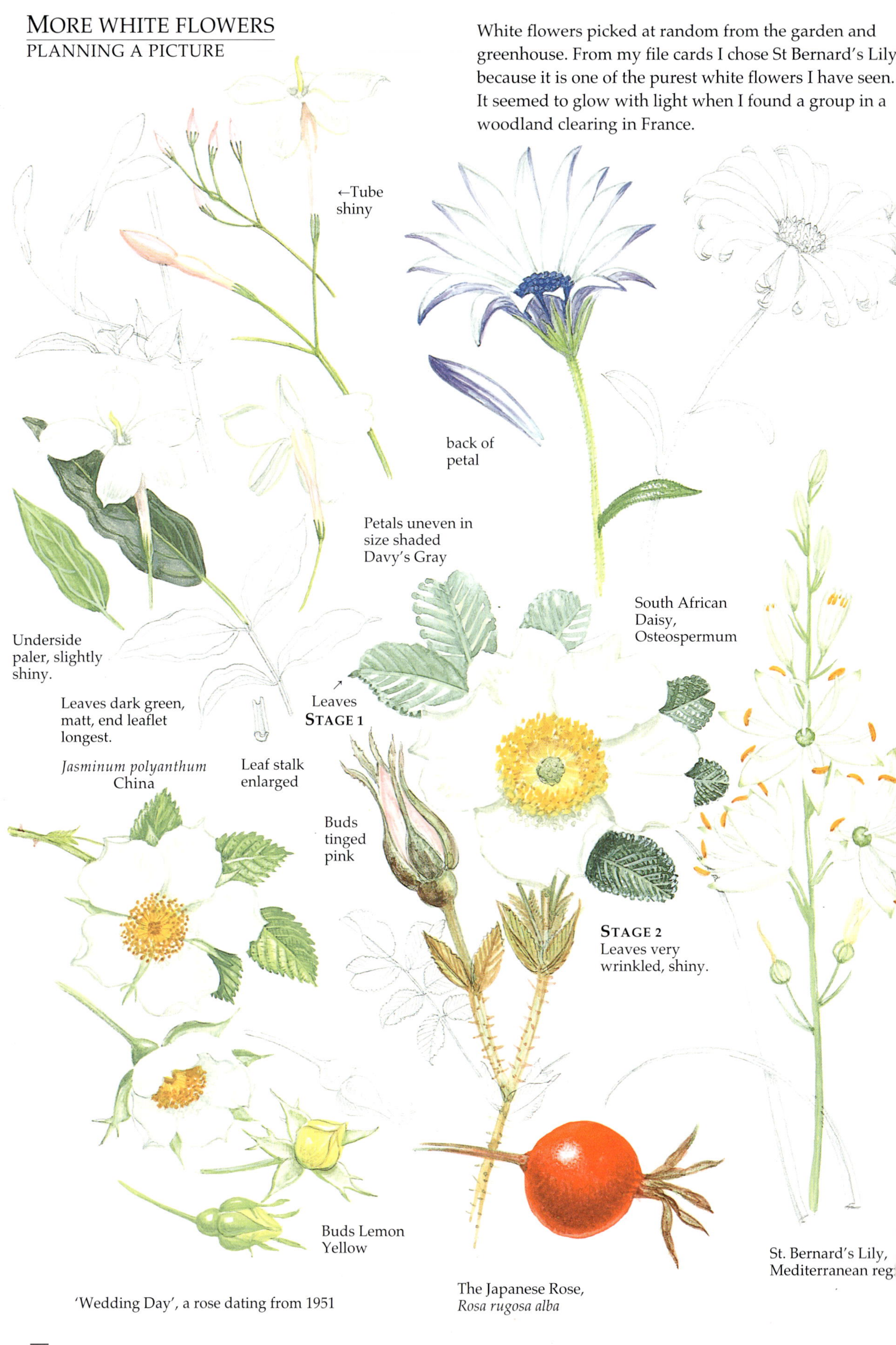

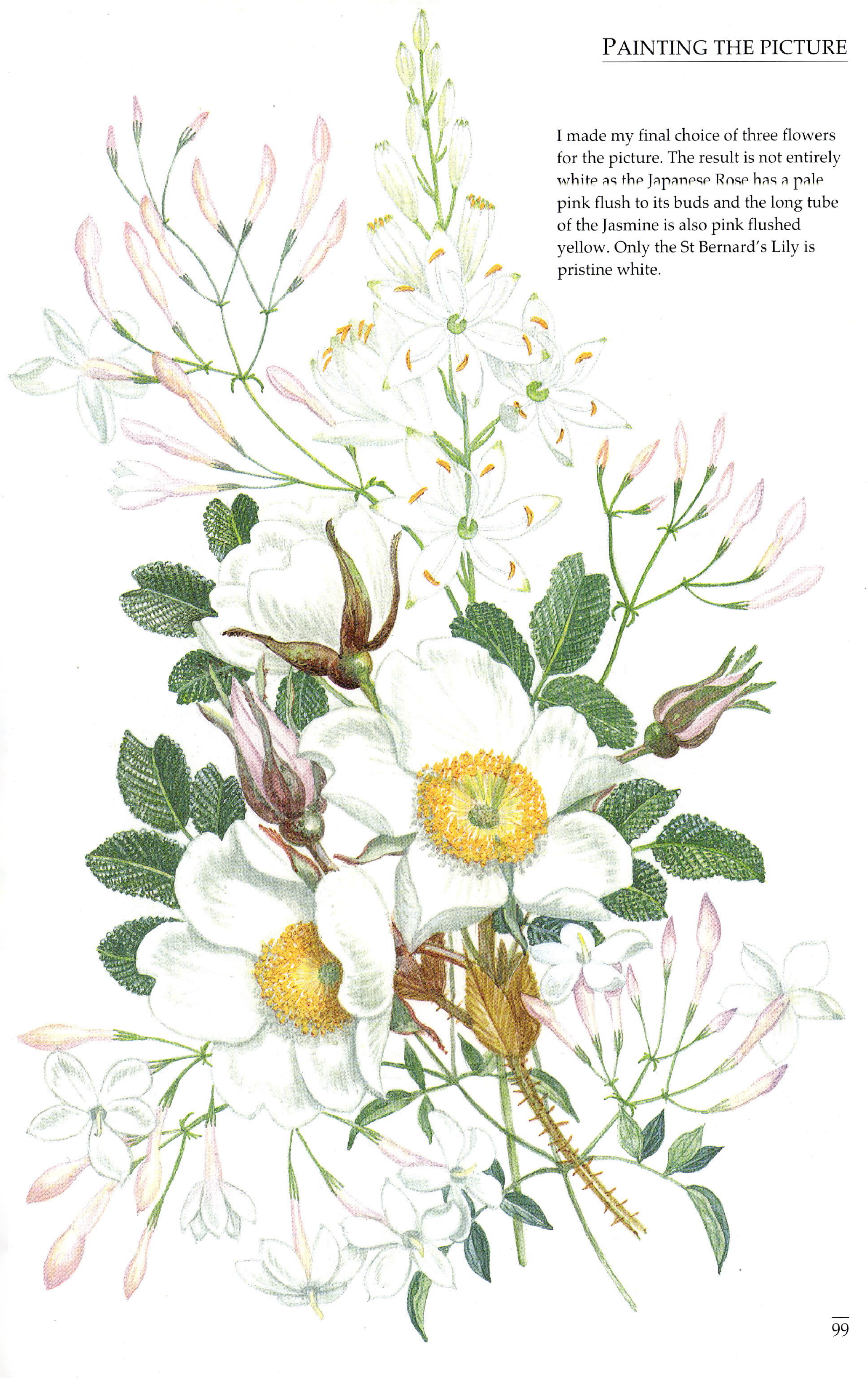

I made my final choice of three flowers for the picture. The result is not entirely white as the Japanese Rose has a pale pink flush to its buds and the long tube of the Jasmine is also pink flushed yellow. Only the St Bernard's Lily is pristine white.

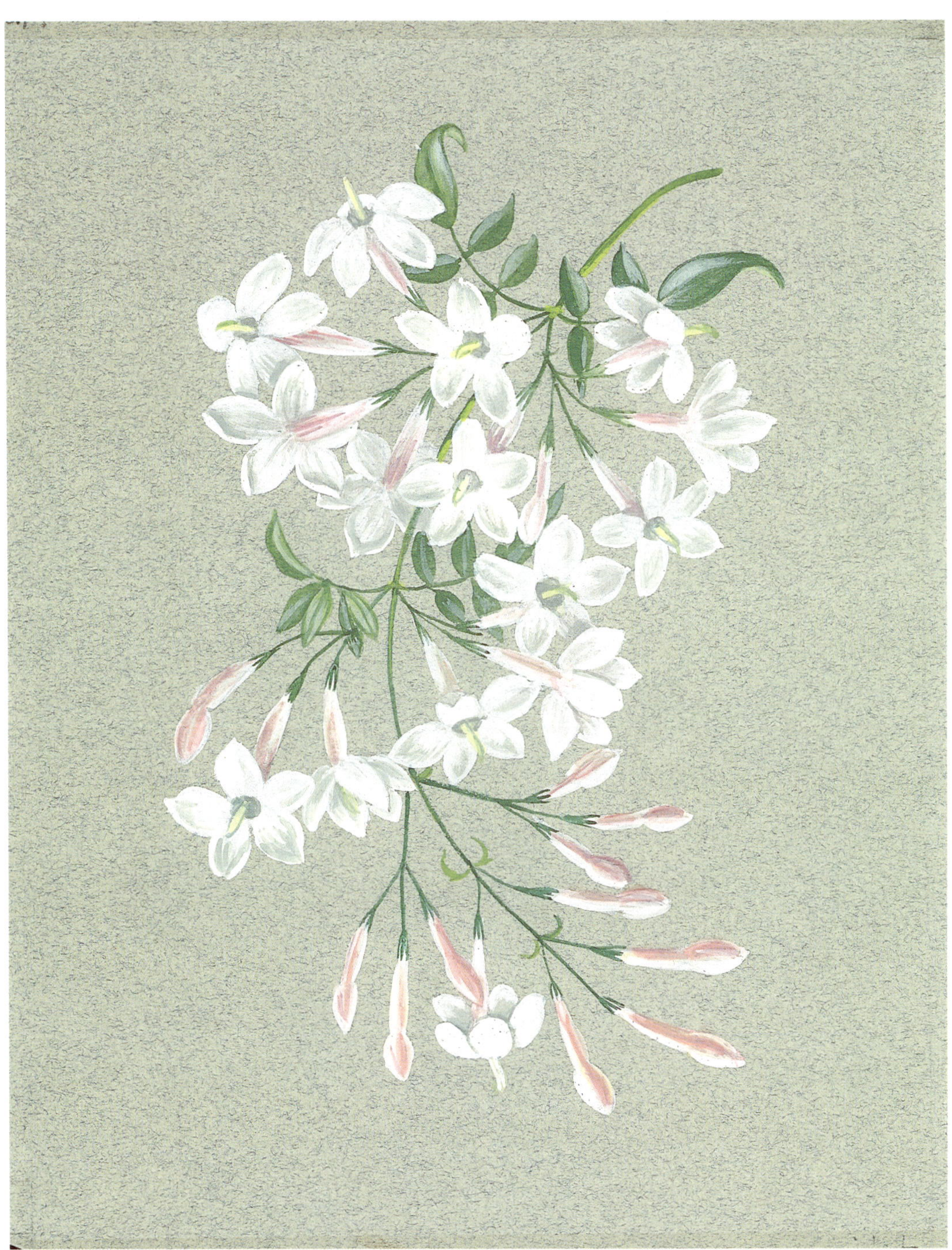

See pp. 12-13 for notes on coloured papers and how to stretch them if necessary. For this and the following three paintings I have used water colours and gouache which is applied exactly in the same way, the only difference being that it is more opaque. Mix some white with both to obtain the palest shades, Zinc White with gouache and Chinese White with water colours. I have illustrated the Jasmine which appears on the two previous pages, to show the different effect of painting on coloured paper.

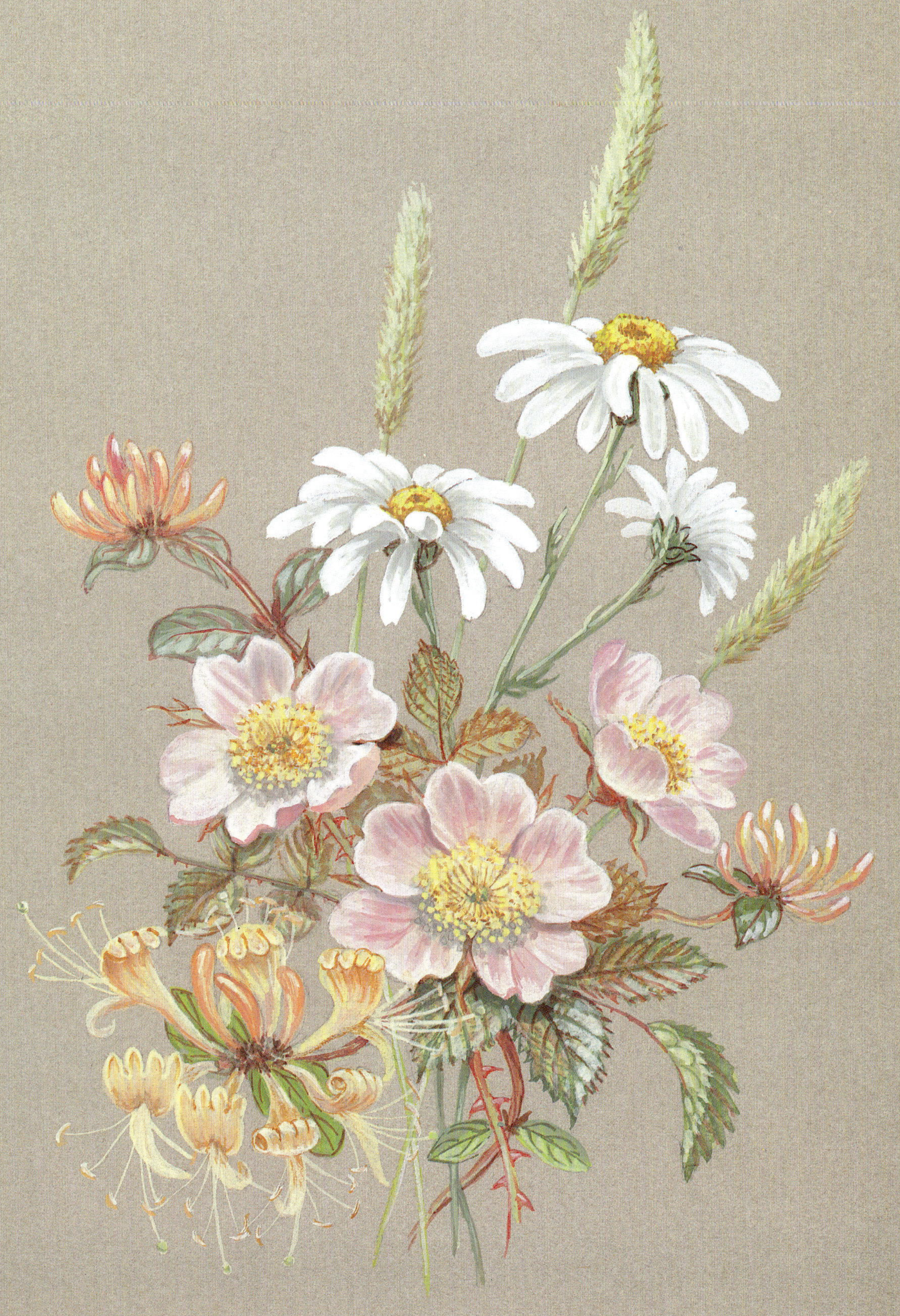

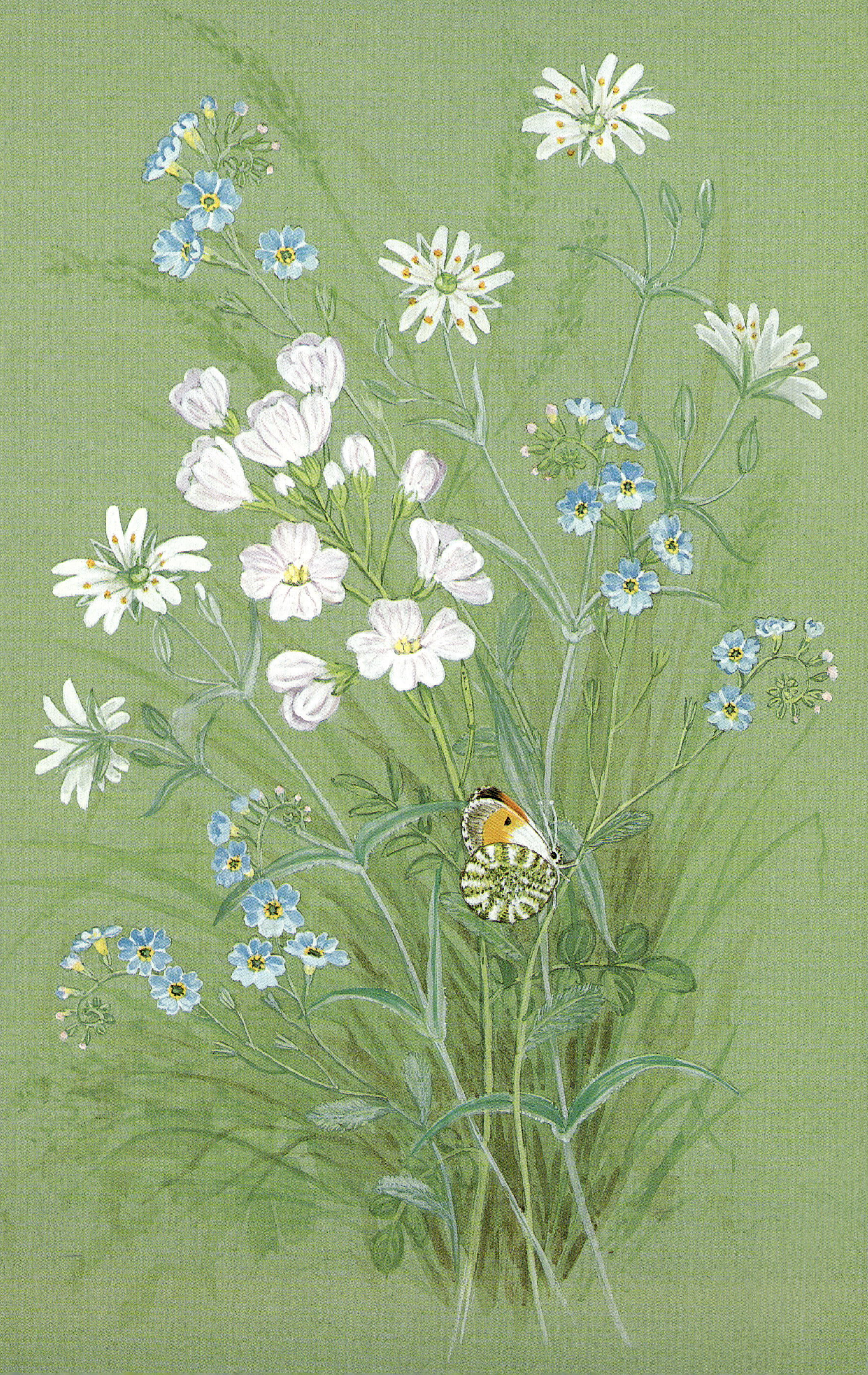

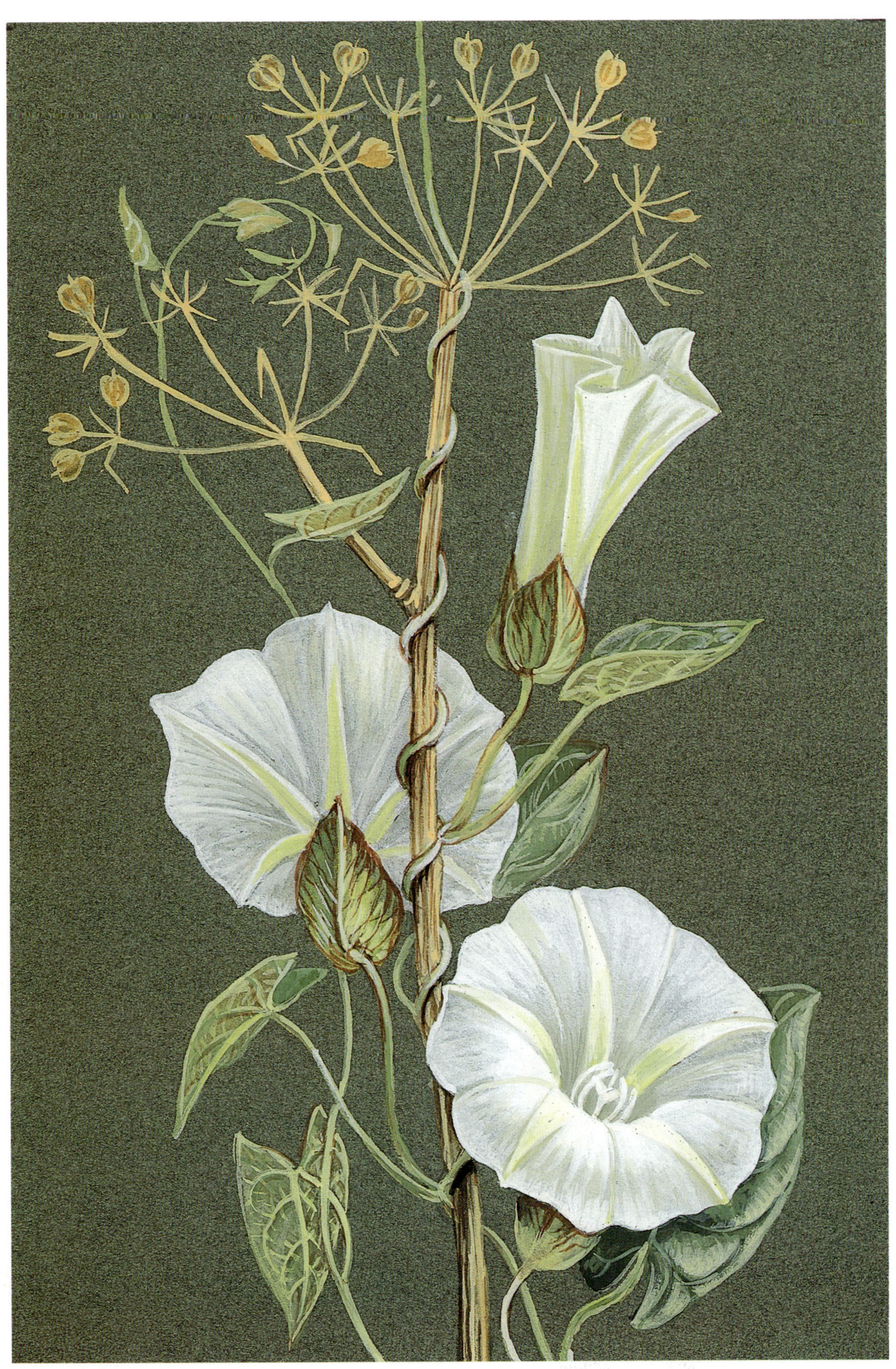

Great Bindweed. Two different styles of painting the same flower are demonstrated here and on p. 96.

SKETCHES FROM ABROAD

THE WILD FLOWERS OF THE FAR NORTH

Many of the flowers of the Arctic Circle, Iceland, Scandinavia and as far south as Scotland have pale cool colours which suit the climate and the clear northern light. White predominates, followed by yellow. You have to travel as far south as the Mediterranean coast to see the hot colours of wild flowers and the exotic trees and shrubs planted in parks and town squares. However, pale shades and the delicate flowers of the north have an irresistible appeal both for the painter and the plant enthusiast.

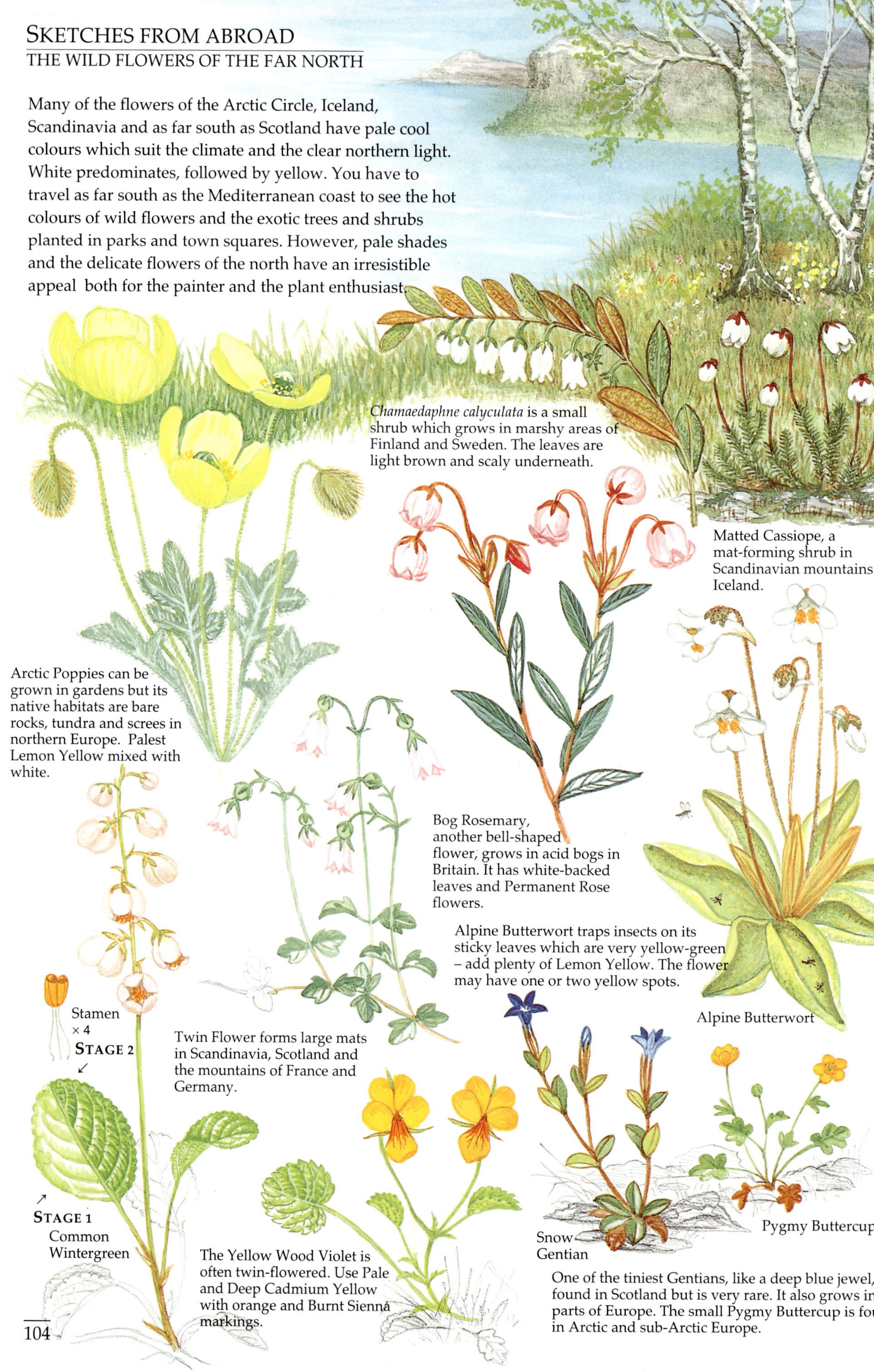

Chamaedaphne calyculata is a small shrub which grows in marshy areas of Finland and Sweden. The leaves are light brown and scaly underneath.

Matted Cassiope, a mat-forming shrub in Scandinavian mountains a Iceland.

Arctic Poppies can be grown in gardens but its native habitats are bare rocks, tundra and screes in northern Europe. Palest Lemon Yellow mixed with white.

Bog Rosemary, another bell-shaped flower, grows in acid bogs in Britain. It has white-backed leaves and Permanent Rose flowers.

Alpine Butterwort traps insects on its sticky leaves which are very yellow-green – add plenty of Lemon Yellow. The flower may have one or two yellow spots.

Twin Flower forms large mats in Scandinavia, Scotland and the mountains of France and Germany.

Common Wintergreen

The Yellow Wood Violet is often twin-flowered. Use Pale and Deep Cadmium Yellow with orange and Burnt Sienna markings.

One of the tiniest Gentians, like a deep blue jewel, found in Scotland but is very rare. It also grows in parts of Europe. The small Pygmy Buttercup is fou in Arctic and sub-Arctic Europe.

These beautiful 'weeds' were once abundant in the cornfields of Britain before being banished by modern farming methods. The wiry stems of the **Cornflowers** were said to blunt the scythes of the reapers and in the 19th century the country poet John Clare wrote that they were 'troubling the cornfields with destroying beauty'. **Corncockles**, tall as the heads of the ripening wheat, were looked upon as noxious weeds as early as the 16th century and banished from the fields by the 19th. Their seeds contain a poison which tainted the wheat flour. Both of these have now changed status from pestilent weeds to popular garden flowers and only rarely are they found growing wild in Britain. But travelling on the small roads of France you can find both of them brilliant among the corn and clashing beautifully with a multitude of **Poppies**, now a rarity in British arable fields.

Another bright ruby jewel of the fields of France and Germany is the small **Pheasant's-eye** with its black-patched petals. It has been re-introduced in Britain, where it was once so abundant in the wild that its flowers were gathered and sold in Covent Garden Market. It probably did little harm but careful seed screening and herbicide sprays have removed it and many more such delightful 'weeds' from our countryside.

Corn Marigold was so pestilent a weed to farmers that King Henry II decreed that it should be destroyed wherever it grew. Occasionally it still appears on disturbed ground, which shows how long its seeds must survive underground. I remember the centre of a newly-built roundabout becoming for a brief period of brilliance a flood of gold, quickly crushed by weed killer before a sombre carpet of grass was laid over their grave. No doubt beds were later dug and planted with well behaved cousins of the banished beauties – the Garden Marigolds.

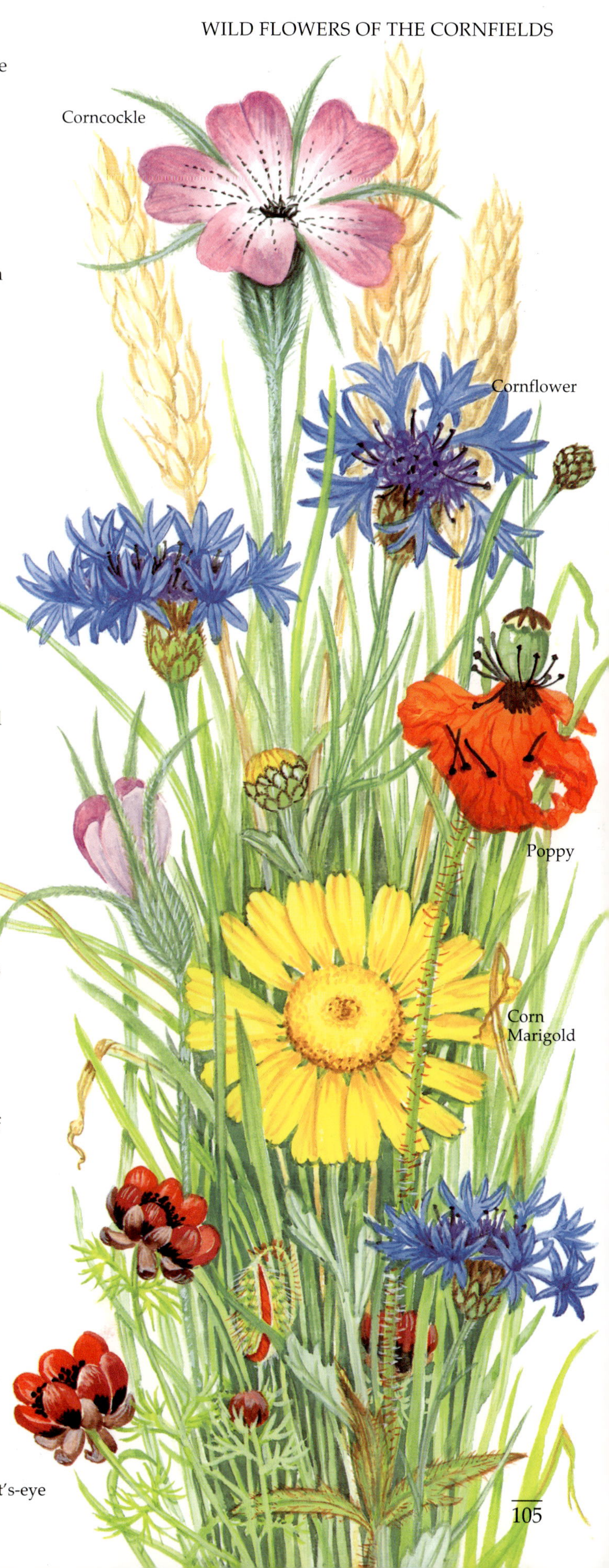

Corncockle – Quinacridone Magenta with pale grey-mauve backs.
Cornflowers – Cobalt Blue.
Common Poppy – Scarlet Lake.
Corn Marigold – Cadmium Yellow Pale.
Pheasant's-eye – Alizarin Crimson with Sepia tinged sepals.

Find Large Venus's Looking Glass at the edge of fields or road sides and you know you are in a different world of flowers. Travelling to southern Europe the flora changes and favourite plants, absent or very rare in Britain, begin to decorate the countryside often in abundance. The Creeping Bellflower, naturalised in Britain, is a tall elegant cool-coloured member of the same family, lovely to look at in the wild but very invasive in the garden.

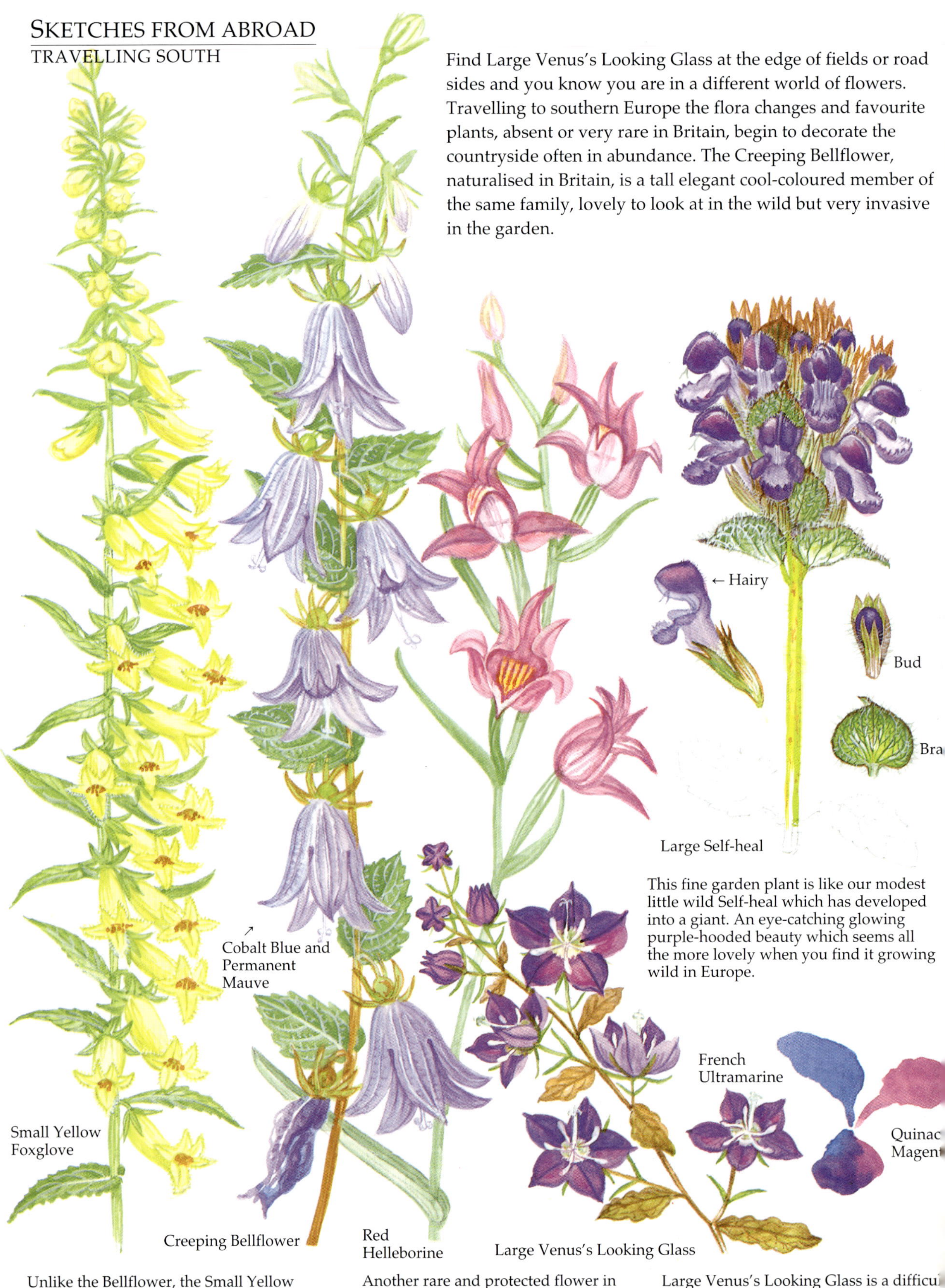

Small Yellow Foxglove

Creeping Bellflower

Red Helleborine

Large Venus's Looking Glass

Large Self-heal

This fine garden plant is like our modest little wild Self-heal which has developed into a giant. An eye-catching glowing purple-hooded beauty which seems all the more lovely when you find it growing wild in Europe.

Unlike the Bellflower, the Small Yellow Foxglove is easy and well behaved in the garden. It is pale Lemon Yellow and grows very upright. Never be tempted to put pretty curves to stems that nature intended should be straight.

Another rare and protected flower in England but widespread on the Continent is the Red Helleborine. This is a typical plant but I found one with 48 flowers on it. The stem is undulating.

Large Venus's Looking Glass is a difficu shade to match in permanent watercolou This and the Self-heal are an even more vibrant purple than 81A in the RHS Colc Chart. The best you can do is mix French Ultramarine and Quinacridone Magenta

Wandering in early summer along the south coast of France from the Camargue westward and south to the Spanish border one finds a wide variety of flowers, some familiar ones which grow successfully in the gardens of Britain and others too tender to attempt to cultivate in the open. Spanish Broom is easily grown and blue Aphyllanthes is a stunningly beautiful plant to see under the Mediterranean sun.

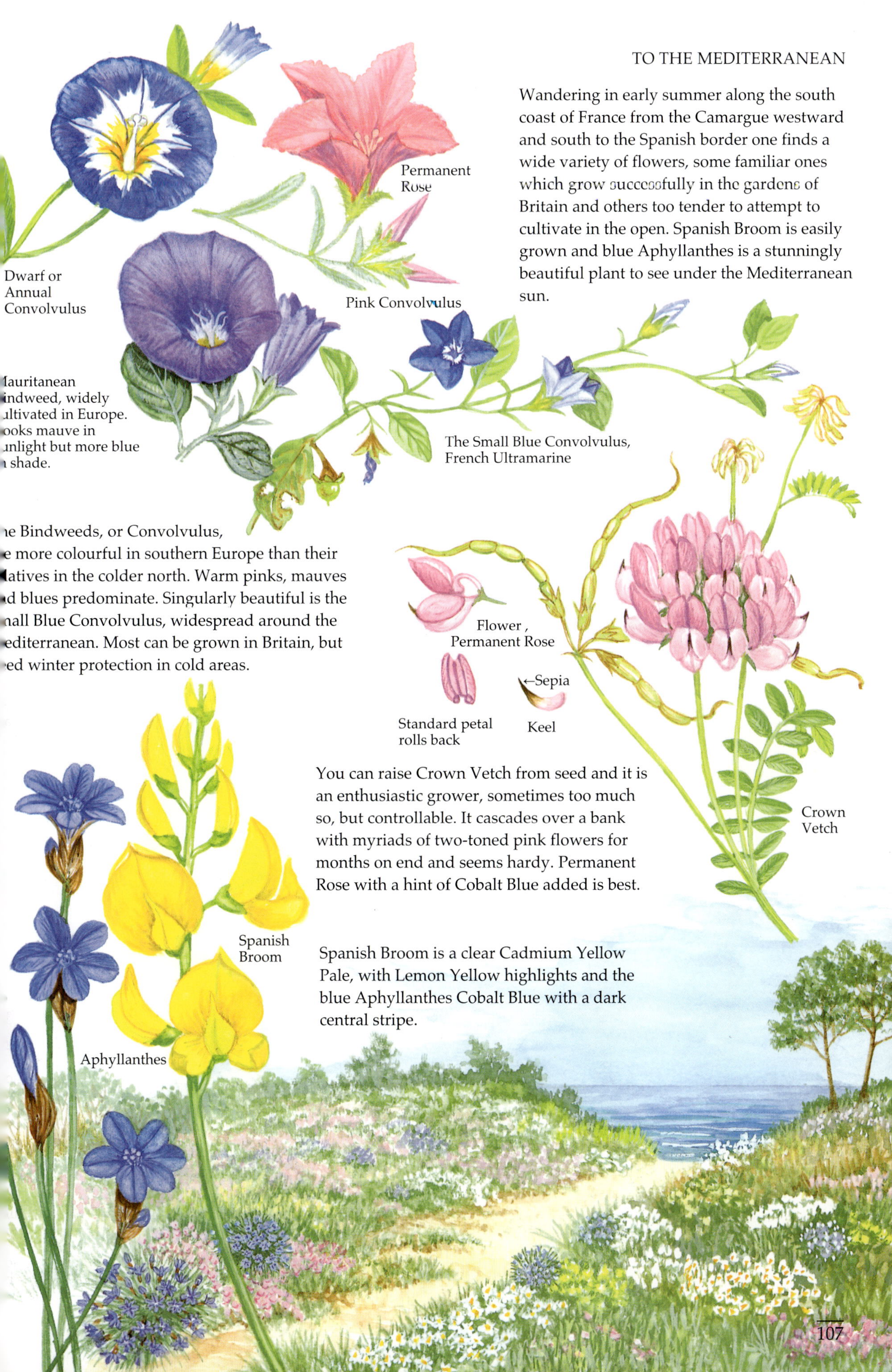

ıe Bindweeds, or Convolvulus, e more colourful in southern Europe than their latives in the colder north. Warm pinks, mauves ıd blues predominate. Singularly beautiful is the nall Blue Convolvulus, widespread around the editerranean. Most can be grown in Britain, but ed winter protection in cold areas.

You can raise Crown Vetch from seed and it is an enthusiastic grower, sometimes too much so, but controllable. It cascades over a bank with myriads of two-toned pink flowers for months on end and seems hardy. Permanent Rose with a hint of Cobalt Blue added is best.

Spanish Broom is a clear Cadmium Yellow Pale, with Lemon Yellow highlights and the blue Aphyllanthes Cobalt Blue with a dark central stripe.

SKETCHES FROM ABROAD

MOUNTAIN FLOWERS

Designing a field guide to the identification of flowers has to be carefully done; before I begin to do the final paintings a list of species, sometimes well over 2000, is drawn up to decide how many will fit on each page with just enough of each flower to show its important features without adding extra size or pages to the book. Only occasionally is there room for a spray of flowers however much I would like to do it. If I cannot get the exact shade I want in permanent water colour I use fugitive ones and diluted inks in the cerise to magenta range. The fact that the paints may fade in time is of little importance once the book is safely printed.

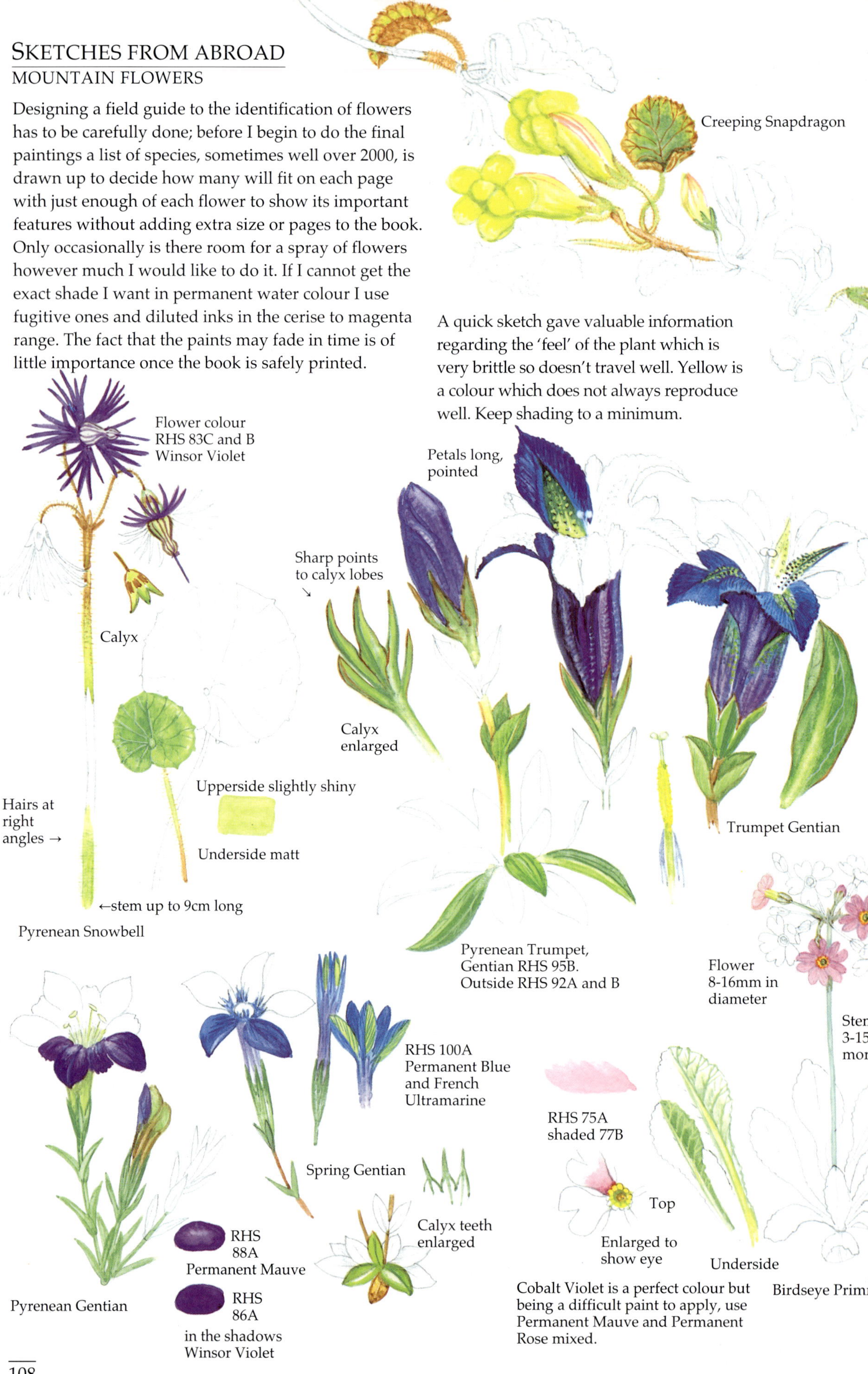

The quest for plants in the mountains of Europe and many days working on paintings from Herbarium collections continues until I have sketched the last one onto my file cards. Then I can design and complete the final paintings. Flowers like the gentians are easy to fit on to one page as they are small and compact unlike any of the shrubs or trees, for instance.

In these cases I carefully select the most easily recognised part of the plant, probably a flower and the fruit which I paint life size with a very miniature version of the tree beside it as the Silver Birch painting demonstrates.

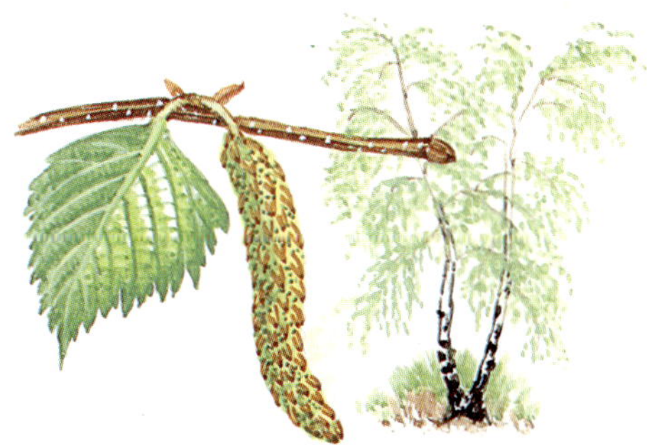

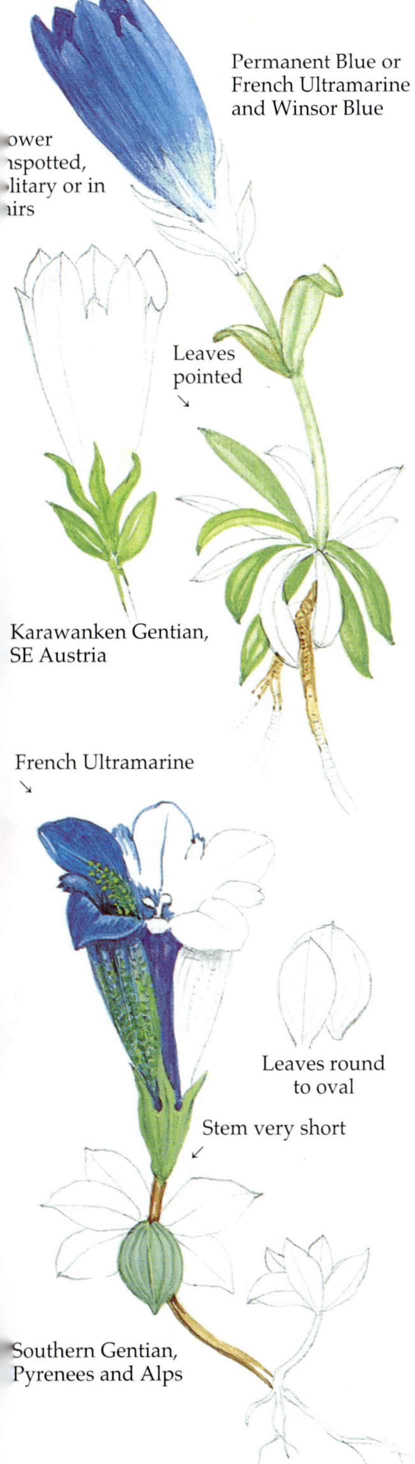

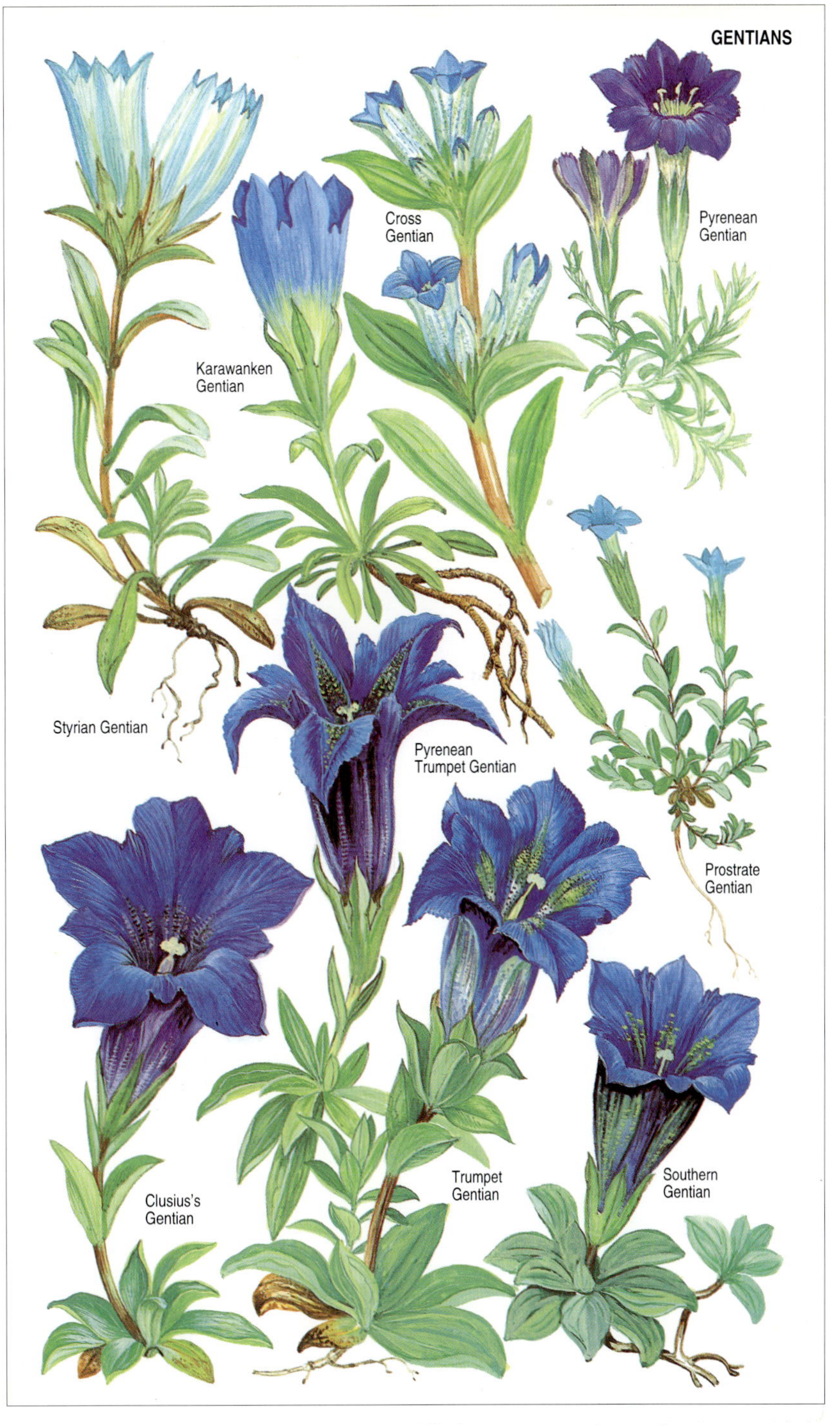

GENTIANS

Styrian Gentian

Karawanken Gentian

Cross Gentian

Pyrenean Gentian

Prostrate Gentian

Pyrenean Trumpet Gentian

Clusius's Gentian

Trumpet Gentian

Southern Gentian

A page from *Alpine Flowers of Britain and Europe* by Christopher Grey-Wilson and Marjorie Blamey.

Lovely flowers to paint though you won't find any of these wild in Britain. Several will grow in gardens, including the well-named Beautiful Flax which always seems to have a shiny halo around it as it faces up to the Mediterranean sun. There are several rusty-coloured Foxgloves, all of which can be grown from seed and they are fascinating to paint with their glowing colour and net-veined flowers. Seed and plants of these and of the Yellow Foxglove (p. 106) can be bought in Britain.

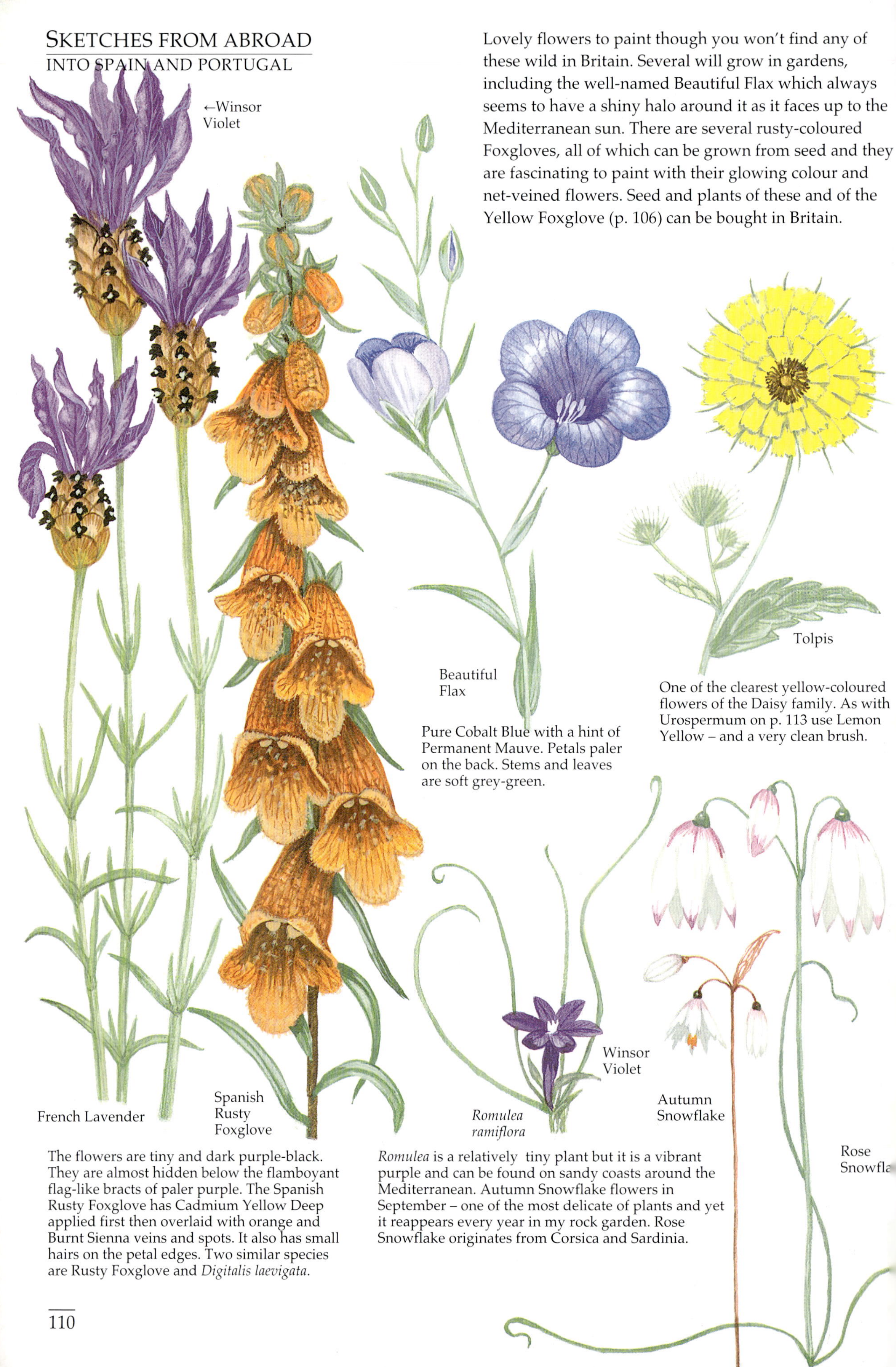

Pure Cobalt Blue with a hint of Permanent Mauve. Petals paler on the back. Stems and leaves are soft grey-green.

One of the clearest yellow-coloured flowers of the Daisy family. As with Urospermum on p. 113 use Lemon Yellow – and a very clean brush.

The flowers are tiny and dark purple-black. They are almost hidden below the flamboyant flag-like bracts of paler purple. The Spanish Rusty Foxglove has Cadmium Yellow Deep applied first then overlaid with orange and Burnt Sienna veins and spots. It also has small hairs on the petal edges. Two similar species are Rusty Foxglove and *Digitalis laevigata*.

Romulea is a relatively tiny plant but it is a vibrant purple and can be found on sandy coasts around the Mediterranean. Autumn Snowflake flowers in September – one of the most delicate of plants and yet it reappears every year in my rock garden. Rose Snowflake originates from Corsica and Sardinia.

Still travelling further and reaching the south coast of Portugal you can find Hoop Petticoat Narcissus spreading over the sea cliffs, some only 5cm (2 inches) tall. Illustrated also are some of the profusion of flowers found there in the warm sunshine of early February, while Britain is still gripped by frosts.

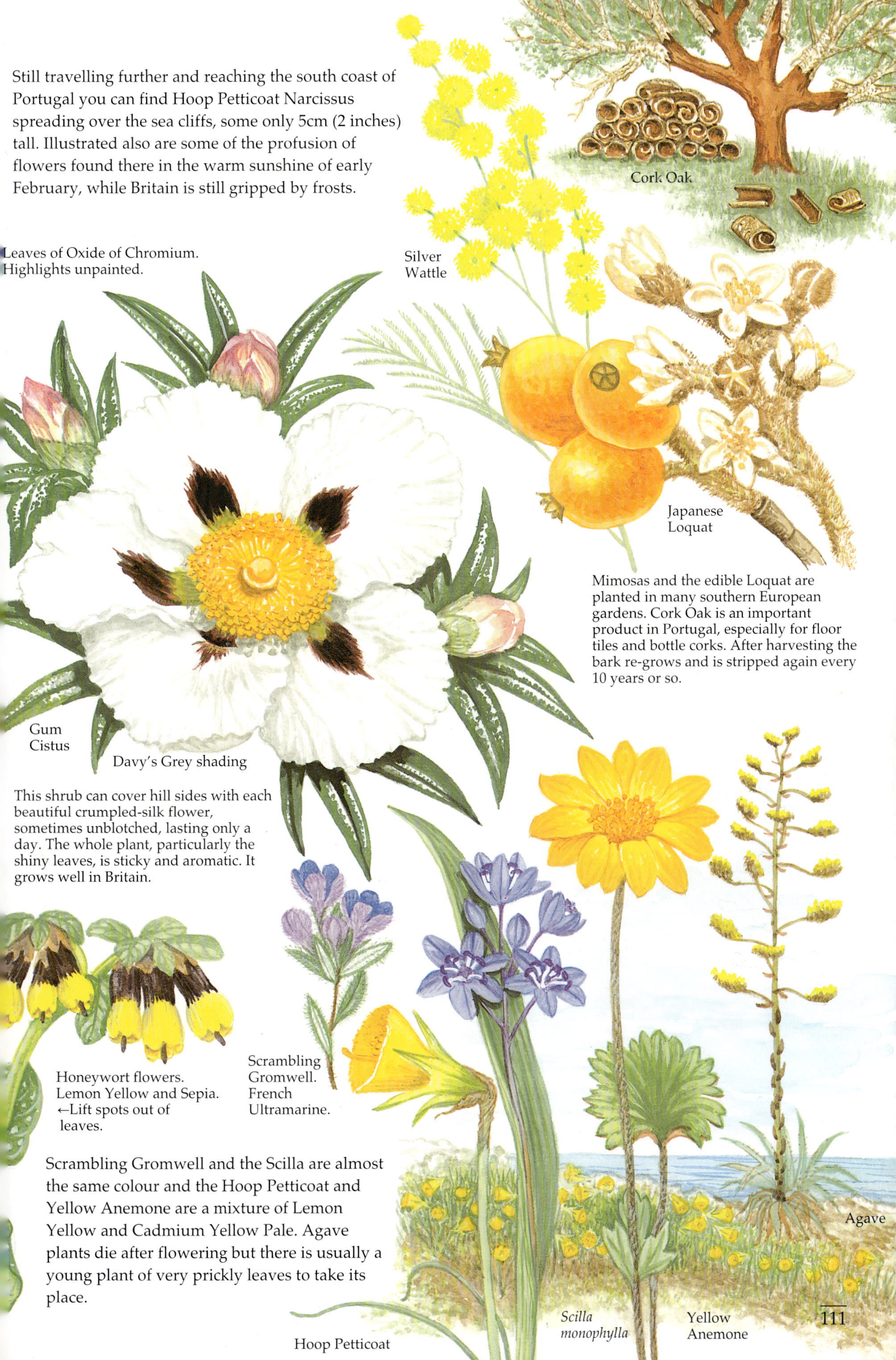

Mimosas and the edible Loquat are planted in many southern European gardens. Cork Oak is an important product in Portugal, especially for floor tiles and bottle corks. After harvesting the bark re-grows and is stripped again every 10 years or so.

This shrub can cover hill sides with each beautiful crumpled-silk flower, sometimes unblotched, lasting only a day. The whole plant, particularly the shiny leaves, is sticky and aromatic. It grows well in Britain.

Scrambling Gromwell and the Scilla are almost the same colour and the Hoop Petticoat and Yellow Anemone are a mixture of Lemon Yellow and Cadmium Yellow Pale. Agave plants die after flowering but there is usually a young plant of very prickly leaves to take its place.

SKETCHES FROM ABROAD

WAYSIDE FLOWERS IN MAJORCA

Wild flowers grow in profusion around and often in the arable fields of Majorca, so there is no shortage of models for the flower painter. I sketched a handful of flowers by wandering only a few yards along a country lane and loved the contrasts and clashes they produced. Later I found where the odd plant of Italian Sainfoin had come from, a whole field of them which, from a distance, looked like small crimson lupins.

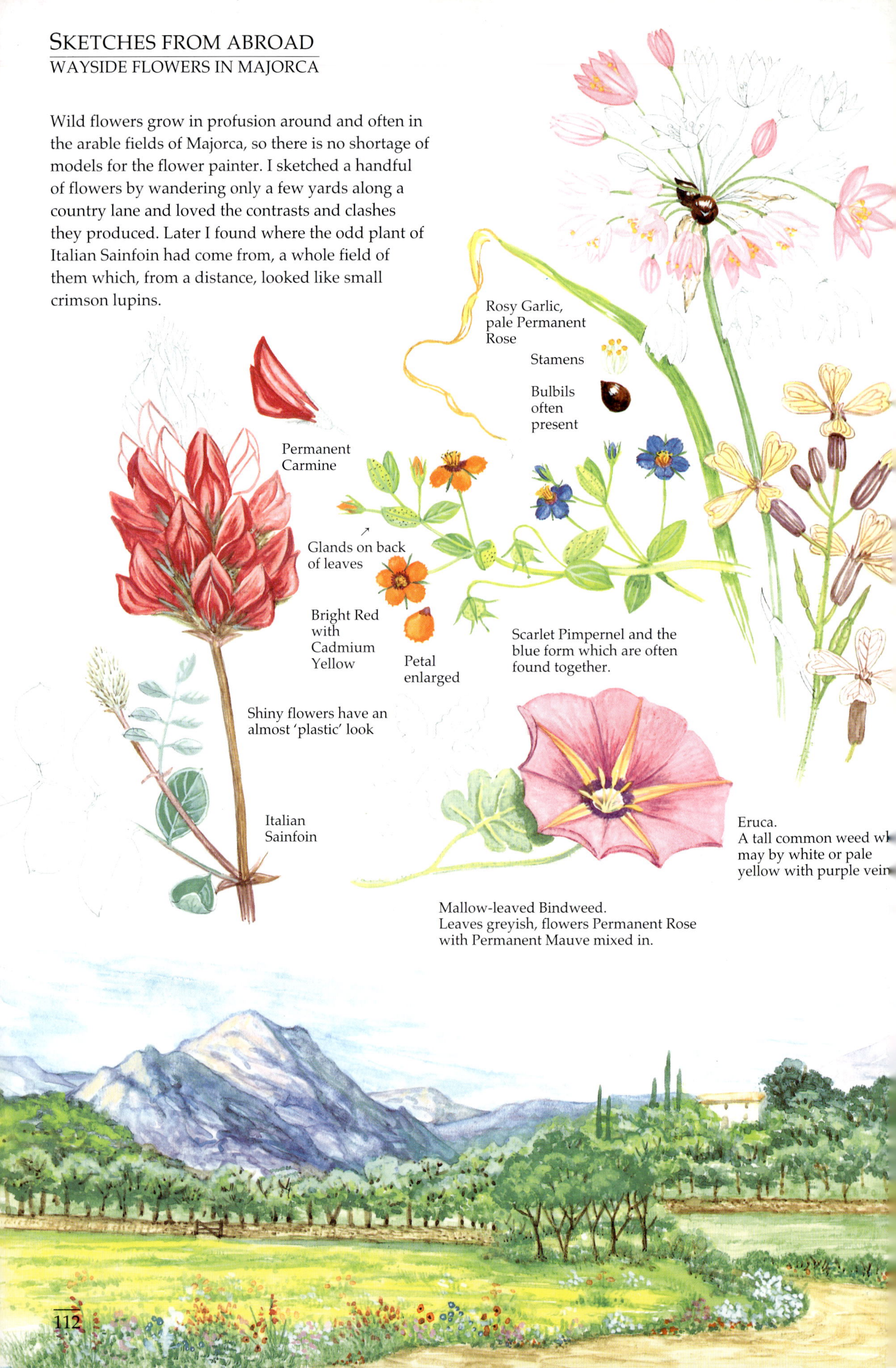

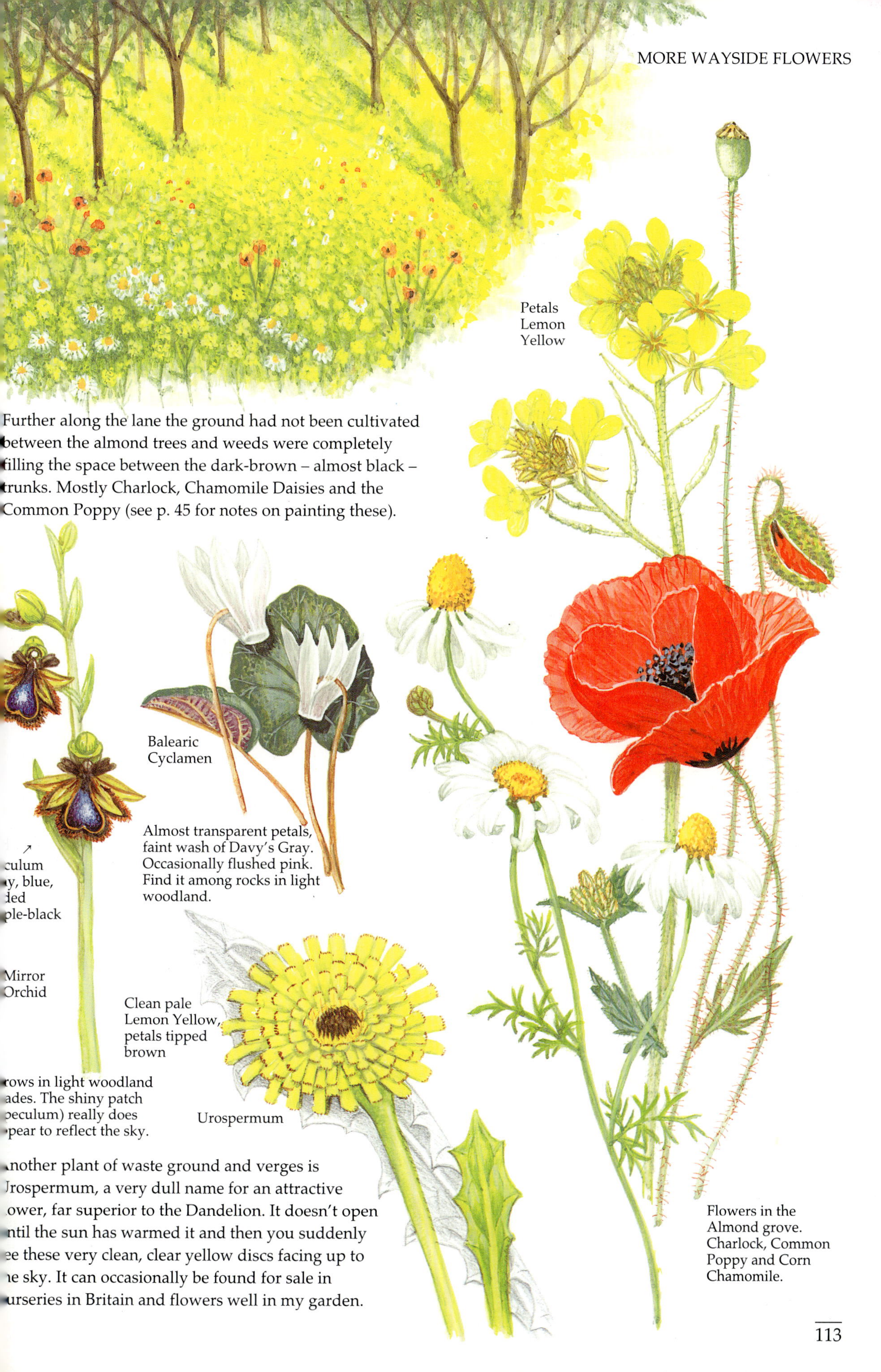

Further along the lane the ground had not been cultivated between the almond trees and weeds were completely filling the space between the dark-brown – almost black – trunks. Mostly Charlock, Chamomile Daisies and the Common Poppy (see p. 45 for notes on painting these).

nother plant of waste ground and verges is Jrospermum, a very dull name for an attractive ower, far superior to the Dandelion. It doesn't open ntil the sun has warmed it and then you suddenly ee these very clean, clear yellow discs facing up to ne sky. It can occasionally be found for sale in urseries in Britain and flowers well in my garden.

Flowers in the Almond grove. Charlock, Common Poppy and Corn Chamomile.

If you walk near the sea around almost any Mediterranean Island you will find many flowers where hotels have not competely eliminated their habitats. As well as the three species of the lovely Rockroses which often fill coastal areas and woodlands, I also found wild Gladioli in the field which bordered the edge of the sea and here and there Tassel Hyacinths. The 'tassel' is a deep purplish-blue, French Ultramarine mixed with Winsor Violet.

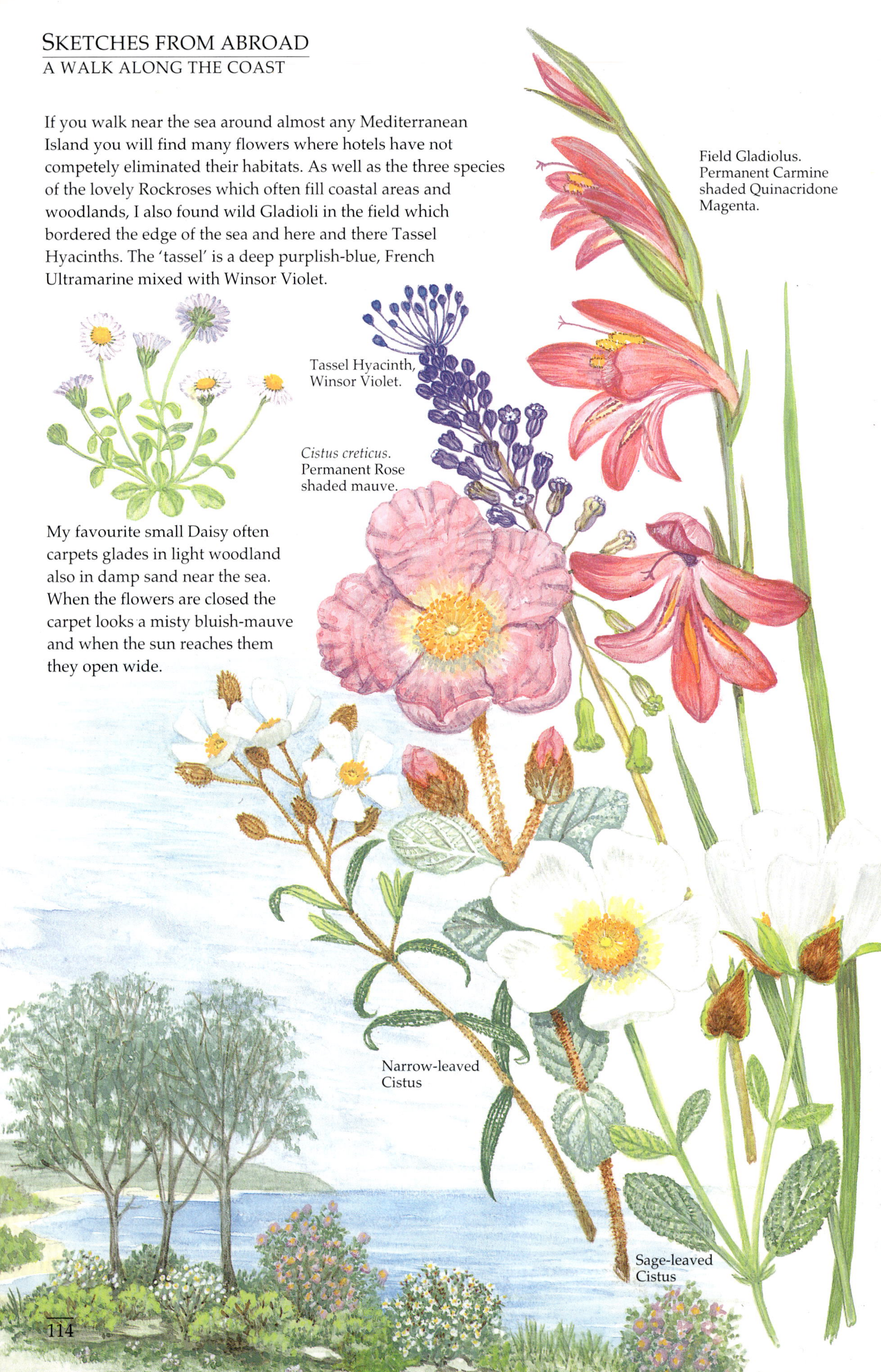

My favourite small Daisy often carpets glades in light woodland also in damp sand near the sea. When the flowers are closed the carpet looks a misty bluish-mauve and when the sun reaches them they open wide.

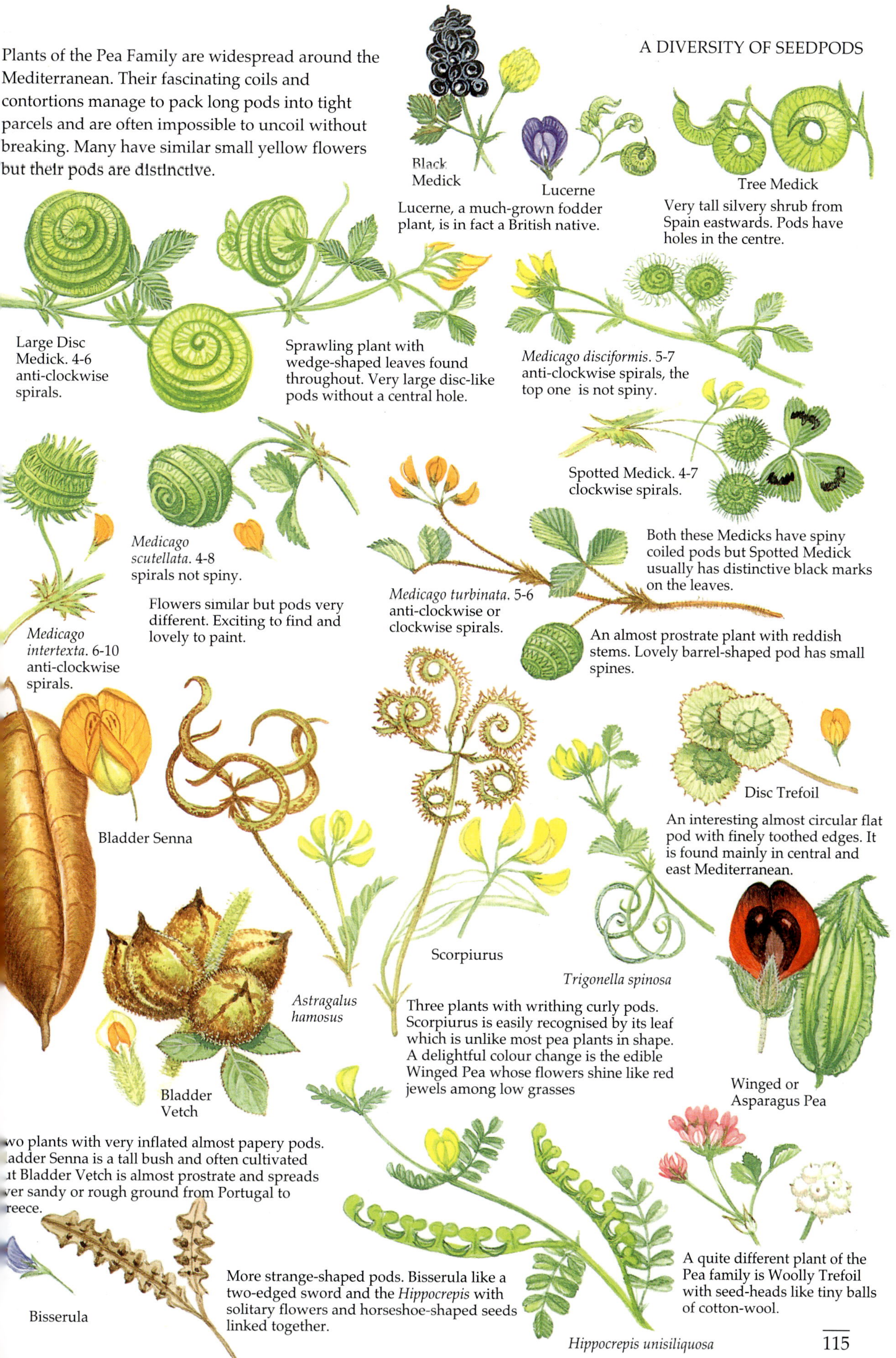

Plants of the Pea Family are widespread around the Mediterranean. Their fascinating coils and contortions manage to pack long pods into tight parcels and are often impossible to uncoil without breaking. Many have similar small yellow flowers but their pods are distinctive.

Lucerne, a much-grown fodder plant, is in fact a British native.

Tree Medick. Very tall silvery shrub from Spain eastwards. Pods have holes in the centre.

Large Disc Medick. 4-6 anti-clockwise spirals.

Sprawling plant with wedge-shaped leaves found throughout. Very large disc-like pods without a central hole.

Medicago disciformis. 5-7 anti-clockwise spirals, the top one is not spiny.

Spotted Medick. 4-7 clockwise spirals.

Both these Medicks have spiny coiled pods but Spotted Medick usually has distinctive black marks on the leaves.

Medicago scutellata. 4-8 spirals not spiny.

Flowers similar but pods very different. Exciting to find and lovely to paint.

Medicago turbinata. 5-6 anti-clockwise or clockwise spirals.

An almost prostrate plant with reddish stems. Lovely barrel-shaped pod has small spines.

Medicago intertexta. 6-10 anti-clockwise spirals.

Disc Trefoil

An interesting almost circular flat pod with finely toothed edges. It is found mainly in central and east Mediterranean.

Three plants with writhing curly pods. Scorpiurus is easily recognised by its leaf which is unlike most pea plants in shape. A delightful colour change is the edible Winged Pea whose flowers shine like red jewels among low grasses

wo plants with very inflated almost papery pods. .adder Senna is a tall bush and often cultivated ıt Bladder Vetch is almost prostrate and spreads ver sandy or rough ground from Portugal to reece.

More strange-shaped pods. Bisserula like a two-edged sword and the *Hippocrepis* with solitary flowers and horseshoe-shaped seeds linked together.

A quite different plant of the Pea family is Woolly Trefoil with seed-heads like tiny balls of cotton-wool.

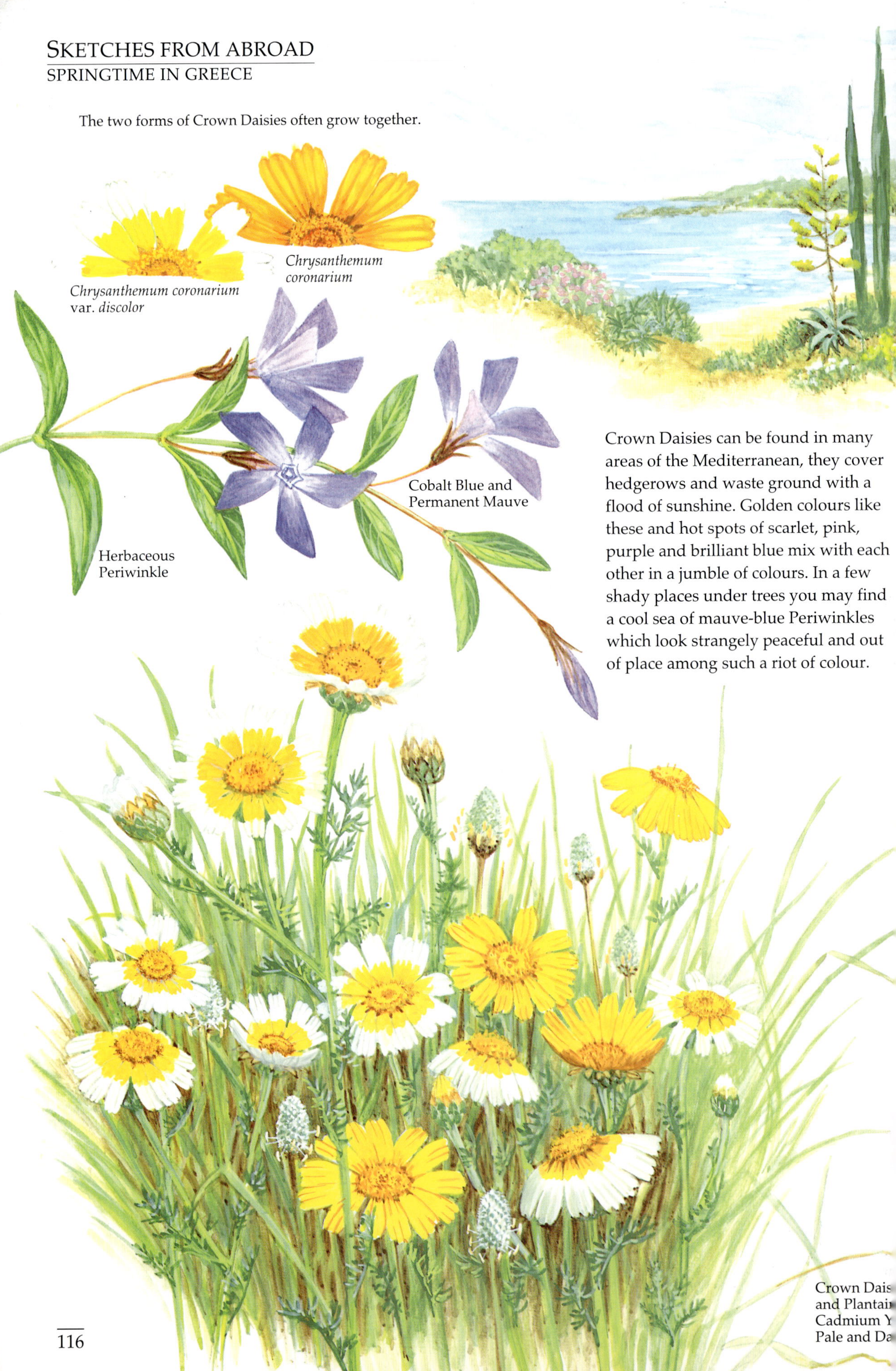

The two forms of Crown Daisies often grow together.

Chrysanthemum coronarium var. *discolor*

Chrysanthemum coronarium

Herbaceous Periwinkle

Cobalt Blue and Permanent Mauve

Crown Daisies can be found in many areas of the Mediterranean, they cover hedgerows and waste ground with a flood of sunshine. Golden colours like these and hot spots of scarlet, pink, purple and brilliant blue mix with each other in a jumble of colours. In a few shady places under trees you may find a cool sea of mauve-blue Periwinkles which look strangely peaceful and out of place among such a riot of colour.

Crown Dais
and Plantai
Cadmium Y
Pale and Da

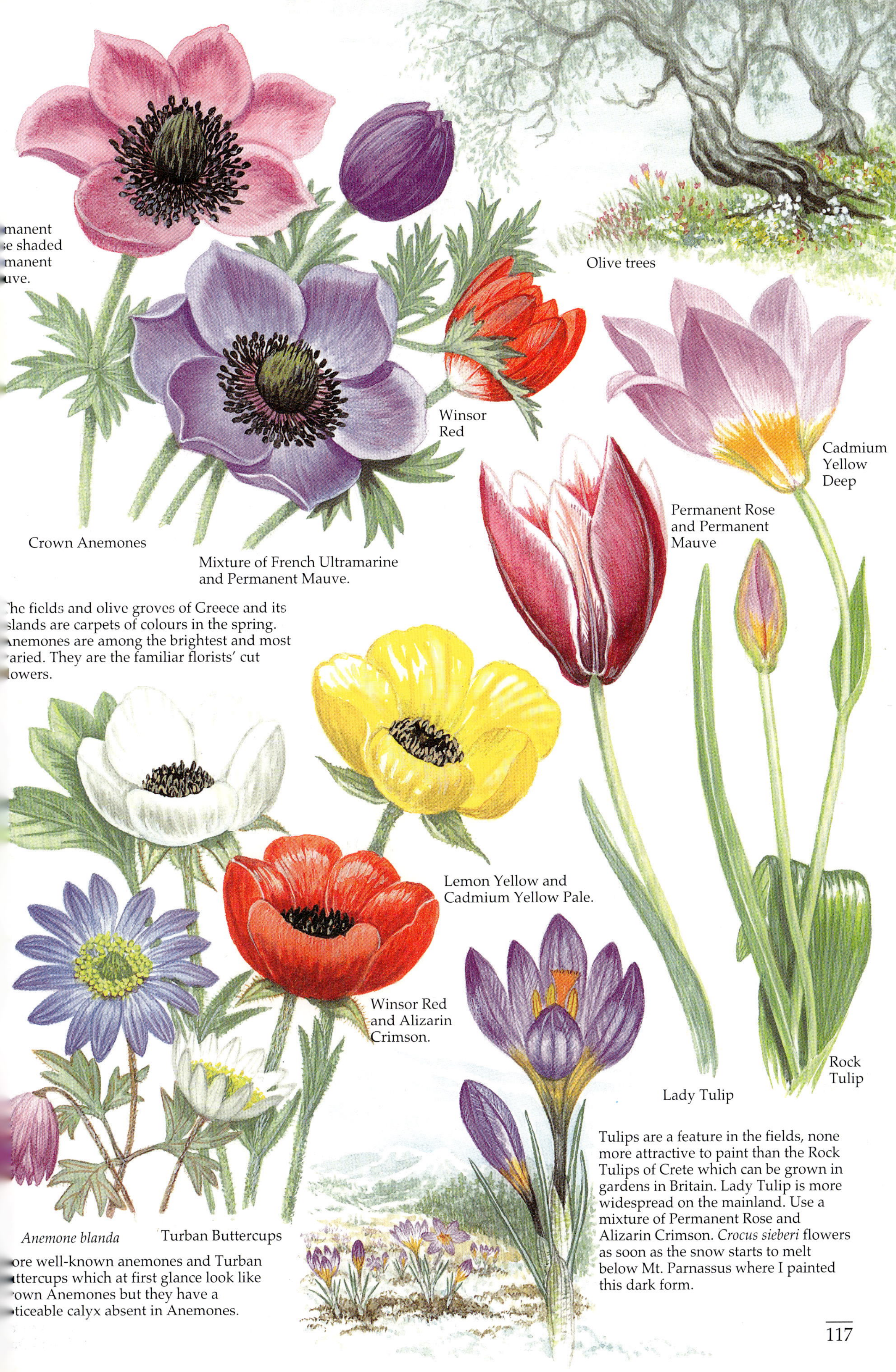

he fields and olive groves of Greece and its slands are carpets of colours in the spring. nemones are among the brightest and most aried. They are the familiar florists' cut lowers.

ore well-known anemones and Turban ttercups which at first glance look like own Anemones but they have a ticeable calyx absent in Anemones.

Tulips are a feature in the fields, none more attractive to paint than the Rock Tulips of Crete which can be grown in gardens in Britain. Lady Tulip is more widespread on the mainland. Use a mixture of Permanent Rose and Alizarin Crimson. *Crocus sieberi* flowers as soon as the snow starts to melt below Mt. Parnassus where I painted this dark form.

Among the flowers in Northern Europe I always prefer the delicate, the soft coloured, the small and simple flowers – Primroses, Oxlips, Harebells and the tiny Twin Flowers – but also Poppies! Having painted the book 'Wild Flowers of the Mediterranean' I still find I prefer the same type of plant in spite of the flamboyant species which surround one there.

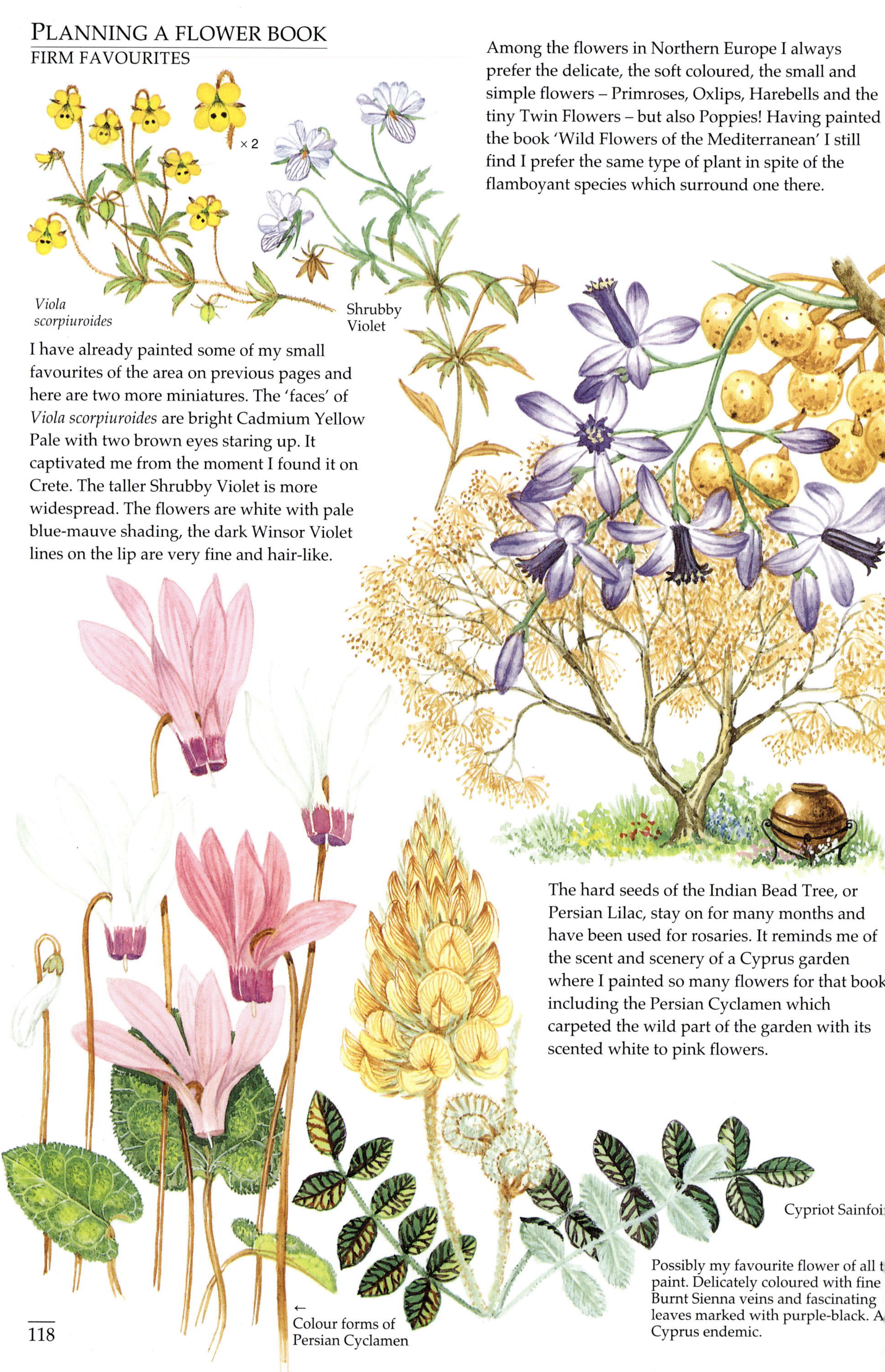

Viola scorpiuroides

Shrubby Violet

I have already painted some of my small favourites of the area on previous pages and here are two more miniatures. The 'faces' of *Viola scorpiuroides* are bright Cadmium Yellow Pale with two brown eyes staring up. It captivated me from the moment I found it on Crete. The taller Shrubby Violet is more widespread. The flowers are white with pale blue-mauve shading, the dark Winsor Violet lines on the lip are very fine and hair-like.

The hard seeds of the Indian Bead Tree, or Persian Lilac, stay on for many months and have been used for rosaries. It reminds me of the scent and scenery of a Cyprus garden where I painted so many flowers for that book including the Persian Cyclamen which carpeted the wild part of the garden with its scented white to pink flowers.

Cypriot Sainfoi

Possibly my favourite flower of all t paint. Delicately coloured with fine Burnt Sienna veins and fascinating leaves marked with purple-black. A Cyprus endemic.

← Colour forms of Persian Cyclamen

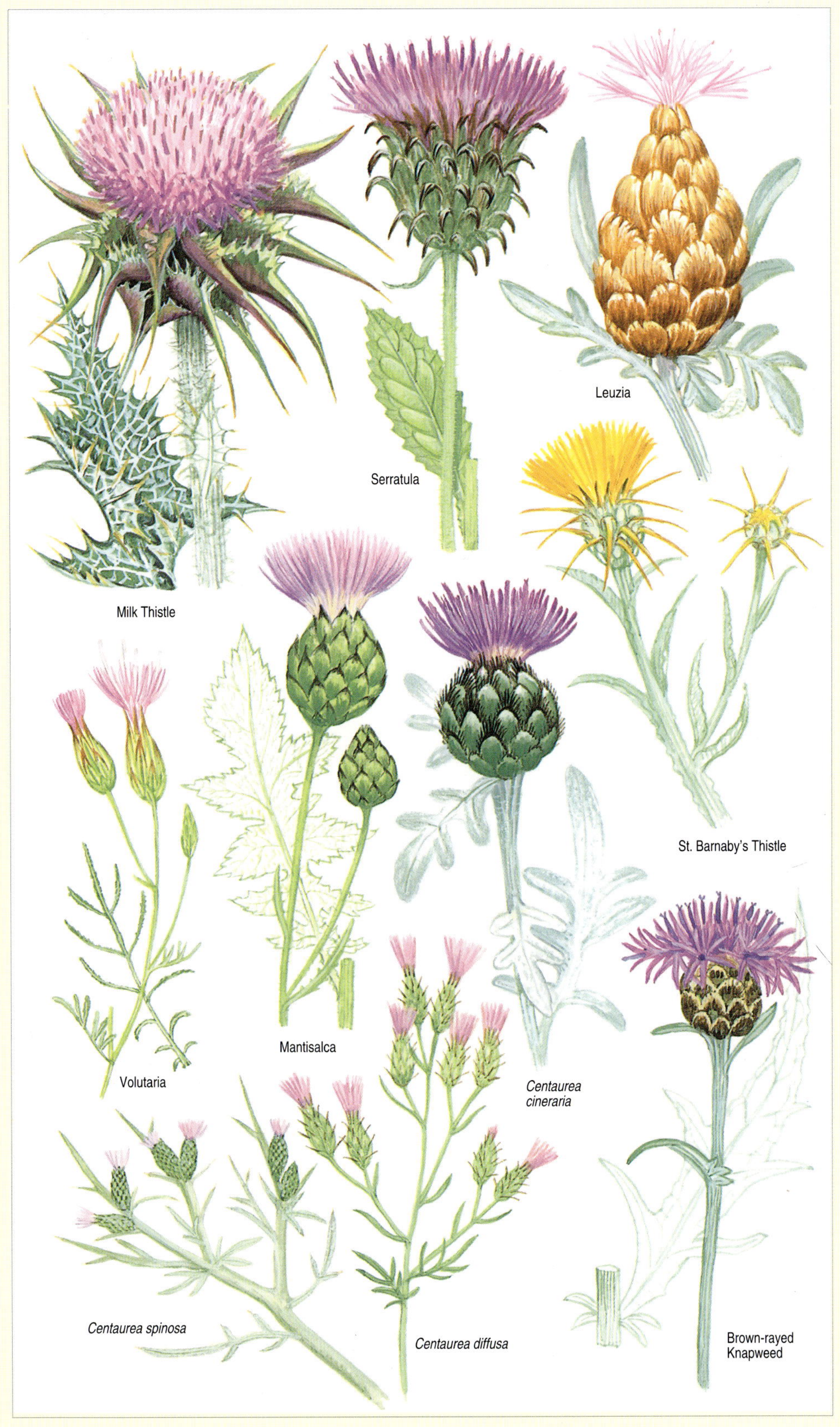

Mediterranean Wild Flowers by Marjorie Blamey and Christopher Grey-Wilson, published by Collins.

Flowers from Far Afield

The Americas

This Red Passion Flower from Brazil is said not to be hardy enough to survive even in the Mediterranean. However it is now flowering beautifully in my cold greenhouse in the west of England, so it is worth growing and is available from specialist nurseries. Its flowers are complicated so I have separated the parts to make it easier.

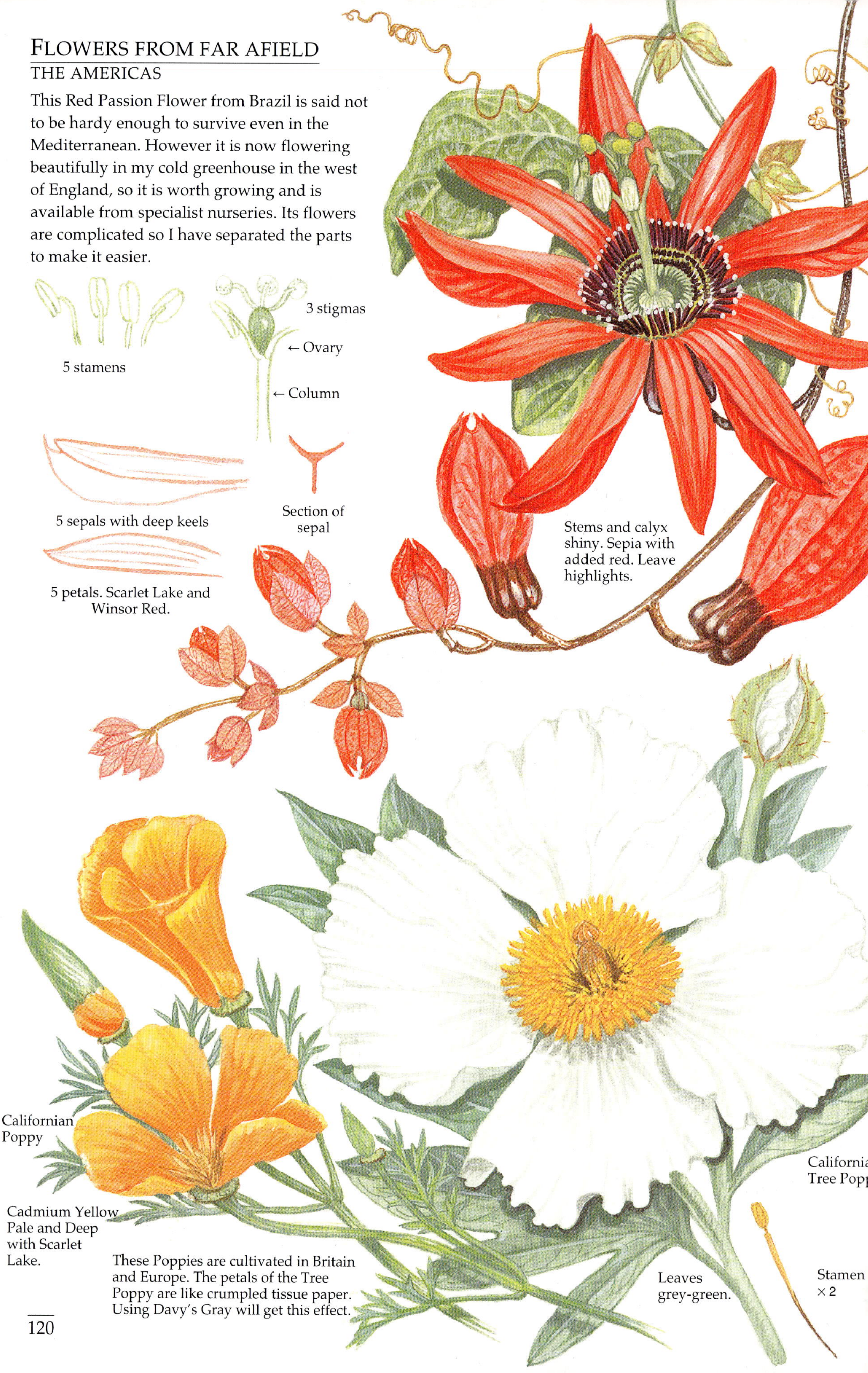

These Poppies are cultivated in Britain and Europe. The petals of the Tree Poppy are like crumpled tissue paper. Using Davy's Gray will get this effect.

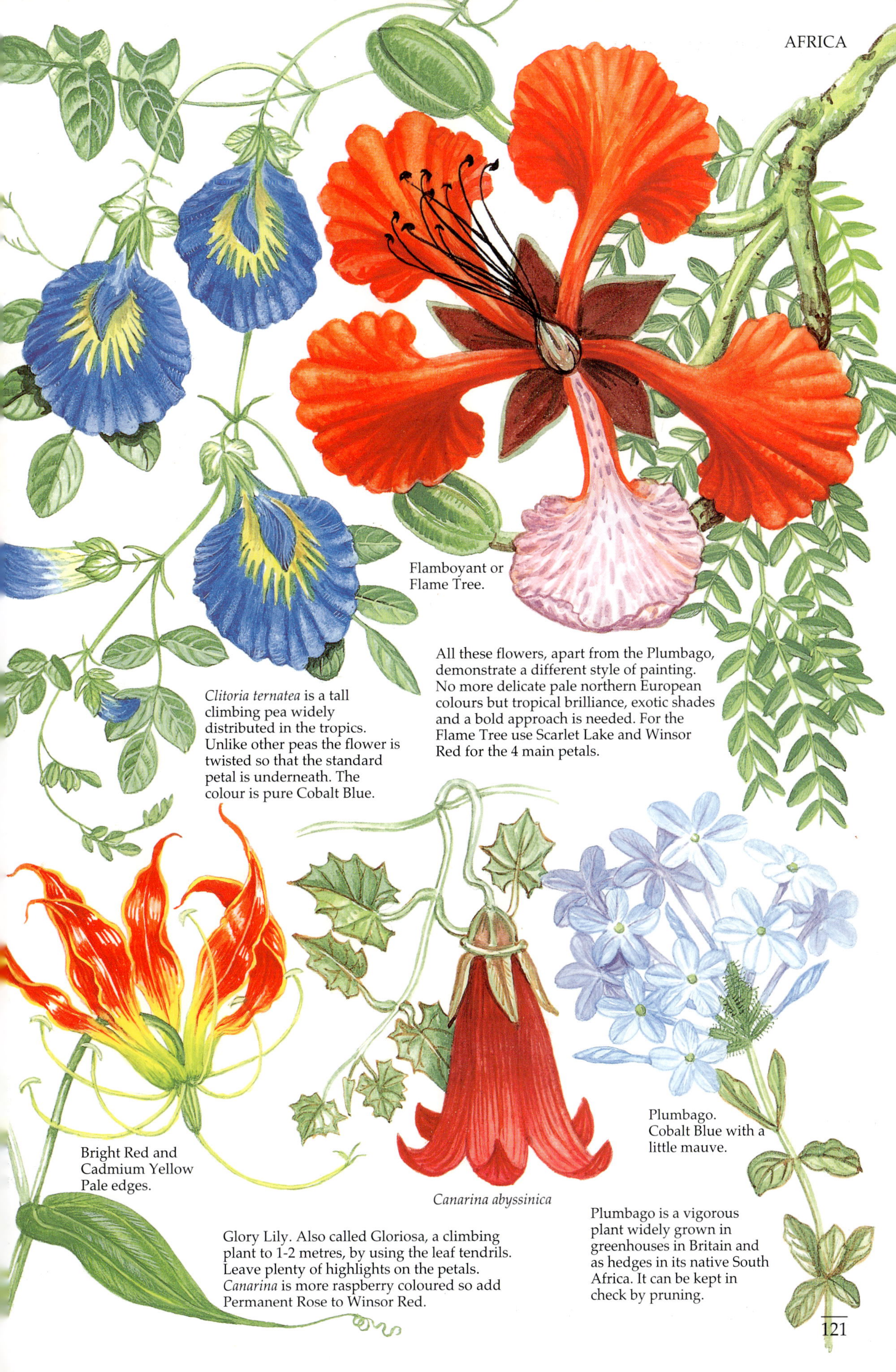

Flamboyant or Flame Tree.

All these flowers, apart from the Plumbago, demonstrate a different style of painting. No more delicate pale northern European colours but tropical brilliance, exotic shades and a bold approach is needed. For the Flame Tree use Scarlet Lake and Winsor Red for the 4 main petals.

Clitoria ternatea is a tall climbing pea widely distributed in the tropics. Unlike other peas the flower is twisted so that the standard petal is underneath. The colour is pure Cobalt Blue.

Bright Red and Cadmium Yellow Pale edges.

Canarina abyssinica

Plumbago. Cobalt Blue with a little mauve.

Glory Lily. Also called Gloriosa, a climbing plant to 1-2 metres, by using the leaf tendrils. Leave plenty of highlights on the petals. *Canarina* is more raspberry coloured so add Permanent Rose to Winsor Red.

Plumbago is a vigorous plant widely grown in greenhouses in Britain and as hedges in its native South Africa. It can be kept in check by pruning.

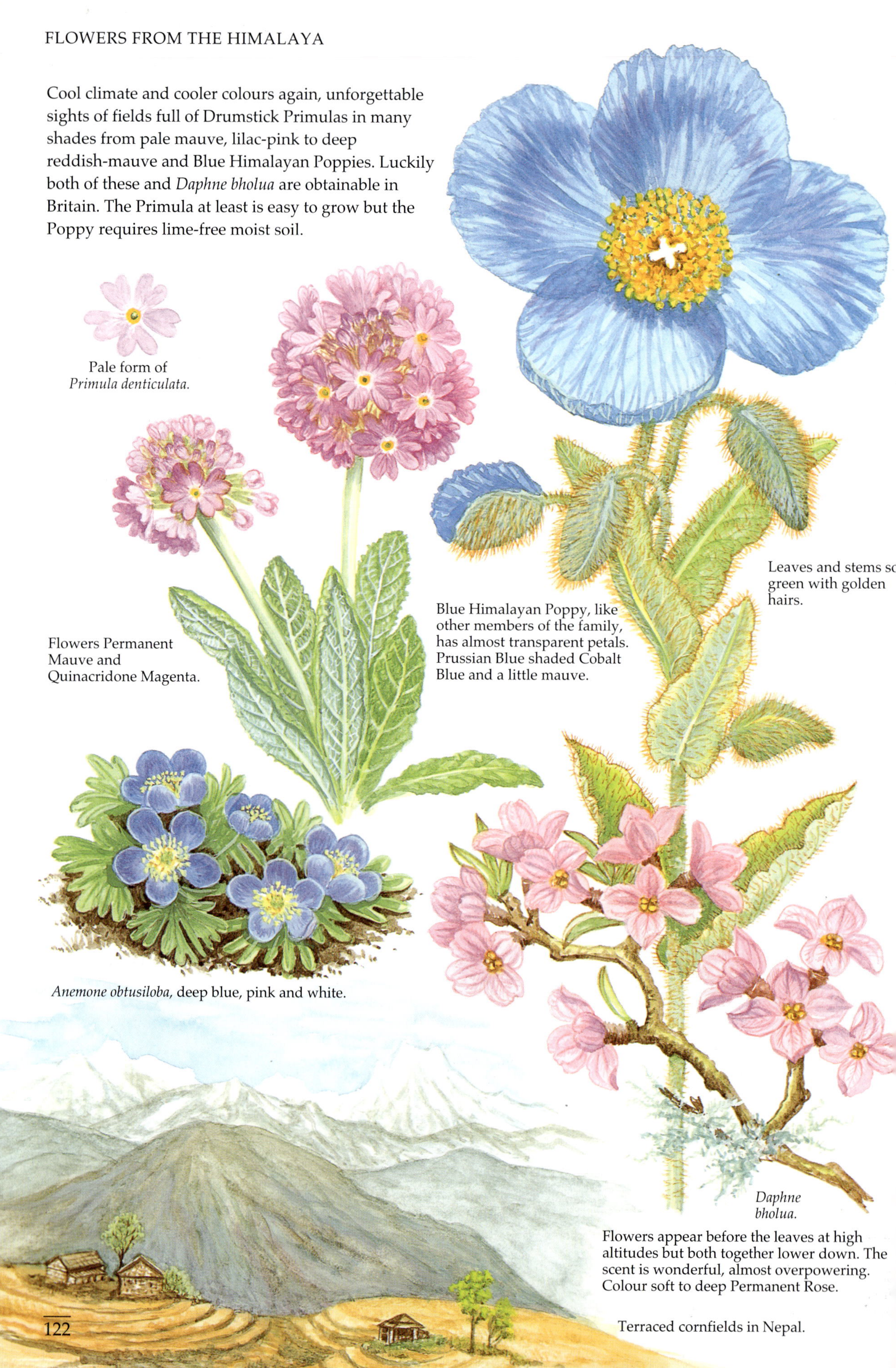
Cool climate and cooler colours again, unforgettable sights of fields full of Drumstick Primulas in many shades from pale mauve, lilac-pink to deep reddish-mauve and Blue Himalayan Poppies. Luckily both of these and *Daphne bholua* are obtainable in Britain. The Primula at least is easy to grow but the Poppy requires lime-free moist soil.
Pale form of *Primula denticulata.*
Flowers Permanent Mauve and Quinacridone Magenta.
Blue Himalayan Poppy, like other members of the family, has almost transparent petals. Prussian Blue shaded Cobalt Blue and a little mauve.
Leaves and stems sc green with golden hairs.
Anemone obtusiloba, deep blue, pink and white.
Daphne bholua.
Flowers appear before the leaves at high altitudes but both together lower down. The scent is wonderful, almost overpowering. Colour soft to deep Permanent Rose.
Terraced cornfields in Nepal.

These flowers from China, Japan and Australia can all be grown in Britain. Campsis, usually the hybrid form Madame Galen, flowers best in a greenhouse. This and the Gentian come from China. Bottlebrush, from Australia, flowers surprisingly well in mild areas. Quince and Wintersweet, both from Japan, are widely planted.

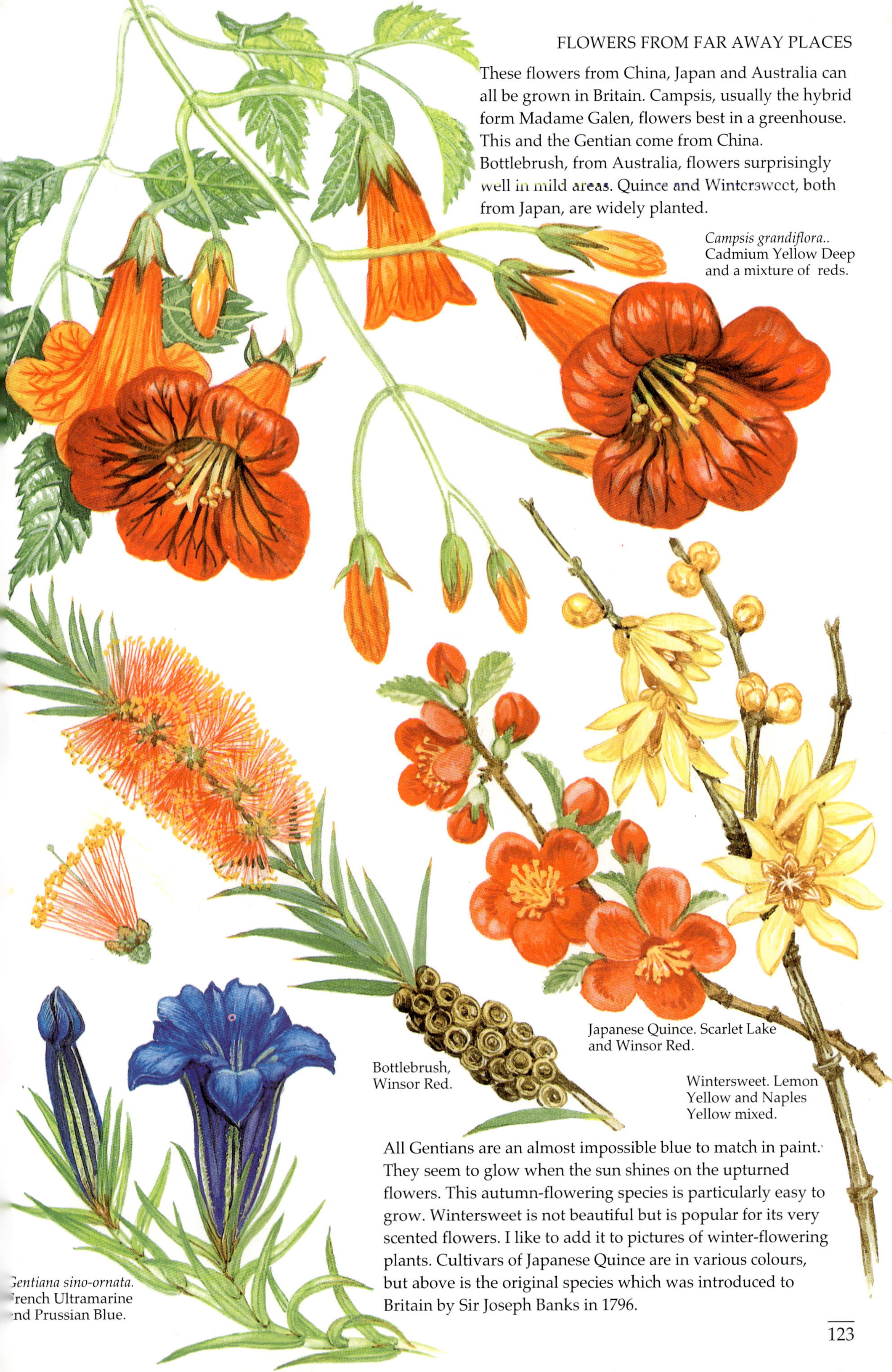

Campsis grandiflora.. Cadmium Yellow Deep and a mixture of reds.

Japanese Quince. Scarlet Lake and Winsor Red.

Bottlebrush, Winsor Red.

Wintersweet. Lemon Yellow and Naples Yellow mixed.

Gentiana sino-ornata. French Ultramarine and Prussian Blue.

All Gentians are an almost impossible blue to match in paint. They seem to glow when the sun shines on the upturned flowers. This autumn-flowering species is particularly easy to grow. Wintersweet is not beautiful but is popular for its very scented flowers. I like to add it to pictures of winter-flowering plants. Cultivars of Japanese Quince are in various colours, but above is the original species which was introduced to Britain by Sir Joseph Banks in 1796.

ADDING WILDLIFE TO YOUR PICTURE

Butterflies and bees can be attractive additions to flower paintings so long as they do not dominate them. One is usually quite sufficient though Buddleia or Hemp Agrimony can be almost covered by butterflies in late summer. It is not difficult to find dead bees or the occasional butterfly in autumn, which can be collected and kept in boxes for future reference.

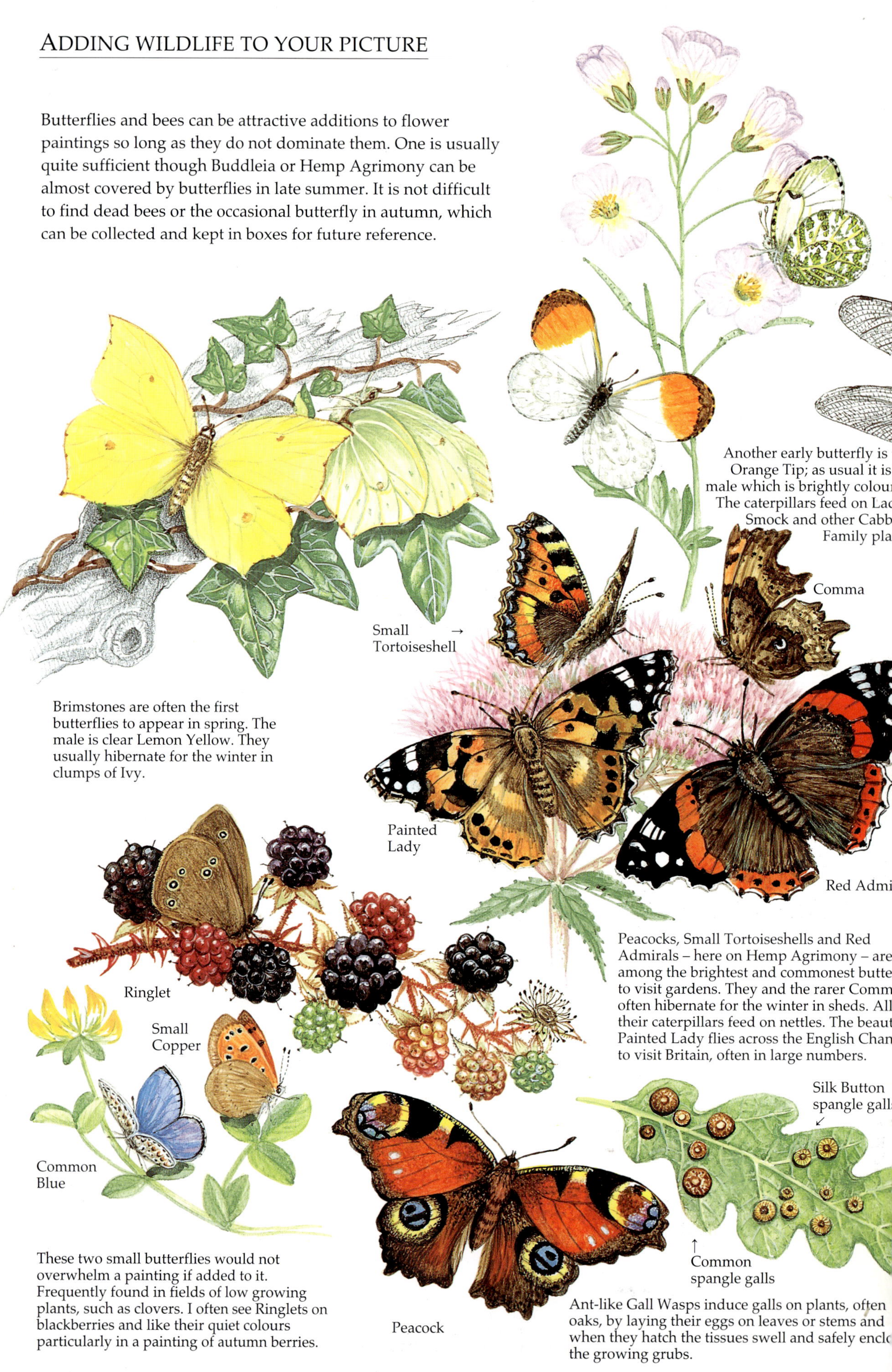

Another early butterfly is t Orange Tip; as usual it is male which is brightly colour The caterpillars feed on Lad Smock and other Cabba Family plar

Brimstones are often the first butterflies to appear in spring. The male is clear Lemon Yellow. They usually hibernate for the winter in clumps of Ivy.

Peacocks, Small Tortoiseshells and Red Admirals – here on Hemp Agrimony – are among the brightest and commonest butte to visit gardens. They and the rarer Comm often hibernate for the winter in sheds. All their caterpillars feed on nettles. The beaut Painted Lady flies across the English Chan to visit Britain, often in large numbers.

These two small butterflies would not overwhelm a painting if added to it. Frequently found in fields of low growing plants, such as clovers. I often see Ringlets on blackberries and like their quiet colours particularly in a painting of autumn berries.

Ant-like Gall Wasps induce galls on plants, often oaks, by laying their eggs on leaves or stems and when they hatch the tissues swell and safely encl the growing grubs.

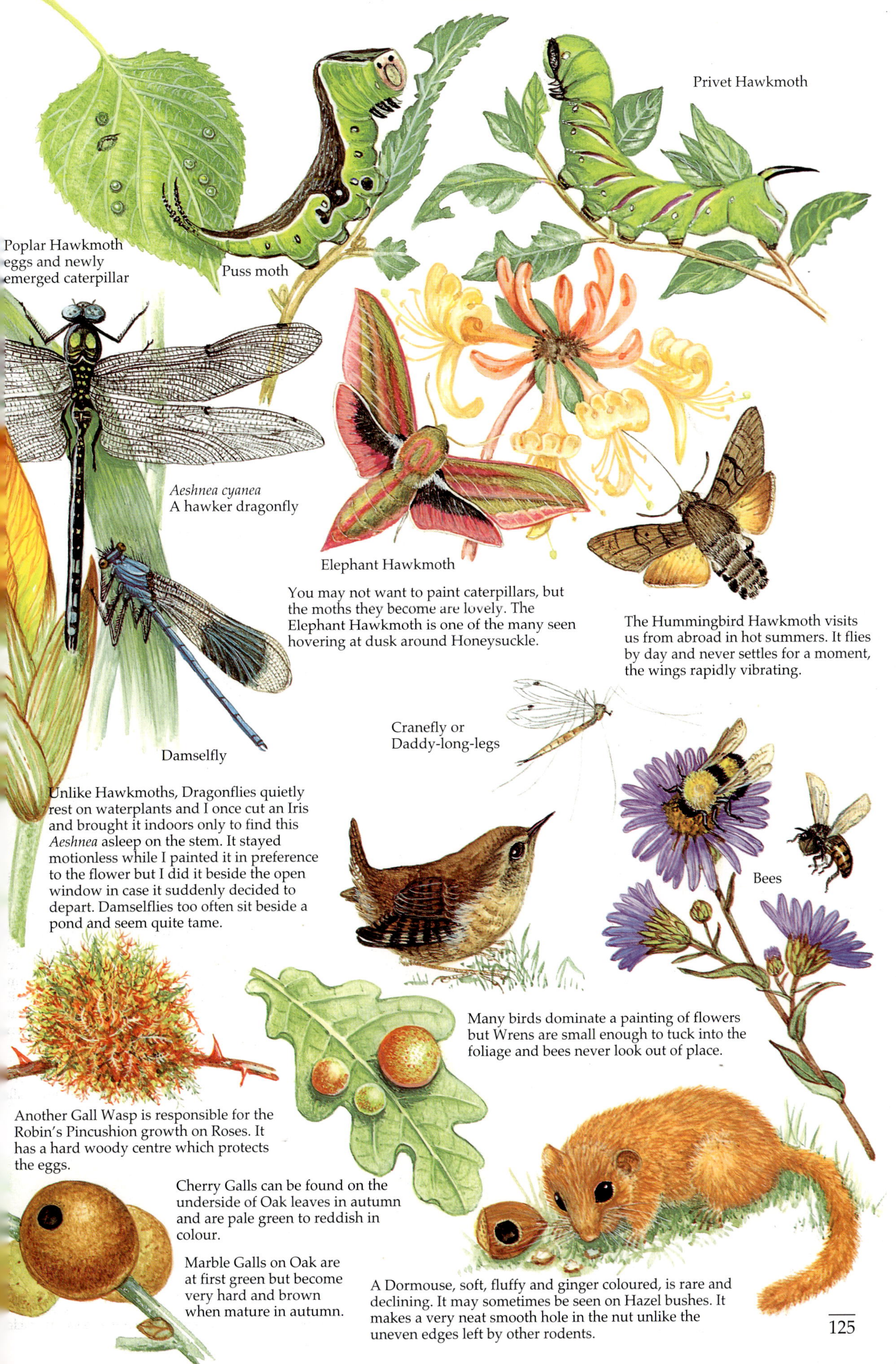

You may not want to paint caterpillars, but the moths they become are lovely. The Elephant Hawkmoth is one of the many seen hovering at dusk around Honeysuckle.

The Hummingbird Hawkmoth visits us from abroad in hot summers. It flies by day and never settles for a moment, the wings rapidly vibrating.

Unlike Hawkmoths, Dragonflies quietly rest on waterplants and I once cut an Iris and brought it indoors only to find this *Aeshnea* asleep on the stem. It stayed motionless while I painted it in preference to the flower but I did it beside the open window in case it suddenly decided to depart. Damselflies too often sit beside a pond and seem quite tame.

Many birds dominate a painting of flowers but Wrens are small enough to tuck into the foliage and bees never look out of place.

Another Gall Wasp is responsible for the Robin's Pincushion growth on Roses. It has a hard woody centre which protects the eggs.

Cherry Galls can be found on the underside of Oak leaves in autumn and are pale green to reddish in colour.

Marble Galls on Oak are at first green but become very hard and brown when mature in autumn.

A Dormouse, soft, fluffy and ginger coloured, is rare and declining. It may sometimes be seen on Hazel bushes. It makes a very neat smooth hole in the nut unlike the uneven edges left by other rodents.

SELECTED WATERCOLOURS FOR FLOWER PAINTERS

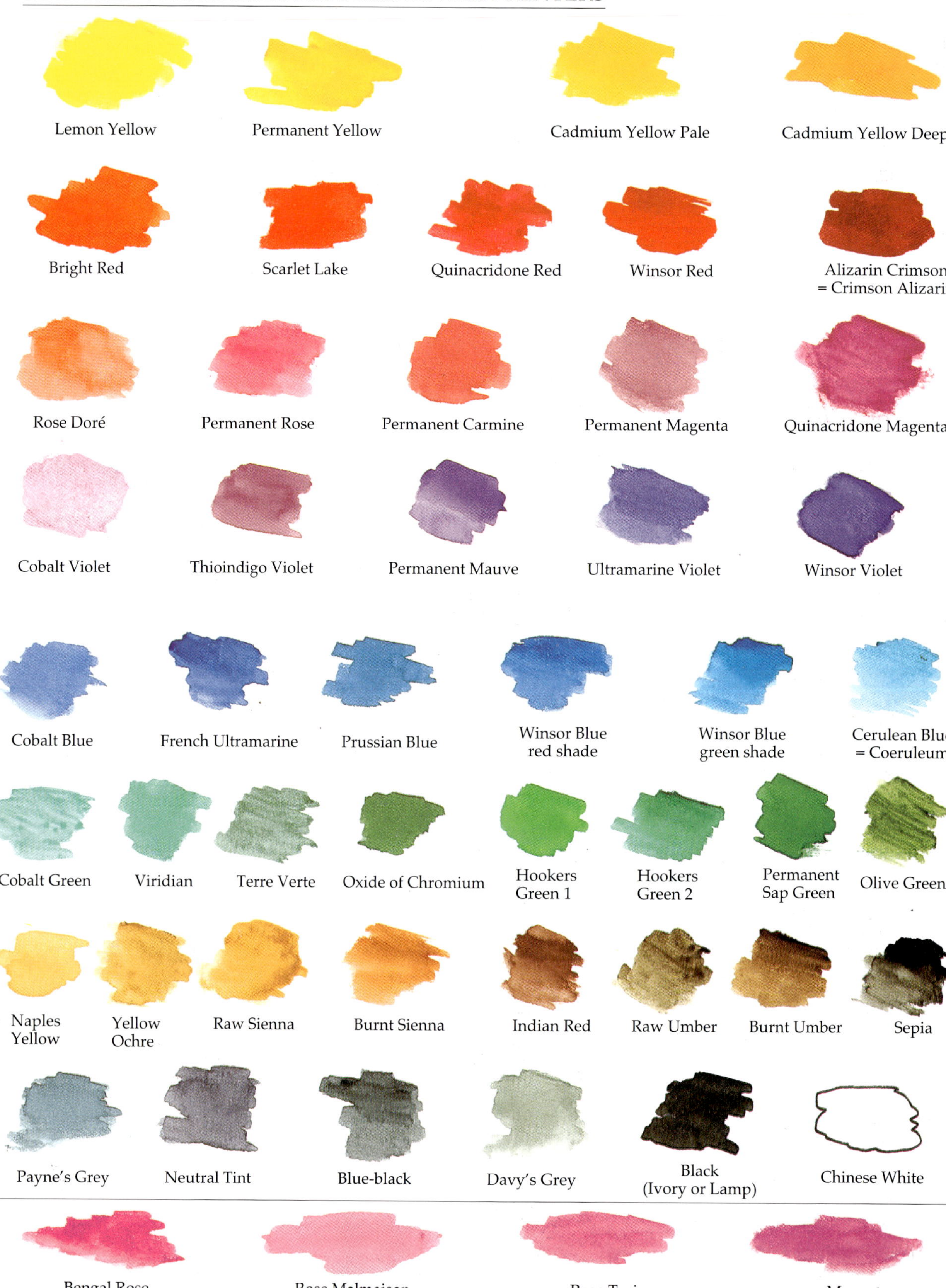

Most of the large range of Gouache paints are moderately to extremely permanent. However, the four colours shown above from the pink-magenta range are fugitive and will fade in time. These vivid – perhaps too vivid – shades have no match in the watercolour range. Used for temporary work or to be reproduced and thus 'fixed' on the printed page, they can be applied in the same way as watercolours – but remember that they are opaque.

General Index

Index of the Flora and Fauna You Will Find in the Book